The new city; principles of planning

Ludwig Hilberseimer

Nabu Public Domain Reprints:

You are holding a reproduction of an original work published before 1923 that is in the public domain in the United States of America, and possibly other countries. You may freely copy and distribute this work as no entity (individual or corporate) has a copyright on the body of the work. This book may contain prior copyright references, and library stamps (as most of these works were scanned from library copies). These have been scanned and retained as part of the historical artifact.

This book may have occasional imperfections such as missing or blurred pages, poor pictures, errant marks, etc. that were either part of the original artifact, or were introduced by the scanning process. We believe this work is culturally important, and despite the imperfections, have elected to bring it back into print as part of our continuing commitment to the preservation of printed works worldwide. We appreciate your understanding of the imperfections in the preservation process, and hope you enjoy this valuable book.

HILBERSEIMER : THE NEW CITY

The New City

PRINCIPLES OF PLANNING

by L. HILBERSEIMER

With an Introduction by Mies van der Rohe

PAUL THEOBALD • CHICAGO • 1944

COPYRIGHT 1944 BY PAUL THEOBALD, CHICAGO, ILLINOIS, U S A
FIRST EDITION

PRINTED AND BOUND AT THE WISCONSIN CUNEO PRESS, INC
TYPOGRAPHY BY O M FORKERT

CONTENTS

WHERE THE GREAT CITY STANDS . . . xiii
INTRODUCTION xv

PART ONE
SOCIETY AND CITIES

City Planning, a Social Task	17
Origin, Growth and Decline of Cities	18
Predomination of Natural Science	18
Peasants and Nomads	19
"Organic" and "Geometric" Settlements	20
Autocratic Cities	22
Free Cities	23
Colonial Cities	28
Political and Economical Means of Existence	28
Early Despotic States	30
Influence of Magic Ideology	31
Place of Refuge	31
Geographical and Topographical Conditions	33
Locations: Insular, Cape and Plain	34
Cities and Defence	40
Rise and Decline of Cities	40
Stages of Economy	41
Cities of the Nineteenth and Twentieth Centuries	45
Growth of Population	46
City and Country	46
Economic Disorder	46
New Types of Cities	47
Three Deficiencies	48
Concentration and Decentralization	49
New Possibilities	51
Integration of Industry and Agriculture	51
Cities and Regional Planning	53
Decentralization Unavoidable	54
A New Spirit	54

PART TWO
ELEMENTS OF CITY PLANNING

Natural and Technical Means	55
The City and Its Different Parts	56
The Individual and Society	56
Location, Layout and Size of a Settlement	56
Traffic Difficulties: a Symptom of Disorder	58
New Suggestion: The Centric and the Ribbon System	59
Ebenezar Howard and Raymond Unwin: The Satellite Town	60
Eric Gloeden: The Coordinated City	61
Martin Maechler: Functional Organization of Berlin	64
Le Corbusier: Une Ville Contemporaine	64
Circular and Street Village	66
Soria y Mata: La Ciudad Lineal	68
Frank Lloyd Wright: Broadacre City	68
N. A. Milyutin: Stalingrad	70
L. Hilberseimer's Planning System	71
Comparison of the Centric and the Ribbon System	72

Conclusion	73
City Planning and Housing	74
Types of Dwellings	75
Minimum Requirements	75
Sunlight and Housing	76
Socrates Perception	76
B C Faust's Theory	77
An Experience of the Pueblo Dwellers	77
Confusion of Today	77
Effects of Different Orientations	78
Room Insolation	78
Types of Sunrays and their Influence	80
Results of our Investigation	81
Protection against Sun	85
Population Density	86
What does Population Density Mean?	88
Latitude	88
Topography	89
Orientation	89
Duration of Insolation	89
Fallacy of Multi-storied Building	91
Relation of Depth to Length	91
Storey Height	91
Differences between the One-Family House and the Multi-storey Building	91
How to achieve Privacy in high Density	92
Influence of Density on the Plan of a Dwelling	93
Mixed Type of Settlement	95
Average Population Density	96
Building and Zoning Laws	96
Minimum Demands	96
Insufficiency of the Present Block and Street System	100
Combination of Blocks	100
The Super Block Residential Area	100
The Super Block Commercial Area	104
Advantages and Disadvantages	104
The Need of a New Settlement Unit	104
Structure, Shape and Size of the New Unit	107
Street System	107
Straight or Curved Streets?	111
The Width of Streets	111
Advantageous Features of the New Unit	113
Flexibility of the Use of the New Unit	113
Simple Industrial Settlements	113
Smoke-pollution and its ill Effects	113
How to Abolish Smoke—by Techno-Chemical Means or by Planning?	115
Influence of Prevailing Winds on Industrial Settlements	115
Four Wind Diagrams	118
Integrated Industries	122
The Commercial Area	122
Adaptability of the Unit to any kind of Terrain	125
Increase of the Number of Units by decreasing Density	125
The City in the Landscape	125
Theory and Reality	128

PART THREE
REPLANNING OF CITIES

Obstacle of Replanning Cities	129
Old Methods	129

The Ever Changing City	130
The City's Environment	130
Application of our Planning Principles	132
A European Industrial City	132
The Cities chaotic Structure	132
Three Schemes	133
The Replanned City	133
The actual Reconstruction	136
An Industrial City in the Middle West	136
The Replanned City Wind Conditions result in a fan-like Arrangement	137
Future Expansion	140
Procedure of Reconstruction	140
Chicago. Its planless and rapid Growth	140
Daniel H Burnham's Opinion	141
Reorganization of the City	144
Heavy Industry	144
Manufacturing Industries with Smoke, and without	145
The Commercial Area	145
Diagrams of the Reorganized City	147
Urbs in Horta	149
Is Reconstruction possible?	149
The Slum Problems	150
How Reconstruction can be achieved	151
"Master Plan for London"	151
Analysis	152
Traffic	152
Industry	153
Railroads	154
Housing	154
Our Diagrammatic Sketch for London	155
Administrative and Commercial Districts	155
The Industrial Area	156
Possibilities of Expansion	156
New York. Manhattan	156
Two Schools of Thought in City Planning	158
Procedure in Rebuilding a City	158
The Purpose of our City Diagrams	160
Administration and Legislation	160
Finance Problems	161
Economy of Planning	161
The Prefabricated House	161
Charles Breese's Proposal	164
Pooling of Ownership	164
Mortgages and their Amortization	164
Rebuilding without Loss in National Wealth	164
Passive Observation or Creative Action?	164
National Planning	165
Planless Decentralization and its Consequences	165
The Region and a Balanced Economy	166
Harmony between the Parts and the Whole	166
Man—the Object of all Planning	166

PART FOUR
THE ART OF CITY PLANNING

The Object in the Art of City Planning and its Means	167
Principles of the "Organic" and the "Geometric"	168
Two Examples	168
Structure and Art	170

Material and Artistic Means	171
Proportion	171
Relative and Absolute Proportion	173
Contrast	173
Cities and Hills and in Plains	175
Perspective	175
Saint Mark's Square	177
Spacial Feeling and Spacial Concepts Gothic	179
The Static Concept of the Renaissance	179
Circular Buildings	179
Circular Cities	179
The Dynamic Concept of the Baroque	182
Free Space. A New City Element	182
Union of the City with the Landscape	186
Classic Revival	188
Beauty at the Expense of Truth	188
The Imitative Spirit of the Nineteenth Century	188
The Esthetic and the Scientific Approach	190
Science and Art	190
Adequacy of the Spatial Concept and of the New City Structure	190
Rational Elements: the Base of Artistic Freedom	191
A Note by the Author	192

ILLUSTRATIONS

PART ONE
SOCIETY AND CITIES

1	Priene, Asia Minor	17
2	Stone-age Settlement at Glastonbury	20
3	Stone-age Settlement at Castellazo di Fontanellato	21
4	Roman Camp	24
5	Timgad	24
6	Versailles	25
7	Peking	25
8	Thera	26
9	Luebeck	27
10	Noerdlingen	27
11	Selinus	29
12	Montpazier	29
13	Philadelphia	29
14	The Acropolis	32
15	Place of Refuge	32
16	Early Settlement of Paris	34
17	Early Settlement of London	35
18	Norma, Italy	36
19	Jerusalem	36
20	Corcula, Dalmatia	37
21	Berne, Switzerland	37
22	Carthage	39
23	Cnidos, Asia Minor	39
24	Ual-Ual, Abyssinia	42
25	Ragusa, Dalmatia	42
26	Carcassonne, France	43
27	Narden, Holland	43
28 and 29	Urban and Rural Sky	48
30	Do Slums Make Criminals?	50
31	A Traffic Jam	52
32	Disorder and Chaos	53

PART TWO
ELEMENTS OF CITY PLANNING

33	The City in the Landscape	55
34	Plan of Priene	57
35	Plan of Noerdlingen	57
36	Traffic Diagram of London	59
37	Raymond Unwin, Diagram of Greater London	60
38	Raymond Unwin, City With Suburbs and Satelite Towns	61
39.	Eric Gloeden, Coordinated System of Different Settlements	62
40	Detail of the Above Plan	62
41	Martin Maechler, Diagram of Berlin	63
42	Le Corbusier, "Une Ville Contemporaine"	65
43	Le Corbusier, Replanning of the Center of Paris	65
44	Circular Village	67
45	Street Village	67
46	Soria y Mata, "La Ciudad Lineral"	68
47	Frank Lloyd Wright, Broadacre City	69
48	N A Milyutin, Proposed Plan for Stalingrad	70

IX

49	L. Hilberseimer, Planning System	71
50	Ludwig Sierks, Centralized Traffic System	73
51	Peter Friedrich, Traffic System in Ribbon Development	73
52	Plan of Apartment Houses	79
53	Sun Charts by Howard T. Fisher	80
54, 55 and 56	Diagrams of Sun Penetration on December 21	82
57, 58 and 59	Diagrams of Sun Penetration on June 21	83
60, 61 and 62	Diagrams of Maximum and Minimum Sun Penetration at Different Seasons	84
63	Diagram Showing Influence of Roof on Density	87
64	Diagram Showing Relation Between Latitude and Population Density	87
65	Population Density at Latitude 51° 30′	88
66	Apartment Houses With Different Densities and Plans	90
67	L-Shaped Houses at a Density of 120 People on One Acre	92
68	Effect of Different Densities on the Plan of Houses	94
69	View of L-Shaped Houses	95
70	Mixed Type of Settlement	97
71	Aerial View of Paris	98
72	Aerial View of London	98
73 and 74	City Streets	99
75	Combination of Eight City Blocks	101
76	Super Block Residential Area	102
77	Super Block Commercial Area	103
78	Henry Wright and Clarence Stein, Radburn	105
79	Raymond Unwin, System of Closed End-Streets	105
80	A New Settlement Unit	106
81	Theoretical Shape of a Settlement Unit	108
82	A New Settlement Unit and the Orientation of Houses	109
83	Details of a New Settlement Unit	110
84	Settlement With Smokeless Industry	112
85	Corcula, Dalmatia	114
86, 87, 88 and 89	Wind Diagrams	116 and 117
90	Integrated Smoke-Producing Industries	119
91	Commercial Area With Residential Sections	120
92	View of a Commercial Area	121
93	Plan of an Industrial City	123
94	Part of a Replanned City on Hilly Grounds	124
95	Diagram of Increased Units	126
96	View of a Settlement Unit	127

PART THREE
REPLANNING OF CITIES

97	American Industrial City Replanned	129
98	New York's Broadway	131
99	European Industrial City	134
100	European Industrial City Replanned	135
101	American Industrial City Present State	138
102	American Industrial City Replanned	139
103	City of Chicago Present State	142
104	City of Chicago. Proposed Replanning	143
105	Aerial View of the Replanned City of Chicago	146
106	City of Chicago Three Diagrammatical Sketches	148
107	The M A R S Plan for London	152
108	A Diagrammatic Sketch for London	153
109	Manhattan A Diagrammatic Sketch of Its Replanning	159
110, 111, 112 and 113	Four Diagrams Showing Procedure of Rebuilding a City	162 and 163

PART FOUR
THE ART OF CITY PLANNING

114	Greek Temple in the Landscape	167
115	Plan of Jueterbog	170
116	Plan of Karlsruhe	171
117	Mansion	172
118	Frauenkirche, Dresden	172
119	St Peter's, Rome	174
120	St Peter's Square, Rome	174
121	Sebenico, Dalmatia	176
122	Prague, The Hradschin	176
123	Melk on the Danube	176
124	Stralsund on the Baltic Sea	178
125	Chartres, Cathedral	178
126	Olympia, Temple of Zeus	180
127	Magnesia, Temple of Zeus	180
128	Priene, Temple of Aesculapius	180
129 and 130	Piazza St Mark, Venice	181
131	Interior of a Gothic Cathedral	183
132	Mediaeval Street	183
133	Michelangelo and San Gallo, Palazzo Farnese, Rome	184
134	Donato Bramante, Plan of St Peter's Church and Square	184
135	Donato Bramante, Santa Maria Della Consolazione at Todi	184
136	Fra Gioconda, Design for an Ideal City	185
137	Plan of Palmanova	185
138	Perugino, Christ Delivers the Keys to St Peter	187
139	Michelangelo, Plan of the Capitol Square	187
140	Michelangelo, View of the Capitol Square	187
141	Bath, Panoramic View	189
142	Bath, View from Hedgemead Park	189

WHERE THE GREAT CITY STANDS.

The place where a great city stands is not the place of stretch'd
    wharves, docks, manufactures, deposits or produce merely,
Nor the place of ceaseless salutes of new-comers or the
    anchor-lifters of the departing,
Nor the place of the tallest and costliest buildings or shops
    selling goods from the rest of the earth,
Nor the place of the best libraries and schools, nor the place
    where money is plentiest,
Nor the place of the most numerous population

Where the city stands with the brawniest breed of orators and
    bards,
Where the city stands that is belov'd by these, and loves them
    in return and understands them,
Where no monuments exist to heroes but in the common words
    and deeds,
Where thrift is in its place, and prudence is in its place,
Where the men and women think lightly of the laws,
Where the slave ceases, and the master of slaves ceases,
Where the populace rise at once against the never-ending au-
    dacity of elected persons,
Where fierce men and women pour forth as the sea to the
    whistle of death pours its sweeping and unript waves,
Where outside authority enters always after the precedence of
    inside authority,
Where the citizen is always the head and ideal, and President,
    Mayor, Governor and what not, are agents for pay,
Where children are taught to be laws to themselves, and to
    depend on themselves,
Where equanimity is illustrated in affairs,
Where speculations on the soul are encouraged,
Where women walk in public processions in the streets the
    same as the men,
Where they enter the public assembly and take places the
    same as the men,
Where the city of the faithfullest friends stands,
Where the city of the cleanliness of the sexes stands,
Where the city of the healthiest fathers stands,
Where the city of the best-bodied mothers stands,
There the great city stands

                                                Walt Whitman

Reprinted by permission of Random House Inc from their Modern Library edition
of Walt Whitman's LEAVES OF GRASS

INTRODUCTION

"Reason is the first principle of all human work." Consciously or unconsciously L. Hilberseimer follows this principle and makes it the basis of his work in the complicated field of city planning. He examines the city with unwavering objectivity, investigates each part of it and determines for each part its rightful place in the whole. Thus he brings all the elements of the city into clear, logical order. He avoids imposing upon them arbitrary ideas of any character whatsoever.

He knows that cities must serve life, that their validity is to be measured in terms of life, and that they must be planned for living. He understands that the forms of cities are the expression of existing modes of living, that they are inextricably bound up with these, and that they, with these, are subject to change. He realizes that the material and spiritual conditions of the problem are given, that he can exercise no influence on these factors in themselves, that they are rooted in the past and will be determined by objective tendencies for the future.

He also knows that the existence of many and diverse factors presupposes the existence of some order which gives meaning to these and which acts as a medium in which they can grow and unfold. City planning means for the author, therefore, the ordering of things in themselves and in their relationships with each other. One should not confuse the principles with their application. City planning is, in essence, a work of order; and order means—according to St. Augustine—"The disposition of equal and unequal things, attributing to each its place."

Mies van der Rohe

1. PRIENE, ASIA MINOR. After a reconstruction by A. Zippelius. See also illustration 34.

PART ONE

SOCIETY AND CITIES

City planning is a social task. It must solve problems of technics, science, space, and architecture. As these problems change with the social pattern of their time, the means of realizing the aims of city planning also change. For those means depend, in any era, on the concurrent status of science and technology. The present problem of city planning cannot be solved by the patterns of the past. To attempt to solve them thus would lead to decorative, not structural, formations. New social demands present new technical problems; new technics entail new problems for society. Society, as a rule, comes gradually to cope with the new problems which technology creates. But there is always a lag. The implications of a new alignment of forces are usually not generally appreciated until after the negative effects of the workings of those forces have become apparent.

City planning a social task

This is especially true in our own time We have undergone a transformation in our technical process. We have not yet learned to attain positive values from that transformation. The nineteenth century was a century of free economy It brought into our world two factors which have profoundly altered society; the machine, and the industrialization of production the machine made possible Machines and industry destroyed the essential structure of rural and urban settlements The disorder in which we live follows as inevitable consequence of a changing world Order will come again and will proceed from the nature of things. It will express itself in city planning as in all other phases of human activity.

Origin, growth and decline of cities

If we are to help direct the forces which will bring order out of disorder, it is profoundly important that we understand the forces which, in the past and in the present, influence the origins and developments of human settlements

All human settlements depend, in their growth and in their decline. on social, spiritual, political, and economic forces These forces are influenced by the status of technics, by the forms of production and consumption, and by the means of transportation available to the settlement builders. This interdependence of social and technological forces is expressed in all kinds of culture and varies only with the variations of the predominant elements

We can see that this is true as we study cities of the past They are unlike cities of today, but they show that, as each new order comes into existence, changes in urban development become both possible and necessary. This process is clear wherever we find settlements of men. Students have tended to limit research to large settlements, regarding them as the best examples of the process of change In reality, however, it makes little difference how large or how small the settlement may be. The thing which does matter is the function and significance of that settlement within a particular economic and cultural sphere.

Predomination of natural science

The rationalism of the eighteenth century paved the way for the predomination of natural science in the nineteenth century The conception of evolution and development. which was characteristic of natural science, became the standard of all research. Culture tended to be confused with civilization, and the progress of civilization was fallaciously identified with cultural unfolding It became accepted theory to view the different phases of the history of mankind as successive developments The culture of Egypt, or the Near East, for example, was considered a primitive precursor of Greek culture,

Greek culture was viewed as the culmination of the cultural development of antiquity The primitive communities of prehistoric times were thus regarded, not as groups of men and women, whose mode of livelihood was conditioned by their environment, but rather as stages in an evolutionary succession

We are correcting some of these misconceptions now We are coming to realize that the history of primitive ages can be adequately read. not through research alone. but through research accompanied by an ideological conception, a philosophy of life. We can. therefore. begin to trace and understand. through all history, the operation of the same interwoven social spiritual, political and economic forces which operate in our world today.

From earliest times. environment, and the activities conditioned by it. have influenced the creative spirit of man and moulded the intrinsic character of the communities he builds Modern ethnology recognizes two basic existant types, the peasant and the nomad, each with his own cultural development. In the communities they created, the earliest human dwellings known to us, these opposite types created opposite forms

Peasants and nomads

The peasant. bound to the soil, is the carrier of a mystic culture in which matter and spirit form an inseparable unity Plants, the peasant's means of livelihood, are the determining elements in this culture. Whether the peasant sows or reaps, the life process of plants suggests to him a synopsis of all life, symbolizes to him the close connection of all things He draws no distinction between matter and spirit, for to him all things, are animate His sense of space. is centrifugal, for all life emanates from a central source. The settlements he built in the center of his fields—his living space—were naturally rooted in the soil, like trees

The nomad. whether hunter or herdsman, is the carrier of a culture of magic, in which everything immaterial is alien. The animals. the basic means of existence for the nomad, are the determining elements here To the nomad the life process of those animals suggests a synopsis of all life which endows their existence with significance and purpose. In this magic culture all is earthly, material. and physical; only that which is apparent is accepted The nomad perceives only reality and is opposed to all that is irrational His feeling for space is centripetal, all life incoming from a domain within a border line His settlements are, therefore, essentially tent settlements, moving from time to time, according to natural necessities.[1]

---
[1] Leo Frobenius and Douglas C Fox, *African Genesis* New York 1937.

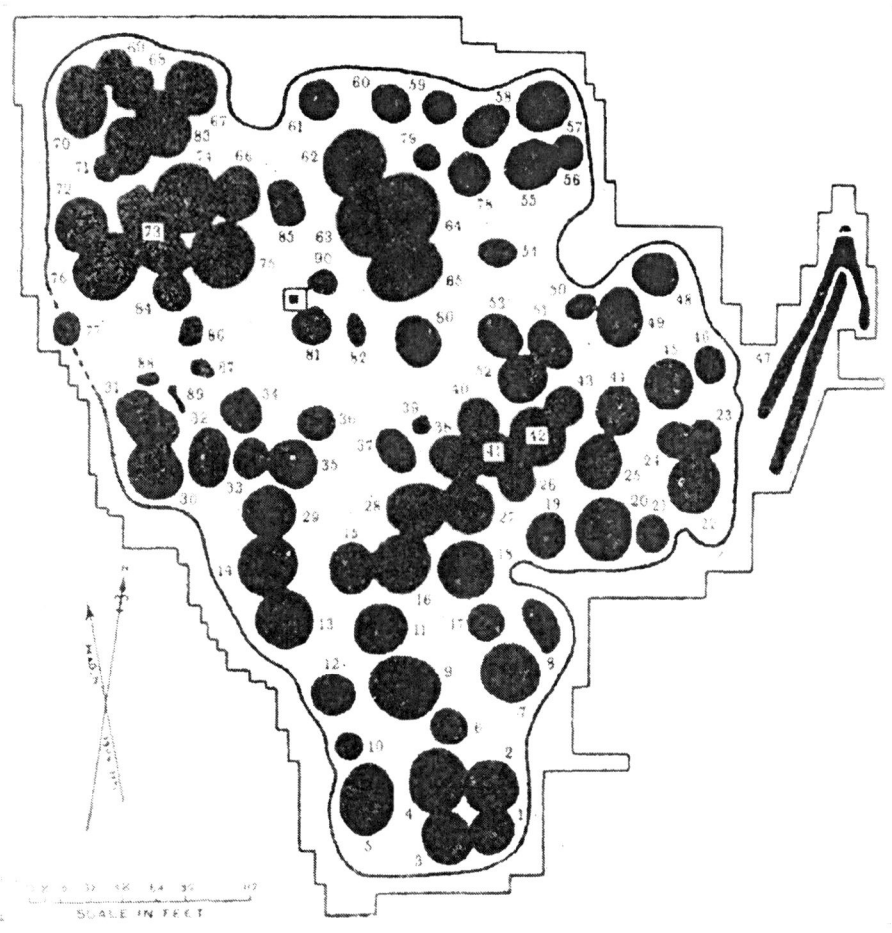

2. STONE-AGE SETTLEMENT AT GLASTONBURY. Plan by A. Bulleid and G. Gray.

We meet these two types again and again in the course of history, regardless of political, economic, spiritual, and cultural circumstances. The elementary reactions of man are unchanging; it is only the expressions of these reactions which changes.

"Organic" and "geometric" settlements

The coexistence of peasants and nomads, of mystic and magic culture, explains also the great contrast between two types of structural form: the "organic" and the "geometric". Historians have too often treated these types as successive rather than coexistent. Yet both are original forms, creating and expressing different concepts of life, no matter how much their elements may have penetrated one another later, and no matter how much they may have been modified by social changes.

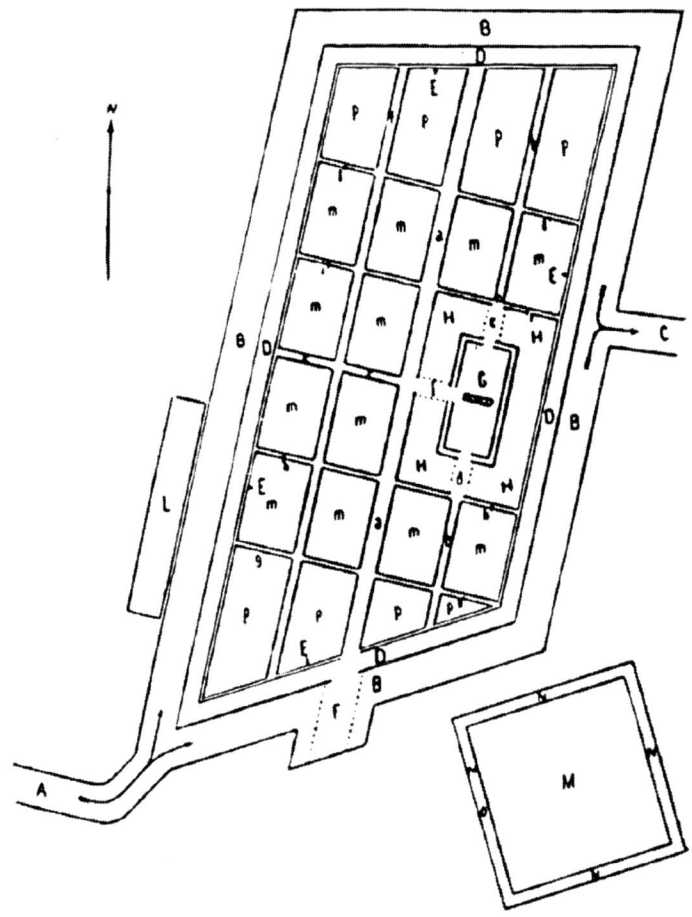

3. STONE-AGE SETTLEMENT AT CASTELLAZZO DI FONTANELLATO.

Both represent particular communal structures, expressing their character symbolically. This contrast between the organic and the geometric is expressed in architectural formations, both in individual buildings and in communal settlements.

The prehistoric towns of Glastonbury *(ill. 2)* and Castellazzo di Fontanellato *(ill. 3)* illustrate these two contrasting types. Glastonbury with its organic layout is a typical expression of a people with a mystic culture, whereas Castellazzo di Fontanellato shows, in its geometrical layout, the characteristics of a people with a magic culture. It is very apparent that the structural differences between these two settlements express contrasting social and spiritual forms of organization.

21

These formative types are rarely presented in pure form in the remnants of habitation accessible to us at present This is partly because the completed structure is not always analogous with the idea which created it It is due, in part, also to the fact that continual contact and mixture of different peoples may blur originally pure forms of expression Social and political influences cause further deviations

Nevertheless, a tendency to organic or geometric formation can always be clearly recognized. Organic settlements are peculiar to free communities They correspond to natural local conditions. Their growth is expressed in their entirety and in all their individual parts Geometric settlements, on the other hand, are the typical form of autocratic communities Here building is subordinated to an abstract planning principle

One may generalize from ample evidence that all mystic peoples, in accordance with their principle of growth, arrive at organic city formations; and that all magic peoples, because of their rational spirit, arrive at geometric city formations

Autocratic cities The tent camp of the nomad antedates and shows in simplest terms the coordinating principle of the geometric city A firmly established tent order was one of the disciplining forces in the life of the nomad. Everybody and everything had a place. No one changed his place without command or urgent reason Because of this fixed order, encampment and decampment could be effected with swiftness and order, the tent and all its contents could be packed and loaded in an hour's time.

The Roman camp *(ill 4)*, with its well established order, is the forerunner of the Roman Colonial City. Timgad *(ill. 5)* in North Africa shows how short a step it was from camp to city. It was founded as a military colony by Trajan It became an autocratic city The square with the official buildings in its center, the colonnaded main streets which end in arched gateways are typical of a Roman imperial city.

Peking *(ill 7)* also was originally a camp city The tent of the commander-in-chief was its center Around this center were the tents of the generals, then those of the subjects, in geometric order The north-south orientation, based on religious conceptions, was carried out so completely in the tent camp that later its layout was adopted for the imperial city But that imperial city was intended to be more than a fortified camp It symbolized the hub of the universe On important festivals, the emperor sat on his throne facing south Before him knelt the worshipping nobles, while the people, all facing north, honored him at the altars and in the remotest hut

Versailles *(ill. 6)*, residence of the French kings, became the prototype of the small capitals of the territorial princes Here the conception of absolute monarchy, represented in its purest form by Louis XVI, found an equivalent expression in the city dominated by the monarch The king was glorified as the representative of the monarchic system. His palace was removed from the city The monarch was the head of the people Therefore, his residence headed the city: and the city itself became subordinate to the soverign palace by a symmetric axial street system.

Characteristic of autocratic states is their location on plains. In such location artificial boundaries, established by a conqueror's claim for domination, replace natural borders Autocratic cities were the creation of a ruler, and they rose suddenly

Organic cities express slow but planned growth They are typically free cities, based on voluntary coalition of citizens Such commonwealths arose for the most part in regions where geographic conditions favored the rise of small integrated states. In Greece and Italy the tribes originally lived in villages When they concentrated in the polis—that is, the city state—they did so chiefly for reasons of safety. The origin of the medieval cities is attributed to the development of craftsmanship and the subsequent rise of markets. Here, for the first time, free labor became an influencing factor in city growth as well as in political power Annual and bi-annual fairs were replaced by the weekly market and concentrated settlements were a prerequisite. Free cities

These cities were so spaced that the rural population from the surrounding countryside could reach them in one day's travel A regional structure was thus developed. characterized by an even distribution of different kinds of settlements A well proportioned pattern of villages, towns, and cities arose. each settlement limited in size and situated with due regard for traffic distances, and well balanced production and consumption relations between rural and urban communities Everything was not only related organically within the different settlements. but was also built with reference to the surroundings of those settlements Topographical influences had much to do with determining their shape.

Thera *(ill. 8)*, on an island in the Aegean Sea, was originally a Phoenician settlement. later developed by Greek settlers To protect it against pirates and invaders, and to afford a free view over the sea, its builders chose a site on the ridge of a mountain. That choice determined the long-stretched and narrow shape of the town. with its one main street leading through its entire length

4. ROMAN CAMP.

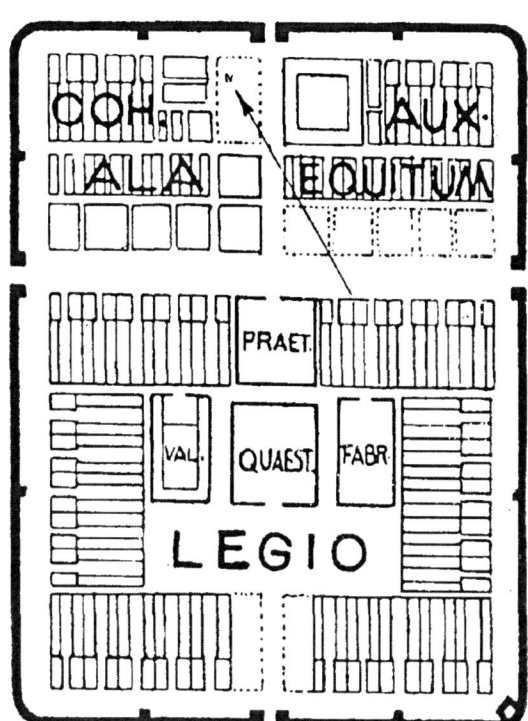

5. TIMGAD.
Plan by
A. von Gerkan.

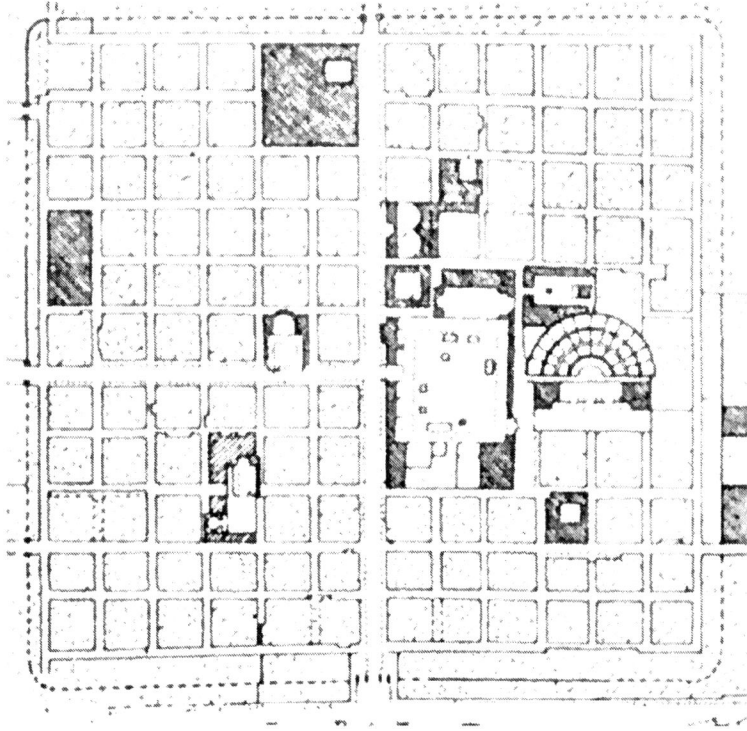

6. VERSAILLES.

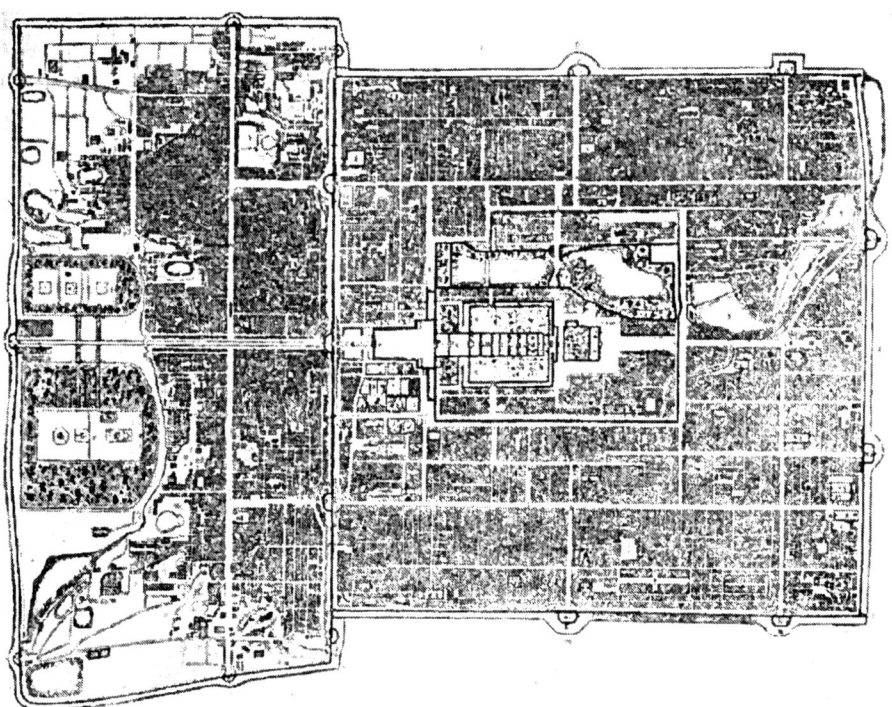

7. PEKING.

8. THERA. Plan by F. Hiller von Gaertringen.

Luebeck *(ill. 9)*, on the Baltic Sea, was built on a flat hill of oblong shape, surrounded by two branches of a river. It was an important city, one of the largest of the middle ages and the founder of the Hansiatic League. Its street system is very clear. Three streets lead through it and are intersected by side-streets, which lead across the city and down to the river.

Noerdlingen *(ills. 10 and 35)*, originally located on a hill, was rebuilt on the plains at the foot of that hill at the beginning of the 13th century. In its new location the city could develop with freedom. During the 16th century it was extended in the shape of a ring around its nucleus. Its shape was almost circular, the circle being the most economical and, at that time, the most efficient form for a fortified city. The street system of Noerdlingen is quite different from that of

9. LUEBECK.

10. NOERDLINGEN. See also illustration 35.

Thera and Luebeck. The nucleus is surrounded by a ring-street from which other streets radiate.

Colonial cities

Geometrical settlements are sometimes found in civilizations with originally organic city formation. This is not difficult to explain. Such settlements—found in Greece, during the middle ages and later in America—were colonial cities, and such cities were always founded and built according to a simple geometric plan.

Selinus *(ill. 11)*, on the southwest coast of Sicily, was founded by Dorians in the middle of the seventh century B.C. After its destruction by the Carthaginians it was rebuilt under the influence of the Hippodamic planning system. The city on the acropolis was divided by a main street and crossed at right angles by side streets. The size of the blocks depended on the plan of the houses which, in their similarity and simplicity, formed a vivid contrast to the splendor of the community buildings and temples.

Montpazier *(ill. 12)*, in the southwest of France, was presumably built according to a design by English planners during the English conquest of the 13th century. The city consists of rectangular blocks with alleys, and two squares—one for the city hall surrounded by arcades, and another for the cathedral—both in the center of the city.

Philadelphia *(ill. 13)* was built after a plan of William Penn. In its rectangular layout it not only expressed the spirit of colonial cities, but symbolized also in the homogeneity of its structure, the democratic character of the new community.

Political and economical means of existence

There are two ways in which man may win his livelihood. One is economic: man may satisfy his needs by the exchange of the products of his labor with others by barter. The other is political: man may sustain his own life by plunder and the exchange of his loot with that of others [1]. The entire course of historical and sociological events is determined by the uses made of these economic political means.

When the peasant, whose occupation binds him to the soil, and who lives by barter, is attacked by the nomad, he fights a losing battle. Economic means are overwhelmed by political.

In very primitive times, the conquering nomads annihilated the vanquished tribes. Gradually they came to realize their potential usefullness [2]. The vanquished tribe was forced to produce goods, at first

---

[1] Franz Oppenheimer *The State* New York 1926
[2] In some parts of the Sahara desert, as an African traveler records, the Arabs and Tibbus, probably, consider certain oases and their inhabitants to be still their property. They appear there at harvest time to claim their tribute, that is, to plunder and to sack. They leave the subdued people to their fate and to their duty of continuing to plant for them.

11. SELINUS.
Plan by M. Hulot.

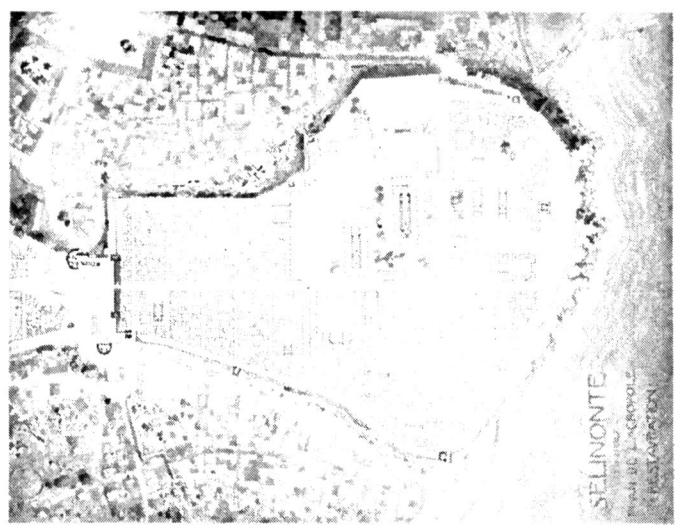

12. MONTPAZIER.
Plan by Parker.

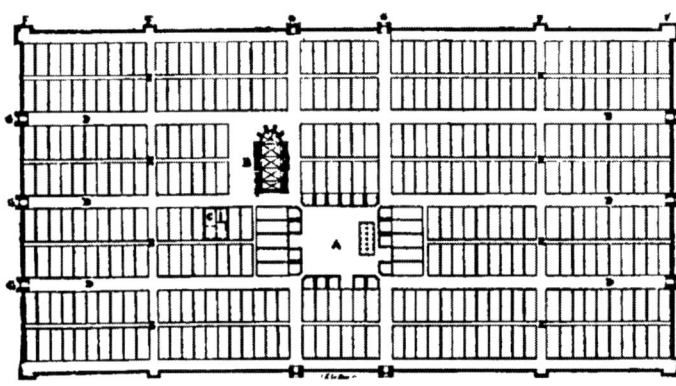

13. PLAN OF
PHILADELPHIA
by William Penn.

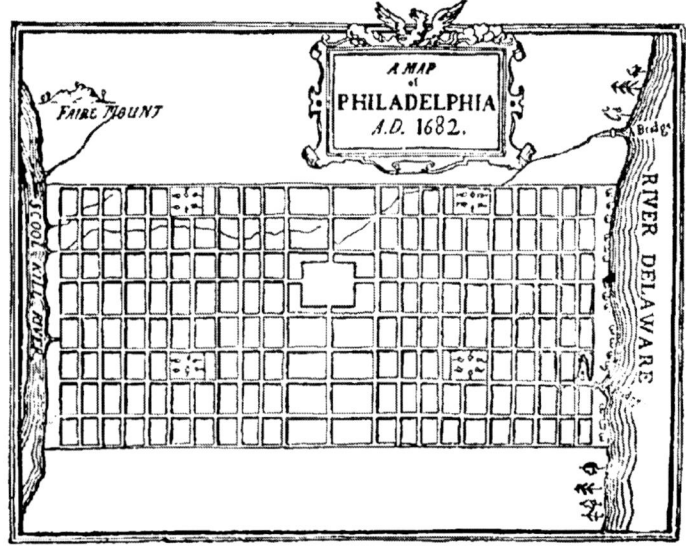

for the victor's consumption, and later for the trade which the victor carried on The victor was soon forced to settle in the conquered territory so as to assure his tribute. The settlements he built, if situated on a vital trading trail, or on a strategically important site, became the centers of later city developments The first cities known to us, in the river valleys of the Nile, Euphrates, and Tigris, were cities resulting from victory and domination. The Romans in their conquests of Gaul, Brittania, and Germania, also used established places of refuge as their permanent camps if they were situated favorably for their purposes These camps frequently gave birth to city developments.

The rise of coastal cities has a like source Pirates progressed from intermittent raids to the founding of trading posts These trading posts arose as free harbors and, with their coastal fortifications, became the nuclei of later seaports. The pre-Grecian settlements of the Aegeans on the islands and shores of Greece and Asia Minor may have originated in this manner and so also the harbor cities of the Phoenicians along the entire coast of the Mediterranean.

A mutual agreement was reached, in time, between victor and vanquished, which gave to the vanquished certain important advantages. He enjoyed the protection of the victor, not only against invading robber tribes, but also against members of his own tribe He enjoyed trade protection, though he had to pay additional tribute for this. Trading centers and cities, governed by overlords and feudal princes, developed from this new cooperative relationship

Early despotic states
The large despotic states arising from victory coordinated, politically and economically, an increased territory which came to comprise a coastal region and, finally, an entire river valley The pre-requisites for a homogeneous and permanent economy of large river domains were thus established in the regions of the Nile, the Euphrates and Tigris, the Ganges and Indus, the Hoang-Ho and Yangtze-Kiang, and other great rivers Only an autocratic system could accomplish this task Huge irrigational systems had to be planned and built Dams, canals, locks, and reservoirs had to be constructed, if secure and permanent living conditions were to be attained.

Such tremendous technical problems required the services of many workers, and these workers were employed without regard for their personal fates. The caste system, serfdom and enslavement, were a necessity for those early states They were all built upon a wide stratum of the original population, and ruled by the conquerors.

But the conqueror—king, priest, or warrior—was also a slave to his calling The life of the ruler, as well as that of all members of the state, depended upon a complicated machinery which had to be maintained even if it meant sacrificing all natural values of life. The problematic nature of civilization is thus shown in its early beginnings

From the predominance of the magic ideology originates the deification of the king To rule was a magic calling The priest-kingdom was probably the first stage of political development The interplay of social and economic and spiritual forces in the determining of human settlements is interestingly shown in this connection. For it is believed that the use of ploughs and draught animals is also based on cult. The chariot of the gods, riding along the Milky Way, was the prototype of the plough Images of such chariots were placed, as holy vessels, on altars. And when the deified kings rode through the streets in triumph, the chariots in which they rode were also modeled upon and made to symbolize the chariots of the gods

Influence of magic ideology

As the culture of the hoe gave way to that of the plough, the magic ideology carried into the fields the idea of holiness The plough being originally a priestly vessel, could obviously be properly handled only by a man, whereas the hoe had been the woman's tool. And therefore, the new tool, which made it possible to grow grain on a large scale to feed the masses concentrated in the growing cities, also profoundly altered the status of women in the social structure It was, in all probability, one of the factors in the social change from the matriarchate to the patriarchate.

For all men in all times, a principal reason for drawing together in settlements has been the need for protection. And that seeking for safety has been one of the most important elements in the rise of cities

Place of refuge

In simplest form the protection for the group was provided by the place of refuge *(ill. 15)*. This was simply a secure place which could be fortified and rendered impervious to attack. People continued to live scattered through the countryside but they could congregate in this stronghold for mutual safety in time of danger [1] Generally only one warden lived in the stronghold He kept record of all who belonged to it, collected taxes from them, and summoned them to arms Because the altar was also protected by being located within the walls of the place of refuge, the stronghold became not only the military, but also the administrative and religious center of the region. When

---

[1] The rural population of Lower and Central Italy retreated to such "Castellos," strongholds, similar to such places of refuge, for protection at night and in times of peril, until the nineteenth century

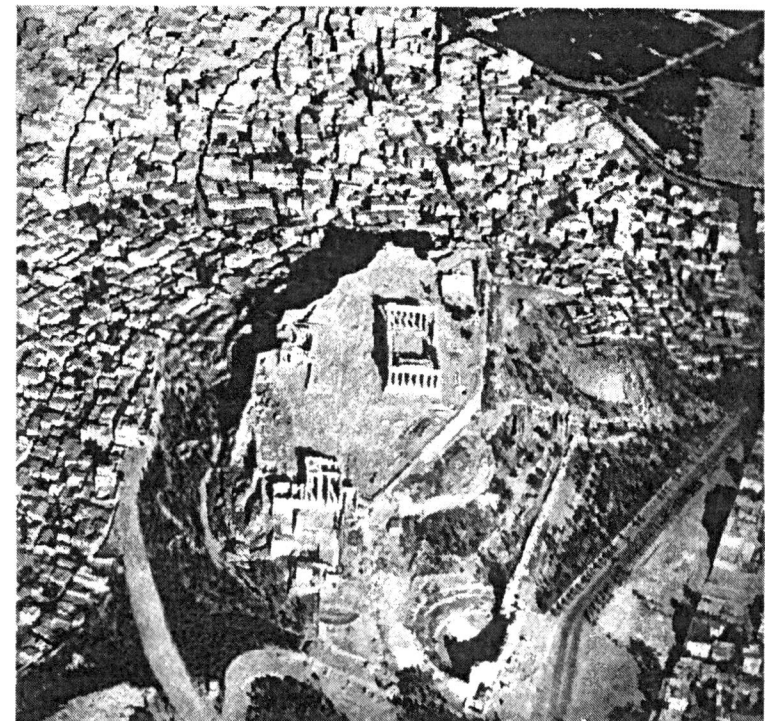
14. THE ACROPOLIS, ATHENS.

15. PLACE OF REFUGE.

favorably located it might develop into a trading post, and then into a city, and thus add economic prominence to its military and religious roles.

Sometimes gradual change of political pattern and power brought an individual to the head of a community The purpose of the stronghold then changed. It might continue to serve as a retreat for the community in time of peril, but it might also become a fortress from which the absolute rulers governed the adjacent territory.

The Acropolis *(ill. 14)* in Athens was originally the place of refuge for its domain It became also the stronghold of rulers first under the domination of Mycenae and under the Pisistratides, then under the Franconian, Catalonian, and Florentine dukes, and finally under the Turks According to the conditions of the times, the Acropolis was now a place of refuge for the people, now the stronghold of rulers, now the site of a temple.

In the Near East have been found ancient cities of autocratic kings fortified from the beginning. The existence of such cities does not necessarily indicate, however, that they were the original settlements on their sites. They should be considered rather as the end of a development whose beginnings are still unexplored and obscure It may be assumed that such cities originated from the same causes which gave rise to those we know from their beginnings Wherever a tyrannous state, or a despotic ruler arose, the place of refuge of the people became the stronghold of the ruler, dominating the city and its territory.

Geographical location and topographical conditions have always been decisive factors in the choice of the site and in the development of settlements. The earliest men probably looked only for the presence of a spring and arable soil. Later settlers looked for a certain type of soil, for evidences of the presence of certain raw materials. They considered whether the location was favorable for trade

The earliest settlements arose, therefore, in valleys, watercourses, and seacoasts—along the natural communication lanes of unsettled regions. According to geographic conditions, certain regions became sparsely settled, others densely populated. The French districts of Arras and Arles, for example, are of approximately equal size. But Arras is fertile and has a large population evenly distributed, whereas Arles is a glacial unproductive country at the mouth of the Rhone— partly swampy, partly rocky—and its population is small and unevenly distributed.

Geographical and topographical conditions

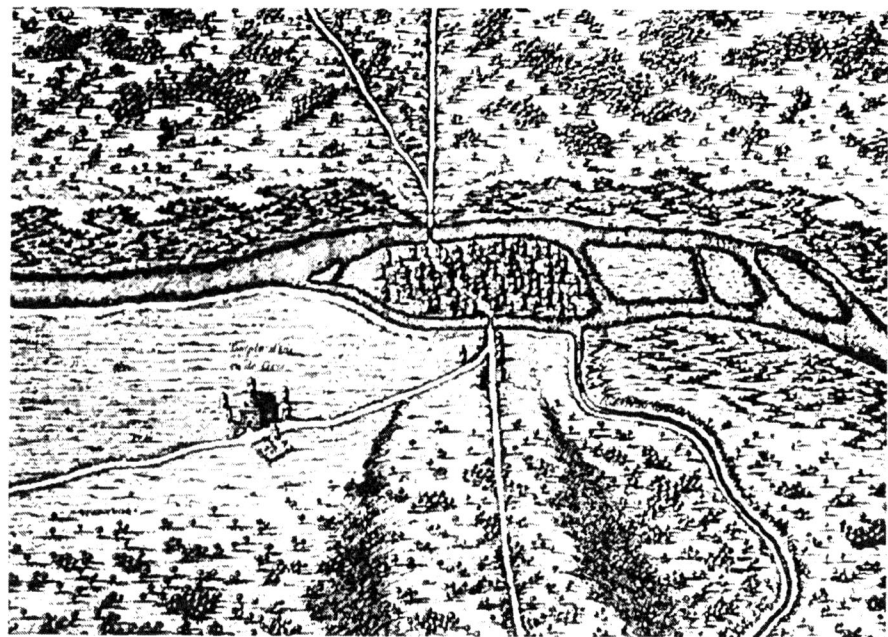

16. EARLY SETTLEMENT OF PARIS.

A settlement favorably located, producing goods peculiar to its region, could grow in power, achieve hegemony. Carthage dominated the Mediterranean, commercially and militarily, for centuries because of its advantageous location in the center of the Mediterranean, its naturally protected position, and the spirit of its population. Constantinople, the communication link between Orient and Occident; London, between England and the European continent; New York, between America and Europe: all these cities have attained their prominence because their geographical location is advantageous.

Topographical conditions have always been especially important in relation to defense. Despite all changes of conditions, the city had to be made as secure as possible at all times. A wise choice of location could make that defense easier.

Locations: Insular, cape and plain

Two principal types of location which have reappeared through all history—the insular position and the cape position—have always been chosen for their defense value.

Advantage was taken of insular formations in rivers, lakes, and seas. Such insular location, naturally isolated, was a primary form of protection. Arne rose on a rocky island of Lake Copias. Paris *(ill. 16)* grew from its nucleus, the fortified fishing island of Lutetia

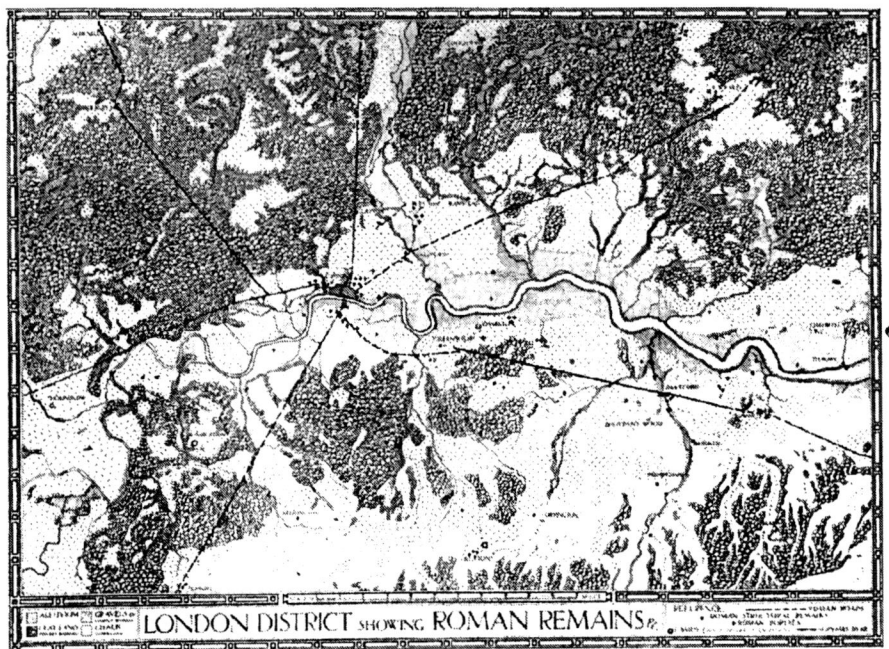

17. EARLY SETTLEMENT OF LONDON.

Parisiorum (the "Isle de la Cité" of today) dominating the valleys of the Seine, Marne, and Oise. As late as the Thirty Years War, the city of Stralsund *(ill. 124)* resisted Wallenstein's siege, not only because of its fortifications, but even more because of its naturally protected insular location. Inhabitants of the Adriatic coastal regions, fleeing the Huns, sought refuge on the islands of a lagoon and built there several island settlements which later became Venice. Because of its singularly protected location, the city escaped the battles between emperor and papacy during the Middle Ages and developed into a trading center between East and West. Insular countries, like insular cities, could also develop undisturbed by continental strife: England and Japan achieved hegemony largely for this reason.

Single elevations, rocky plateaus, sometimes mountains, offered similar insular protection in plains and hilly landscapes. The Greeks and Romans chose such elevations for their first settlements: Athens *(ill. 14)* rose on the Acropolis; Rome on the Palatine. Both settlements were in the immediate vicinity of the sea and yet at a sufficient distance from it so that protection against attacks from pirates could be secured. London's *(ill. 17)* location was, in a sense, also insular. It was built on a swampy site where the river Thames empties into the ocean and at floodtide makes a lake. Two opposite flat hills, rising

18. NORMA, ITALY.

19. JERUSALEM.

20. CORCULA, DALMATIA. See also illustration 85.

21. BERNE, SWITZERLAND.

from the banks of the river, converged there, forming a ford, where London Bridge is today

The cape location, like the insular, provided protection which increased with the narrowness of the connection between cape and mainland Such a site could be made invulnerable by special measures of defense. Cape locations vary according to topographical conditions Norma *(ill 18)*, in Italy, situated on a steep promontory, shows clearly the advantage of a sheltered cape location The Greek city of Thera *(ill. 8)*, safely situated on the top of a mountain, which is connected with another mountain only by a narrow approach, could be easily defended Jerusalem *(ill 19)* lies on a plateau, between the deep valleys of Ben Hinnom and Kidron which form natural boundaries

Peninsulas, formed by river bends, offer similar protection, as can be clearly seen in the city of Berne *(ill. 21)* which rises at a U-bend of the river Aare Berne's growth necessitated renewing its fortifications three times, until the city finally occupied the entire peninsula

Cape formations are also caused by the junctions of two rivers. Such a location is particularly advantageous when, as in Belgrade, at the junction of the Save and Danube, the cape rises high above the flatland This exceptionally well sheltered location made Belgrade a fortress from the first. A cape location is well suited also for the foundation of seaports. Their protection can be relatively complete, as was the case in Corcula *(ills. 20 and 85)* on the Adriatic Sea. In rocky coastal regions promontories offer protection and also form natural harbors. Carthage *(ill. 22)* was situated on a promontory which formed two harbors, one on each side, thus allowing sailing vessels to enter whatever the direction of the wind. Many harbor cities rose in Greece and Asia Minor on such naturally protected sites. Cnidos *(ill 23)* in Asia Minor, perhaps the best example of rational city planning by the Greeks, was one of them.

The exceptional location of Constantinople on the Sea of Marmara, where an inlet extends into the interior and forms a cape, is paralleled by New York's location at the mouth of the Hudson. The comparison between these two cities, one so old, the other so new, shows that geographic locations and topographical formations are important factors in the growth of great cities, no matter in what period these cities develop

When the populations increased, natural protected sites of cities often became inadequate. Then the city descended from its eleva-

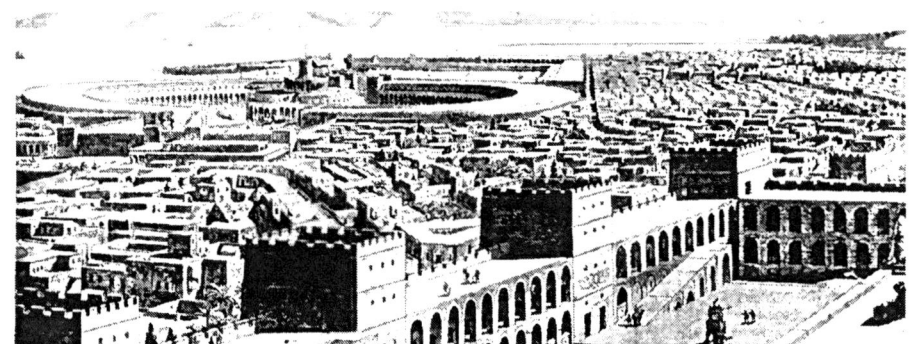

22. CARTHAGE. A reconstruction by M. Aucler.

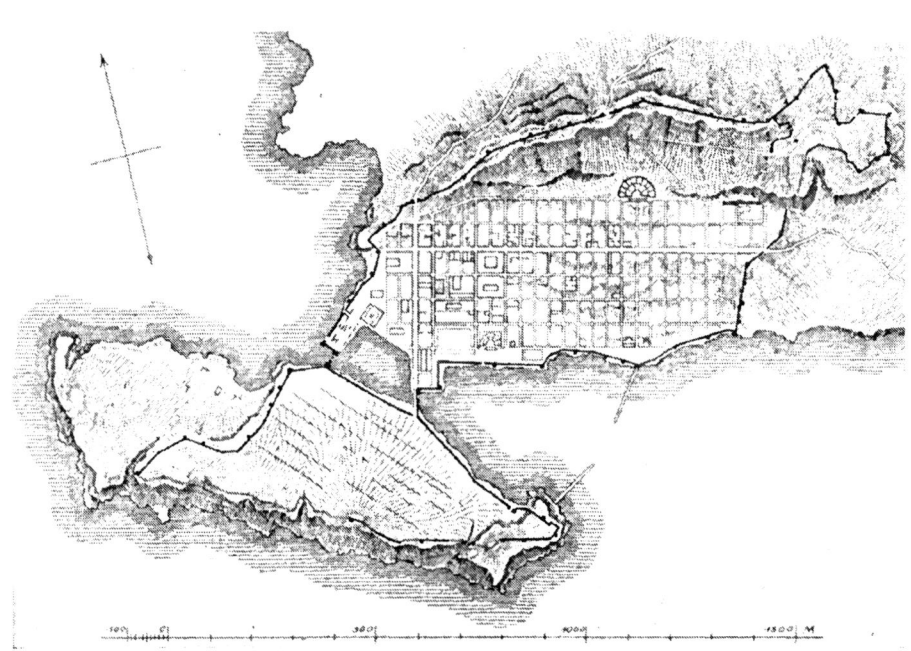

23. CNIDOS, ASIA MINOR. Plan by A. von Gerkan.

tion into the plains and man-made defense had to replace the defense provided by nature The oldest settlement of the Phrygian city of Apamea, Kelaenae, was situated on a high hill, but the later city, built by Antiochus Soter, spread over a plain crossed by rivers The hill was then used as a stronghold and artificial defenses were erected around the city.

Cities and defense

The type of man-made defenses has varied with the changes of offensive and defensive weapons, and these changes have, in turn, influenced the structure of the city as demonstrated in our illustrations 24, 25, 26 and 27. When firearms were invented, protection of the city confined within its walls became difficult. As firearms were perfected, those walls had to be replaced by forts outside the city. The city area was thereby increased. Modern aerial warfare has made all city concentrations dangerous. Protection in the future must be accomplished by disurbanization and dispersal.

Rise and decline of cities

The factors which led to the rise of a city may have already borne in them the seeds of its later retrogression and even decay For their change also brought about changes in the conditions essential to the city's life The shift of power and of sovereignty caused the growth of cities; it also caused their ultimate decline, as the many ruined cities of the Near East give abundant evidence. New religions gave rise to new temples, around which new cities grew while the older cities of extinct cults dropped into oblivion

When a new king ascended the throne in Egypt, for example, he erected a new palace and built a new city for his court and his administration This new city had, of course, no relation to the city which developed from a place of refuge. The reasons for its founding probably rooted in the magic ideology, the ancient rituals, based on animism, which caused primitive man to shun all the belongings of the dead When a deified ruler died, it was only natural and fitting that his entire city be abandoned and left to decay.[1]

The change of trade routes and communication lines, the increase of the size of ships, the formations of sandbanks in harbors—these also were circumstances which, creating at one time the conditions under which cities could grow, created at other times the conditions which made those cities decline Old trading centers and their cities and markets have lost their importance, even in our own day, because the railroad and the automobile have so widened the transportation radius. New centers and new markets have arisen, and with them new cities

---

[1] A Japanese custom, which prevailed into the nineteenth century, is equally interesting In Japan, the house of a deceased person was abandoned and no longer lived in

have come into commercial importance Soon we shall see new shifts conditioned by the airplane Many a seaport will decline, while those cities at junction points of airlines will gain importance as they become traffic centers for passengers and freight.

A city which owes its origin and development to its natural resources. or to a particular type of production, may sink to unimportance if its resources become exhausted, or its peculiar production processes are suspended. It may be abandoned and left to ruin while new resources and new methods of production give rise to new cities

We can distinguish four distinct economic stages in human development the comprehensive household economy, the city economy, the national economy; and finally the world economy. *Stages of economy*

The original basis of the household economy was production within the family, which later was extended to kinfolk and finally replaced by a highly developed slave economy. All goods were consumers' goods. used in the community where they were produced Everything was made in the home, whether that home was the most primitive household or a gigantic establishment manned by slaves as it came to be among the Romans or under the socage tenure of the Middle Ages

Something new came into the picture when hired labor began to be used An augmented form of the comprehensive household economy was created. The workmen came to the house merely to work Sometimes they did not even do this; the material necessary for their labor was sent to their homes This form of paid home production was usually based on the condition that the worker possessed tools—such as mills, looms, ovens.

Home production for wages was the beginning of skilled trades and of the city economy, with its division of labor The householder no longer conducted the entire productive process within his family, or on the manor, or with the help of slaves and serfs. One man produced the raw material, others made the product That product, however, passed through all stages of its manufacture in the same workshop.

City economy was based on the cooperation of the city and its vicinity. Most of the city's products were consumers' goods, used either in the city itself or in the surrounding countryside Only a small portion of the product was used for barter with other cities, and a still smaller portion—and this only much later—with other countries

Under the national economy, a fundamental change was effected. Most consumers' goods became trading goods. They were no longer

24. UAL-UAL, ABYSSINIA.

25. RAGUSA, DALMATIA.

DEVELOPMENT OF THE FORTIFIED CITY.
Ual-Ual (ill. 24) shows the primitive ditch and earthen wall. Ragusa (ill. 25) stone walls crowned with parapets for the defenders. Carcassonne (ill. 26) stone walls connected with towers to enable the de-

26. CARCASSONNE, FRANCE.

27. NARDEN, HOLLAND.

fenders to fight the attackers from two sides. Narden (ill. 27) shows how earthen walls again appear as it was discovered that they were a better protection against cannon balls.

made by an artisan for a definite customer, but were produced for unknown customers in a very expanded market. The price, once composed only of the cost of the raw material and labor, was increased by the return to the middleman, who neither produced nor consumed the product himself, but only sold it. At first, this method of distribution caused little change in the original process of production, but it was the precursor of present-day industry. As the factory system developed, the decentralized industries gave way to centralized production units, concentrated into huge industrial areas with an increased division of labor. This centralization and expansion changed the worker's position. The increasing division of the labor process and the greater mechanization lessened the importance of skilled labor. Unskilled labor or women and even children could now take its place. The necessity for disposing of the rising tide of goods and capital created the conditions for a world economy.

These individual phases of economy find expression in the pattern of their cities. The changes in production patterns had been brought about by the expansion of the economic sphere, from the household to the city, to the nation, to the world. The change was accelerated as needs became more diverse, and technology and transportation made rapid advances. The movement must, therefore, be regarded, not as an evolutionary succession of events, but as the characteristic expression of a certain stage of civilization, in every cultural sphere. With the increase of population and rising standards of living, the domestic agricultural produce and raw materials flowed out to trading centers and overseas markets. Exchange of domestic products of industry for raw materials and agricultural products from overseas ensued. The rising trade served not only to procure the necessities of life for the native population, but also to satisfy demands for luxury which domestic raw materials could not meet. The trade relations of the city of Assur on the Tigris, later the capital of the Kingdom of Assyria, with its colonies in Asia Minor, explain the development in the exchange of industrial produce for raw materials during the third millenium B.C. Trade was conducted over rivers and canals as well as over land routes. The so-called "Cappadocian" clay plates tell of an extensive money and credit system. The merchants were organized into a guild and regular postal communications existed.

Closely related to these trade relations and trade settlements was the expansion of living space. New settlements, new cities, grew up. New land was seized for colonies. The process is as characteristic of the past as of the present.

The city-economy ultimately expanded its economic sphere of influence New forms of production required a larger economic field The territorial state was developed in response to this economic need. The production in this territorial state continued to expand until the borders of the territory once more impeded full economic development Territorial economy engendered national economy and a corresponding national state

Freedom of trade and a spirit of liberalism broke the restraints left over from feudalism. Individual economic enterprise developed freely. All countries partook of this development, though the conditions in which it operated were, of course. varied Centralized national states were established all over the world. And because the impulse bringing them into being was the same the world around. the cities which originated from the national economy, or which were transformed by it, all presented the same characteristics To understand these characteristics one must understand the nature of the processes which created them

The division of labor. begun in the medieval city and continued in the territorial economy, reached its highest degree of development in the rising national economy, and ultimately in the world economy The new forms of production, based on the machine and its specialized division of labor, divided the process of production to an extent hitherto undreamed of At the same time, it concentrated producers at the place of production This concentration of labor implied the development of a labor market to meet the demands of industry It inevitably led to the formation of the large settlements which we think of as the modern city.

Meanwhile the railroad came into existence and the development of even the remotest parts of the country became possible With the new steam propelled ships. these railroads became part of a system whereby goods could be transported to and from all parts of the earth. The masses concentrated in the large cities. where domestic agriculture was non-existent or inadequate, could be supplied with food at comparative ease.

The world in which we live today is divided into large areas, some furnishing raw materials and food products in exchange for manufactured goods, some, as large industrial nations. trading the products of their factories for foods and raw materials. A world-wide finance economy provides credits for the development of manufacture and thus creates the pre-requisite for the growth of vast private enterprises. The result is the disappearance of the obligations which once bound

Cities of the nineteenth and twentieth century

society together. The workman becomes part of the labor process. He is directed by the industrialist, who is the only remaining link of communal relationship. And as the development of industry moves forward even that link becomes weakened. Ultimately even the industrialist is no longer an individual. He is replaced by the large corporation financed by banks or capital stock. A freedom from responsibility and obligation, unknown in other economies, develops under the protection of such anonymity.

Growth of population

The industrial development which we have just outlined was possible only because population, during the nineteenth century, increased tremendously. During the twelve preceding centuries, Europe's population had remained relatively constant. It stood at about 180,000,000. In the nineteenth century that population increased almost threefold. Improved hygienic conditions and the discoveries of natural science, especially medicine, were largely responsible for that increase. Infant mortality dropped, the life span increased. With the conquest of the world market, industry created the basis of existence for the masses of people it needed for large-scale production.

City and country

Migration to the city was one of the demands which this newly developed industry laid upon the people. It was necessary to draw into urban concentrations increasing numbers of the rural inhabitants. During the nineteenth century this was accomplished without draining away the population of rural areas. The number of people engaged in agriculture remained comparatively stable. Into the growing cities was drawn the surplus of the country population. For some time it seemed that this capacity of the city to absorb surplus population was unlimited. The absorption process was simplified by the fact that the new industry required only a small number of skilled workmen. It could use great numbers of the unskilled and semi-skilled, and the need for skill constantly decreased as specialization and mechanization moved forward. The city, which had been merely a trade market, had become a vast labor market as well. And its establishment as a labor market tended to draw into it more and more people.

Economic disorder

Under responsible and far-seeing leadership, such a huge development could have established a true national economy which, by raising living standards, could have created security for everyone. The means to accomplish this end were at hand. But those who guided the development of this individualistic economy had, unfortunately, no aims beyond the advantages of the individual, or the leading groups. Their fundamental creed was that the welfare of the entire community could be best served by the self-interested pursuit of individual ambitions.

This free economy also attempted to create a world economy, an expansion of the market based on private initiative. But because this international economy, like the free national economy, was not founded on actual human needs and their satisfaction, it was also doomed to failure Expansion of production was achieved by wasteful exploitation of natural resources The forms of finance economy, being closely linked with this development, settled more and more into the policy of self-interest The machine, and the steadily advancing specialization it made possible, created an almost unlimited capacity for production This capacity has been wrongly used and wastefully used and never fully used at all. This is the source of our economic disorder. That disorder is aggravated by the fact that most of the countries which were buyers and bases of raw material have themselves become industrialized and are now competitors seeking markets for their own surplus production And here are the roots of the economic catastrophe which is shaking the social structure of our time

This inorganic economy has, inevitably, brought about the equally inorganic development of the city. Cities which rose with this industrial development show the planlessness of their epoch

New types of cities

Two forms of industrial production can be distinguished, and each type influences the settlement forms to which it gives rise. Prime production is the first of these It rises where natural resources exist and it is relatively stable. Manufacture is the second Because it is largely dependent on transportation facilities, it rises at favorably located transportation centers Both forms require large aggregations of workers. Prime production, because of its greater stability, is not necessarily confined to large cities But manufacturing, being subject to considerable fluctuations of production, depends on the labor market and must, therefore, seek the large city where that labor market exists Thus two new types of cities have arisen which have little in common with earlier urban settlements· the purely industrial city, located at the source of raw materials, inhabited almost exclusively by workers: and the manufacturing city, which harbors not only large aggregations of workmen but also a great army of office workers Variations occur in the latter type according to the importance of a given settlement in either industry or trade.

Drawn by the call of developing industry, moving easily over the new transportation routes, more and more people crowded into the cities Populations grew to hundreds of thousands—to millions This huge massing of population presented problems with which the city was completely unable to cope. No plan for their orderly assimilation has

28 and 29. URBAN AND RURAL SKY.

A survey of the possibilities of war-time gardening within the area of Chicago shows the wide-spread contamination by excessive sulphur dioxide. Of this sulphur dioxide the report states: "It may burn the leaves of plants and limit the success of gardening." But what of the people living within these areas?

been even attempted. The great cities of our time are the product of empirical growth rather than of planning principle.

Three deficiencies — The inadequacy of these cities can be traced to three principal deficiencies brought about by the rapid and random growth of urban settlements *(ill. 32)*.

In the first place, no effort was made to locate industry in proper relation to residences. No thought was given to prevailing winds. Therefore, the smoke, soot, and fumes of our industrial cities constitute an evil with grave consequences to the health of the people who live there *(ills. 28 and 29)*.

In the second place, houses in the residential districts were built without the slightest thought to the need for sunlight on the part of the people who would live in those houses. The population density is highest in the worst and unhealthiest parts of the city. Recreational areas in those sections are direly needed. As they exist at present such residential districts are a danger, not only to the people who live there, but to the whole community. Crime and health statistics are witness to this fact *(ill 30)*.

In the third place, the disorder within the city area, the indiscriminate conglomeration of industrial, commercial, and residential districts, gives rise to almost insoluble traffic problems. Far more traffic conveyances than should be needed must be used. And even then traffic facilities continue to be inadequate. The antiquated street system, faithfully followed, adds danger for pedestrians and motorists alike and this danger mounts as traffic increases. Accidents occur and no way is found to prevent them or to relieve the inconveniences and confusions of transportation *(ill 31)*.

Recent technical achievements—electricity and the automobile—are tending to decentralize urban settlements just as the railroad and steam power formerly tended to centralize and concentrate them. Population which had been moving steadily into the city had somewhat reversed its course even before the advent of electricity. Suburban railroads began to carry people outside the city limits. New settlements arose along these lines, ever more distant from the city center. When the automobile came this exodus from the city increased in tempo.

Concentration and decentralization

Just as the technical means of our time tend to grow beyond the city and tend to disperse it, industry itself tends toward the same decentralization. Henry Ford has long recognized this trend. In *My Life And Work*, written in 1923, he says "The belief that an industrial country must concentrate its industry is, in my opinion, unfounded. That is only an intermediate phase in the development Industry will decentralize itself. If the city were to decline, no one would rebuild it according to its present plan. That alone discloses our own judgment on our cities. We have learned much through the concentration of the population. But therefrom stem all the

49

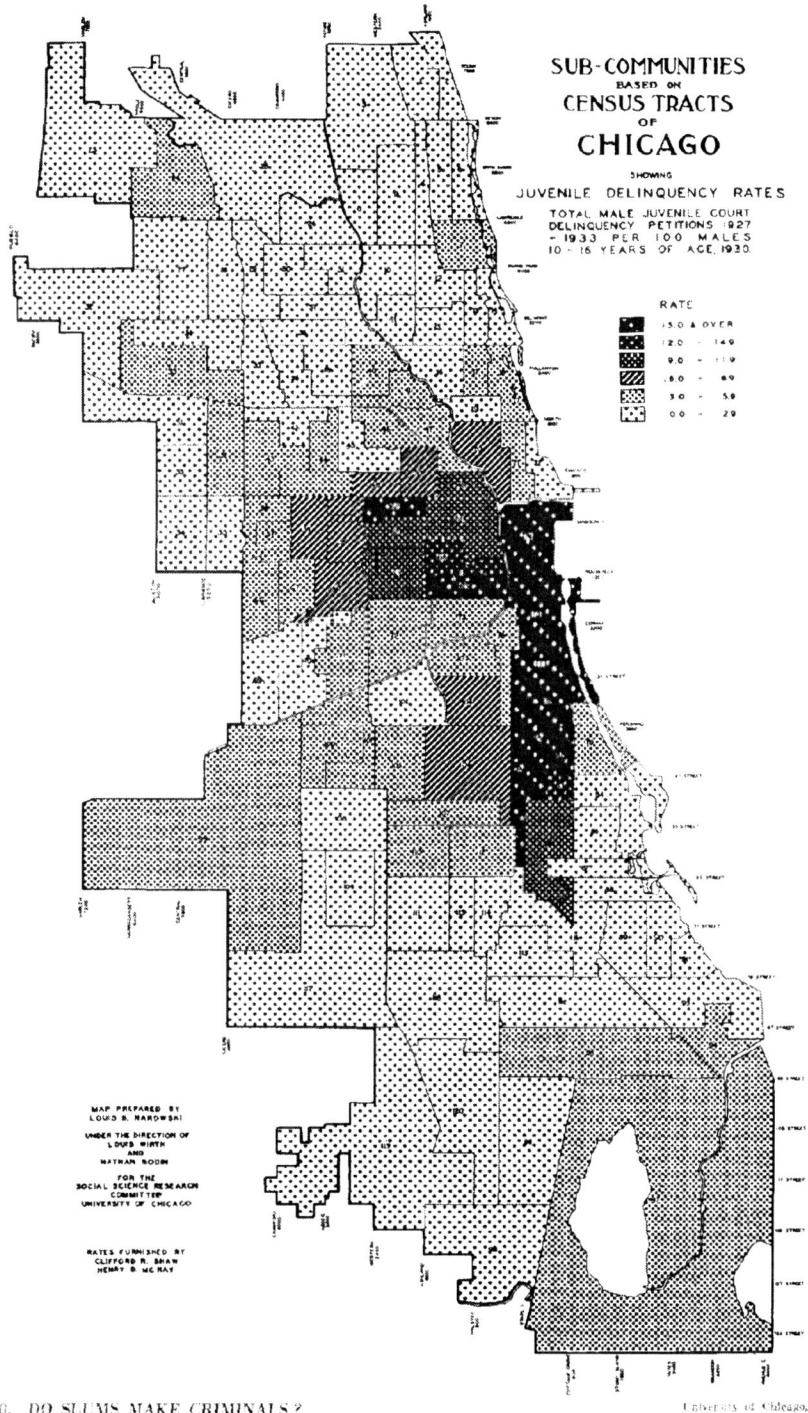

30. DO SLUMS MAKE CRIMINALS?

This map, prepared by the Social Science Research Committee of the University of Chicago, answers the question in the affirmative.

nuisances from which we suffer in the metropolis Working conditions and one's attitude toward life in the city are so unnatural that the instincts advise rebellion. Finally the general expenses in private life, as well as in business, grow so heavy in the metropolis that one can hardly meet them The maintenance of this investment, the expense of maintaining order, and providing transportation in these over populated districts are much greater than the communal advantages achieved through them"

Resettlement in the country as the exodus from the city gathers momentum has obvious and far-reaching benefits for human beings Gardens and small farms may give the security and the health which are lacking within the city walls Fresh air and sunshine come once more within reach In the future. large cities with high population density will no longer be needed As production methods advance, it will be increasingly possible for production plants to divide into small units and be dispersed over a wide area, perhaps the entire country Production would then become not only less expensive but also more efficient, for manufacture in the large city has come to be increasingly uneconomical and wasteful of energy and time

New possibilities

Today even the smallest settlement can be supplied with water, electricity, and heat, light, and power at rates lower than those of metropolitan utilities. Large settlements, with vast undeveloped areas, require extensive and expensive supply and drainage lines and unnecessarily extended transportation systems.

The tendency is toward the reestablishment of industry in rural areas with the accompanying development of self-sustaining communities which balance industrial and agricultural production.

It should be remembered that advancing technics result in the same large-scale production and displacement of labor in agriculture as they do in manufacturing and industry New problems arise. The country can no longer absorb the unemployed from the cities, the cities cannot absorb the unemployed from the farms An integration of industry and agriculture is feasible, but it must be as flexible as possible to meet our every requirement. It could then become the basis of real economic security.

Integration of industry and agriculture

Another force profoundly affecting city-planning today and tending also to accelerate decentralization is military necessity. The need for protection against attacks from the air is leading to the dispersal of residential settlements and industrial plants. Urban settlements are being spread out into the country so that city and countryside are merged

31. A TRAFFIC JAM.

The nation's loss from motor vehicle accidents in 1943 was 23,300 persons killed, and 800,000 injured. Sixty thousand of the injured were left some permanent impairment.

The death toll, though impressive, is 18 per cent less than the 1942 loss of 28,309; and 42 per cent below the 1941 all-time high of 39,969.

The direct economic losses resulting from 1943 traffic accidents are estimated at $1,200,000,000. This includes wage losses, medical expenses, overhead costs of insurance and motor vehicle property damage.

The 1943 traffic toll is the lowest since 1925, when it was 21,900. But, despite the sharp curtailment of motor vehicle use in 1943, the year's mileage was 84 per cent above 1925 levels, indicating a reduction in mileage rate of 42 per cent. Compared to 1942, and making the same allowances for travel change, the 1943 death toll is actually 5 per cent higher.

—From the preliminary 1944 edition of "Accident Facts" issued by the National Safety Council.

These decentralizing factors, which are changing the structure of the settlement, will influence all cities and all metropolitan centers. They will not eliminate metropolitan centers altogether. Such centers, evidence of the achievement of a nation, will continue to remain as economic, cultural and administrative focal points. Concentration and decentralization are not mutually exclusive. They can be combined so that each fulfills a useful function. The metropolis can well be made an economic and a cultural center without crowding into it vast numbers of people.

32. DISORDER AND CHAOS.

The problems of city planning in our day are so complex and so all-comprehensive that individual cities can no longer hope to solve them alone. This is coming to be realized here and there. In 1921, for instance, the Garden-City Society in England proposed to establish settlements in the coal regions of South Wales and Kent. The Society tackled its problem on a wide and systematic scale. It undertook exhaustive researches concerning natural resources and auxiliary resources, available and possible communication lines, and the composition, movement, and expansion of the population. Upon such researches was to be built a regional plan for the economic development, not of a single settlement or group of settlements, but of a wide regional unit. That process is suggestive of the trend of future planning. City planning must become more and more the regional planning of interdependent economic units.

Cities and regional planning

With the decentralization of the city and of industry, the exodus of large groups of population sets in. To find expedient measures for this movement is the real task of planning in our time Administrative measures in city and regional planning can be successful only when they have a comprehensive national basis. The whole nation must be considered as one economic unit in which each section fulfills its respective function in relation to the whole. Within the large unit, city and country—industry and agriculture—must perform productive tasks in the interest of all people. When we understand that city and country are parts of one organism, the economic disruption between city and country will disappear. The present destructive division, with its very unfavorable results, will be replaced by constructive partnership.

Decentralization unavoidable

The process of decentralization is still going on. It is beyond our power to stem or to reverse it. It will affect the life of the city as profoundly as the railroad and the steam engine once affected it. But we can, if we understand the implications of this process and realize the possibilities of the new development, direct it into proper channels It is of vital importance that we do so.

A new spirit

Now as always, the conditions essential to the life of a city are dependent on social, spiritual, political and economic forces Each change of these forces effects change in the structure of the city. We are at present in the midst of a process of profound and far-reaching change, which will inevitably exert its influence upon our cities

But city planning is not merely the expression of changing social patterns; it is also a positive force in the development of those patterns. It is a social and an economic task It may thus function creatively to build the structure of the future in which the economic philosophy is based not on arbitrariness but on the necessities of life for men—a structure in which people and nations and regions may find complete development within a world-wide federation

Gradually modern technics will achieve their true importance and be recognized as the indispensable tool of man rather than his master.

Technical and economic problems may seem to occupy the center of the stage today It nevertheless remains true that their adequate solution depends upon the resolving of momentous social problems The solutions we seek for our cities must be based upon economic realities. They must also be infiltrated with a new spirit

33. THE CITY IN THE LANDSCAPE.

PART TWO

ELEMENTS OF CITY PLANNING

The rapid and planless growth of our cities, during the last hundred years, was, as we have seen, responsible for their malformations. We have customarily assumed that control of such growth is impossible. Social and constitutional progress lags far behind the achievements of technology, and in our cities this lag is evidenced by discrepancies between the means available and actually retained—a discrepancy which causes many difficulties of our cities. Everywhere natural means have passed into disuse; technical facilities have been substituted for them. And our cities have become increasingly complicated in their structure because we have allowed technic to become a supporting rather than a creative factor in their planning.[1]

Natural and technical means

---

[1] By systematically neglecting the simplest elements of city planning, we have provided a large and profitable field to all the palliative devices of engineering: where we eliminate sunlight we introduce electric light; where we congest business we build skyscrapers; where we overcrowd the thoroughfares with traffic we burrow subways; where we permit the city to become congested with a population whose density would not be tolerated in a well designed community, we conduct water hundreds of miles by aqueducts to bathe them and slake their thirst; where we rob them of the faintest trace of vegetation or fresh air, we build metalled roads which will take a small portion of them, once a week, out into the countryside. It is all a very profitable business for the companies that supply light and rapid transit and motor cars, and the rest of it; but the underlying population pays for its improvements both ways—that is, it stands the gratuitous loss, and it pays "through the nose" for the remedy.

These mechanical improvements, these labyrinths of subways, these audacious towers, these endless miles of asphalted streets, do not represent a triumph of human effort, they stand for its comprehensive misapplication. Where an intentive age follows methods which have no relation to an intelligent and human existence, an imaginative one would not be caught by the necessity. By turning our environment over to the machine we have robbed the machine of the one promise it held out—that of enabling us to humanize more thoroughly the details of our existence.

Lewis Mumford: *Sticks and Stones*, New York, 1924.

To solve so complex a problem we must go back to fundamentals. We must learn to see the intricate simply, even naively. We must disentangle the chaos in our conceptions. We must define our purposes. Only then can we plan and build our cities to our satisfaction. Only when our aims are clear in our own minds can we proceed to find ways and means to fulfill those aims.

The city and its different parts

A first step in this clarifying process is recognition of the fact that the city should be organized into industrial, commercial, residential and recreational areas, and that all these areas must be connected with each other by transportation facilities. The essential task of city planning is the proper placing and the organic order of the various elements of the city.

The individual and society

The second step in our approach to city planning is the acknowledgement that, inasmuch as society is composed of individuals, city planning should meet the requirements of the individual as well as of society as a whole. City planning must take account of both individual and collective needs and their inter-relations. Sometimes the requirements of the individual are identical with those of society; but more often the two kinds of need are divergent. Any permanent solution in city planning must, therefore, balance individual needs with the needs of society, resolving insofar as possible the inherent conflict between individualism and communalism.[1]

Location, lay-out and size of a settlement

The task of planning a settlement is more than the determination of its site, its size, and its lay-out. Whatever plan is proposed must be modified by geographic location. Topographical conditions, existing natural resources, production possibilities, must be taken into account, as must also the relation of the site to transportation facilities. Sometimes military or political considerations are important. Economic considerations are always of great weight, for the settlement planned will be dependent upon the means of existence available to its people. They may make their living by industry alone, or by industry combined with agriculture or horticulture, and their mode of livelihood must be reflected in their community's plan. The size and layout of a settlement is also influenced by the particular kind of industry established there. Any settlement, to be effective, should be large enough to make possible the maintenance of communal hygienic,

---

[1] "If I might pursue the figure of speech, I might say that the whole collectivist error consists in saying that because two men can share an umbrella therefore two men can share a walking stick. Umbrellas might possibly be replaced by some kind of common awnings, covering certain streets from particular showers. But there is nothing but nonsense in the notion of swinging a communal stick, it is as if one spoke of twirling a communal moustache."—G. K. Chesterton, *What Is Wrong With The World*. New York 1910.

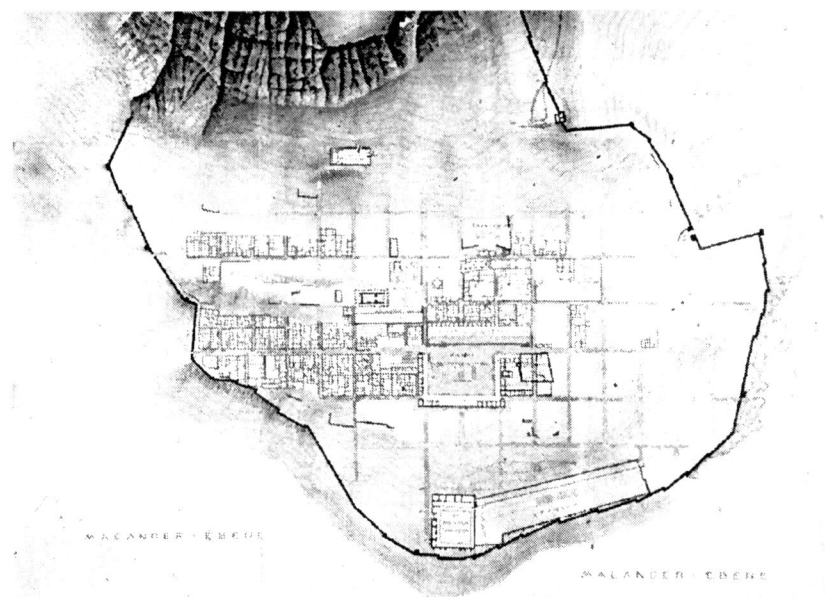

34. PLAN OF PRIENE, ASIA MINOR. See also illustration 1.

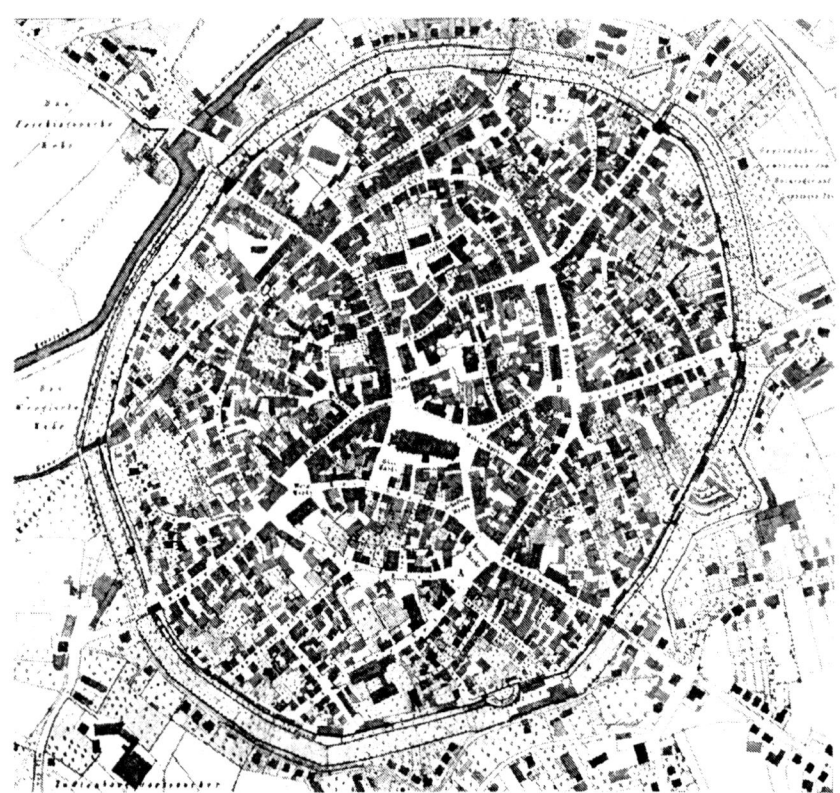

35. PLAN OF NOERDLINGEN. See also illustration 10.

technical, and cultural institutions within it. To industrial settlements will be added economic and cultural centers. Eventually the planning of metropolitan centers may be required to relate and connect the small settlements, by means of transportation facilities. into one homogeneous formation.

The lay-out of an industrial city will differ from that of an administrative or commercial city. Harbor cities will be structurally unlike university towns, state or national capitals. But no matter how much these various urban structures may differ, the same principles of city planning will determine their lay-out and structure

Traffic difficulties; a symptom of disorder

All existing cities have their orientation toward a center This orientation was sound as long as the population and the area of a city did not exceed certain limits In communities where people traveled on foot, the marketplace was logically the center around which the city expanded concentrically This was true whether the cities were of the so-called organic type like Noerdlingen *(ills 10 and 35)*, or of the geometric type like Priene *(ills 1 and 34)*

In the sprawling modern city of mechanized transportation. however, the structure of the centric pedestrian city is no longer adequate or logical As all means of transportation converge toward an arbitrary center, their zones of influence overlap and traffic hazards steadily increase At the city's periphery, meanwhile, a notable shortage of transportation facilities prevails The traffic diagram of London *(ill 36)* shows both the typical congestion in the center and the lack of transportation facilities at outlying points

Study of the ratios between increasing population and increasing traffic give interesting results. In 1871 a certain metropolis, with a population of one million, had ten million passengers annually on its public carriers. In other words, the people of that city made each year ten trips per capita. In 1924 the population of that metropolis had increased to four million and the number of passengers to 1,372,000,000 The people now made 343 trips per capita. While the population had increased four-fold, the number of passengers had increased nearly forty-fold This tremendous increase in traffic is accounted for only partly by the increase in population and the consequent expansion of the city area. The city's disorganization was an even more important factor in the over-burdening of inter-urban traffic No attempt was made in the growing city to establish convenient relations between residential and industrial districts. Industrial districts were scattered at random As the city of free economy became a labor market, workers had to make frequent changes in their

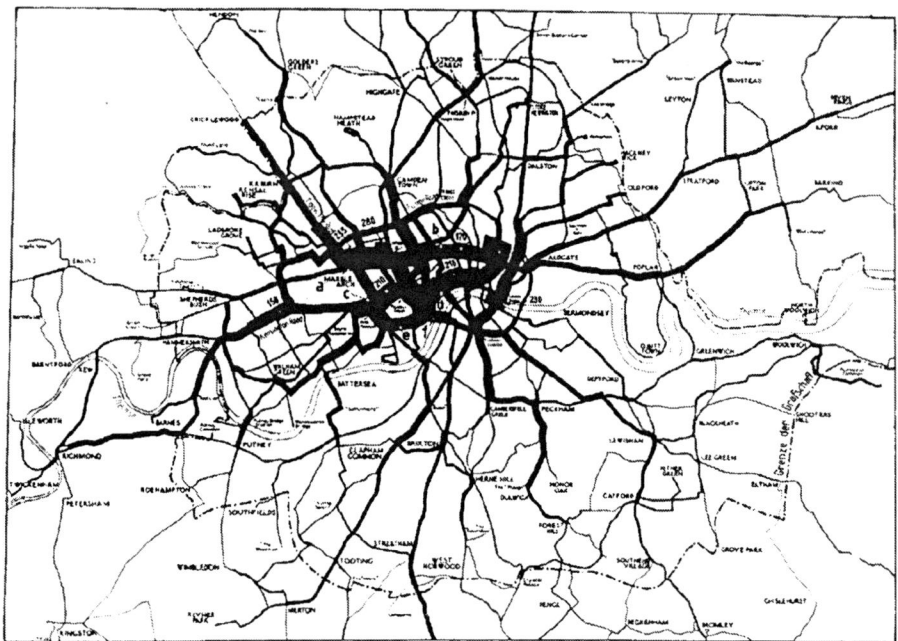

36. TRAFFIC DIAGRAM OF LONDON.

The figures indicate the number of busses passing through the central arteries in one hour.

places of employment. Paradoxical conditions arise as a consequence. Hundreds of thousands of workers who live at one end of the city work at the opposite end.[1] Over-burdening of inter-urban traffic lines naturally results, and existing mal-conditions and disturbances are aggravated. Some students of the situation believe that permanent improvement can be achieved by reorganizing the traffic system. But that alone would not remove the cardinal structural defects which are the outcome of social and economic conditions. Such a solution would be like treating the symptoms of a disease instead of the disease itself.

During the last half century certain principles have been suggested and general solutions sought for the problems involved in city planning, which aim not at the mere treatment of symptoms but rather at the reorganization of the city and its structural formation. They presuppose a fundamental replanning. Two distinct groups of propositions have been advanced. One is based on the old centric system.

<small>New suggestions: The centric and the ribbon system</small>

---

[1] A commuter who spends one hour each way five days a week fifty weeks a year for thirty-six years winds up having devoted the equivalent of nine full working years to travel in uncomfortable circumstances through unattractive surroundings with which he has always been roughly familiar.—*Fortune*, May 1943. New York.

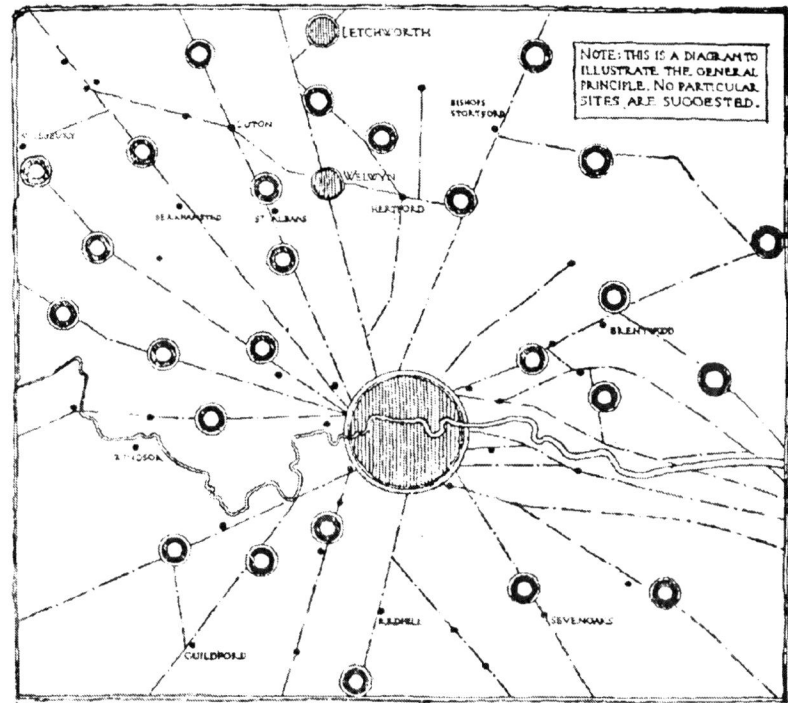

37. RAYMOND UNWIN, Diagram for Greater London.

The other suggests the development of a new linear or ribbon system. It is worth while to study the virtues and the faults of both approaches to our problem.

In making such a study let us recognize at the outset that both proposals seek to clarify and simplify the relationships between areas, to place a definite limitation on size, and to solve the traffic problem.

Howard and Unwin: The satelite town

The system of satellite towns developed by Raymond Unwin is the best known example of the solution proposed by the first group. Unwin's plan is based upon the ideas of Ebenezer Howard, who tried to bring about an integration between industry and agriculture in his plans for the development of "Garden Cities."[1]

Unwin *(ill. 38)* advocates that only those institutions which are indispensable for the settlement should remain in the city center. Around this center and directly connected with it, should be residential districts for the people who work there. Satellite cities should be located at a suitable distance from these residential districts. These satellite cities, relatively independent, should each consist of four parts. One part would serve industrial purposes, the other three would be residential districts. Each part would accommodate four to six thousand

[1] Ebenezer Howard: *"Tomorrow, A Peaceful Path to Real Reform,"* London, 1898; and *"Garden Cities of Tomorrow,"* London, 1902.

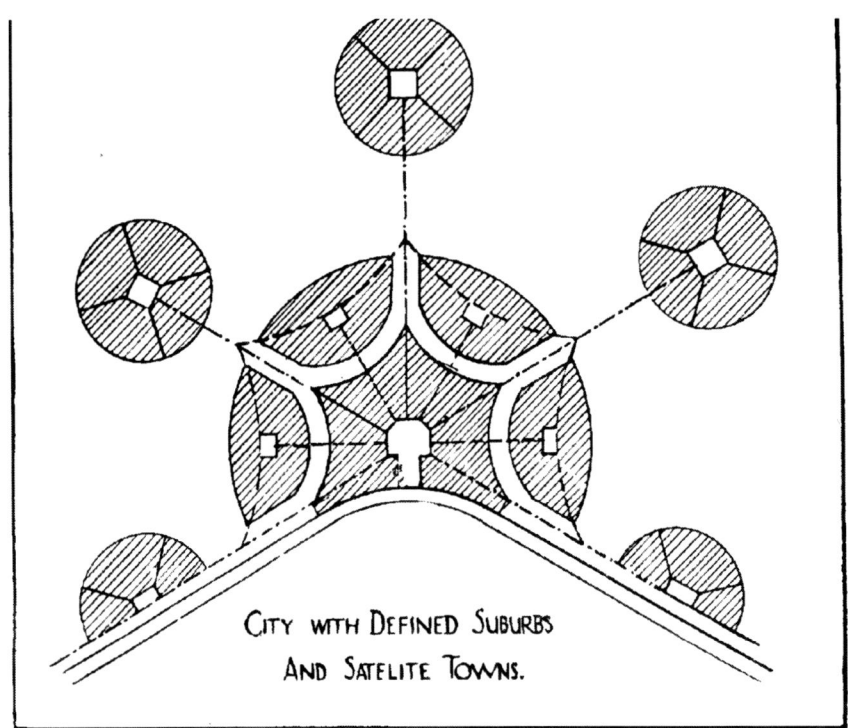

38. RAYMOND UNWIN, City with defined suburbs and satellite towns.

inhabitants, "in order to maintain a local market, adequate for the supply of daily needs." "Three of such units," Unwin notes, "so arranged that all can use one shopping center, would be sufficient to maintain a really adequate number of shops, and besides would allow the maintenance of a recreational center with institutes, theatres, and the like." These partially independent satellite cities would not need local means of transportation. They would be connected with each other and with the city itself by a transportation system.

Open spaces would be provided between the center of the settlement and the various satellite cities, and also between the satellites. These free spaces would serve as recreation areas and would provide space for future expansion. The possibility of future growth, however, is imperfectly solved by this plan. Such growth could disturb the equilibrium of the settlement and might thus jeopardize the entire system.

An application of the satellite system, modified by existing conditions, is Unwin's diagram for Greater London *(ill. 37)*. The diagram shows how satellite towns could be arranged around London.

Eric Gloeden *(ills. 39 and 40)*, worked along somewhat similar lines to those of Unwin, but arrived at a different solution. He no longer

Gloeden: The coordinated city

61

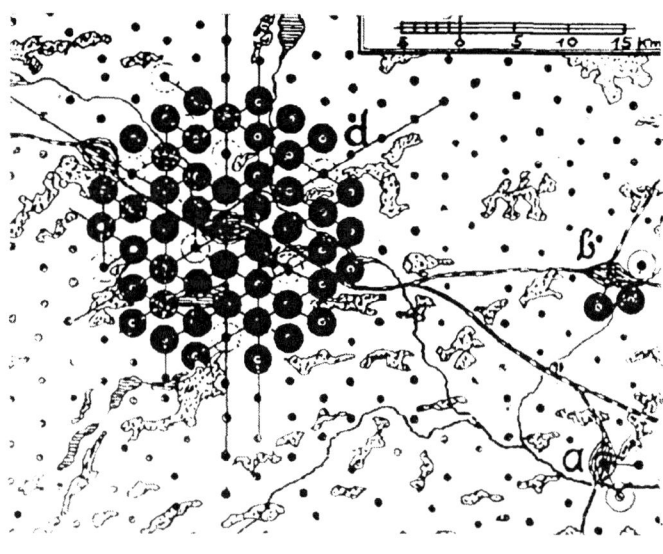

39. ERIC GLOEDEN, Coordinated system of different settlements.

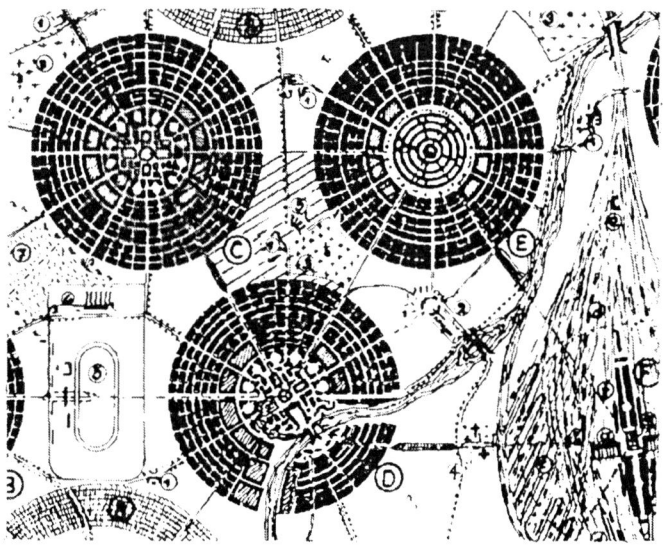

40. Detail of above plan.

advocates a definite center for his settlement. The center of the city, instead of being dominant, becomes "first among equals." New settlements are grouped around the original settlement, separated from it and from each other by vacant spaces. Each of these new settlements is a homogeneous whole, so limited in size as to make local mechanical traffic unnecessary. The settlement units proposed by Gloeden are considerably larger and much closer together than those which Unwin suggests. The number of their inhabitants is determined by the nature

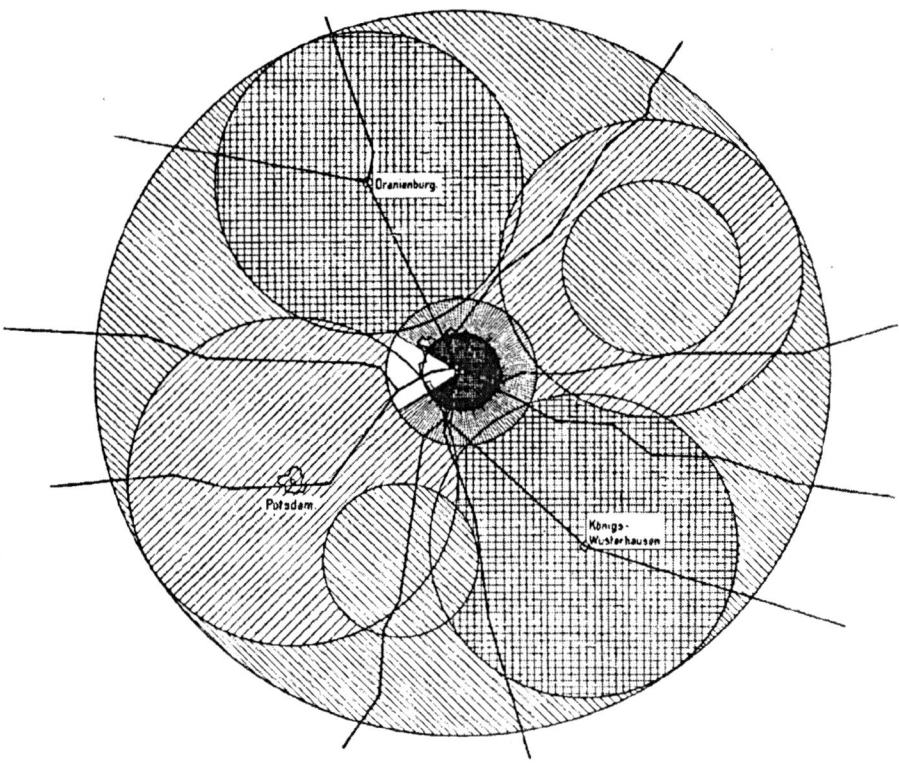

41. MARTIN MAECHLER, Diagram of Berlin.

of the activities assigned to them. With such specialization in the city units, a new city type develops, having clearly marked characteristics of its own. The physiognomy of one settlement would be very different from that of its neighbor settlements.

According to this plan, no settlement is to exceed a population of 100,000. Its radius is to be not more than three quarters of a mile. The proposed area is one and three quarters square miles. About ten to fifteen minutes' walk, therefore, will bring the remotest resident to the center of his settlement. That center is to serve the purposes of production, trade, or administration. A belt of woods and fields between the various units will be at least one-third of a mile wide. Expansion will be accomplished, not by enlarging the existing units as it would be under the Unwin plan, but by adding new units. These new units will be connected with each other by a railroad system. Any number of them may be added as necessity arises.

The disadvantage of Gloeden's plan is that it calls for the location of the industrial area in the center of the settlement. Residential districts located around this center and the residential districts of nearby units would inevitably suffer from the noxious gases and fumes of industry if they were situated in the "shadow" of the prevailing winds

Maechler: Functional organization of Berlin

Martin Maechler *(ill. 41)* based his diagram of the proposed reorganization of Berlin on the centric system. An area of thirty miles radius is projected, with the city hall as its center. This area is divided on the basis of the different demands of economic, social, and cultural life. Efficient arrangement of the areas of industry, commerce, recreation, education, and residence is provided

Berlin is the seat of administration and industry but its dominant function is commerce. The city's center is, therefore, given to commerce. That center occupies a circular area with a radius of five miles. This circular area is encompassed by a ring-like area with a radius of seven miles. Expansion of the commercial area is thus foreseen and provided for. From the West, a sector of 60 degrees cuts into this area. In it are located administrative and representative edifices, hotels, institutes of art, science, research, and education. In a large outer ring, are the residential, industrial, and recreational areas. Adjacent to the industrial areas are residential districts for their workers. Between the industrial areas, and along the rivers, in a northeast-southwest direction, lie the residence areas of people employed in the commercial and administrative area

Such a city formation obviously requires the comprehensive transportation system which is necessarily connected with the centric system. One of the weaknesses of this plan is evident at this point Maechler tries to solve the traffic problem by planning a central station, a junction for the main railroad lines leading from North to South and from East to West. He makes this station the focal point of all suburban lines, and thus affords convenient transportation facilities for the whole city

Le Corbusier "Une ville contemporaine"

Le Corbusier's "Une Ville Contemporaine" *(ill. 42)* is likewise based on the centric system. It illustrates how a metropolis could be developed and arranged architecturally. Le Corbusier's principles are these: to de-congest the centers of our cities; to augment their density, to increase the transportation facilities; and to have areas for parks and open spaces. In the center of his city is the hub of traffic, the central station, which is largely a subterranean building. Its roof is two storeys above the ground level of the city and it forms an aerodrome for aero-taxis. This aerodrome is connected with the subway

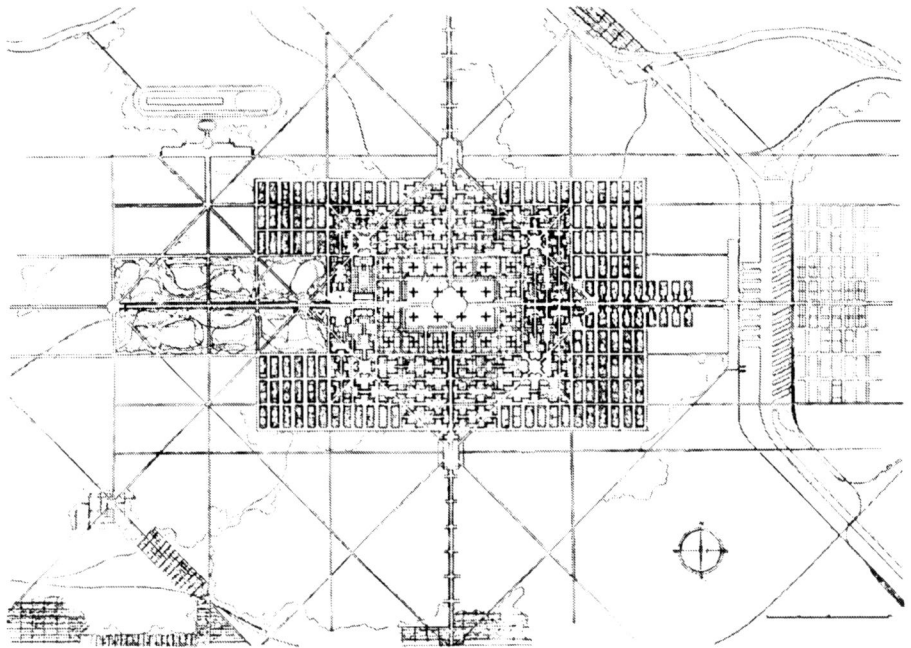

42. LE CORBUSIER, "Une Ville Contemporaine."

43. LE CORBUSIER, Replanning of the center of Paris.

lines, the suburban lines, and the main lines. The platforms for these lines are located in three storeys under the ground level of the city. This traffic center is also the crossing point of the two main highways. It therefore connects all main traffic facilities.

The business area surrounds the traffic center. Here in order to increase the open space, Le Corbusier arranges this building vertically. Twenty-four skyscrapers are provided. Each has a capacity of from ten to fifty thousand people. The entire area, therefore, can accommodate from four to six hundred thousand employees. Each skyscraper is surrounded by parks and has a direct connection with the subway.

Next to the business area is the residential area with its apartment houses. Eastward from the center is the industrial area, separated from the residence area by a park. In the open country around the city are the suburbs, built as garden cities after the scheme of the satellite system.

Le Corbusier later applied his system of skyscrapers in his proposition for the reconstruction of the center of Paris *(ill 43)*, to show how an existing city might be rebuilt. Le Corbusier's plan may be considered as the most perfect application of the centric system to a large community. It shows, not only all the advantages, but also all the disadvantages of the centric system. Above all it shows that working areas cannot be connected in such a way that means of transportation can be eliminated.[1] But whatever are the weaknesses of his plan, Le Corbusier did find a new relationship between city plan and buildings, a new scale of measurement. He gained open space by concentration and thus brought openness into the city.[1]

Circular and street village

During the last few decades, a new plan of urban organization has been evolved which seems better adapted to our present-day demands than the centric system. As the centric system developed from the ancient circular village *(ill 44)* which grew out of the need for defense, so also has the ribbon development grown out of an ancient fore-runner—the one-street village *(ill 45)* where houses were built on both sides of a single thoroughfare, where gardens lay behind the houses, and fields stretched beyond the gardens.

---

[1] In *La Ville Radieuse*, Le Corbusier presents a city diagram based on the linear system but does not take all the advantages which this system of planning offered. If he had conceived them he could have established a rational relationship between the various parts of the city, and by connecting them in walking distance he could have eliminated entirely local means of passenger transportation.

44. CIRCULAR VILLAGE. The origin of the centric system.

45. STREET VILLAGE. The origin of the ribbon system.

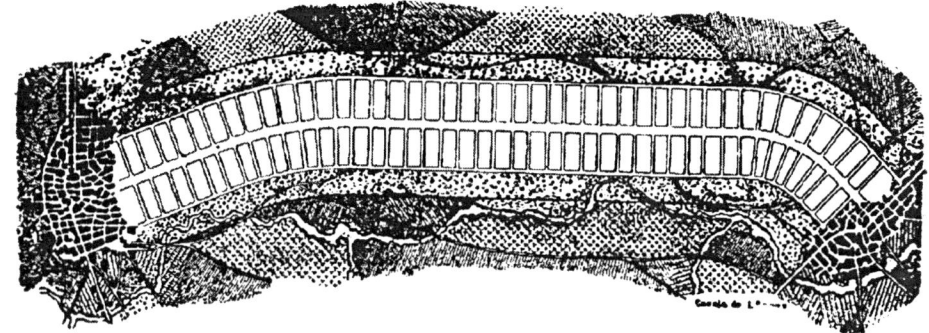

46. SORIA Y MATA, La Ciudad Lineal.

Soria y Mata: "La Ciudad Lineal"

In its present form, the ribbon system of town development traces its origin to the Spanish writer Soria y Mata[1] who suggested, as early as 1882, that cities be built along their main arteries of communication. He claimed that the city of the future would be so built, and suggested that such a city might so expand that at its ends might lie Cadiz and St. Petersburg, or Peking and Brussels. "If you lay railroads and streetcar lines, gas, water, and electric mains along one principal channel and place, at fixed intervals, some small buildings, intended for local administrative offices, all the problems will be solved which the concentration of population in the centric city brought about. The expansion of such a city would be simple: at any point along the line where it is necessary or topographically possible a new town could be started at an angle to the main line, like the branch of a tree."

The scheme of Soria y Mata was originally intended to connect two densely populated cities *(ill. 46)*. A thoroughfare was to be run between them. On both sides of this main channel residential zones were to be placed in the adjoining countryside. "The character of infinity, typical of the ribbon town which can be elongated on two sides while it is limited in depth, makes it an ideal form for civilization and culture," he said. Soria y Mata did not know the automobile and never dreamed of its influence on city planning. But by separating the street system of the residential area from the main thoroughfare he found the solution for the problem the motor car would some day cause.

Wright's "Broad Acre City"

Frank Lloyd Wright's "Broadacre City"[2] *(ill. 47)* shows how the present-day highway could well form the vertebrae of such a ribbon settlement, and how such a settlement could be connected with the countryside, combining agriculture with industry. His model shows

---
[1] Soria y Mata: *La Ciudad Lineal*, Madrid 1931.
[2] Frank Lloyd Wright: *Broadacre City*, Taliesen, 1940.

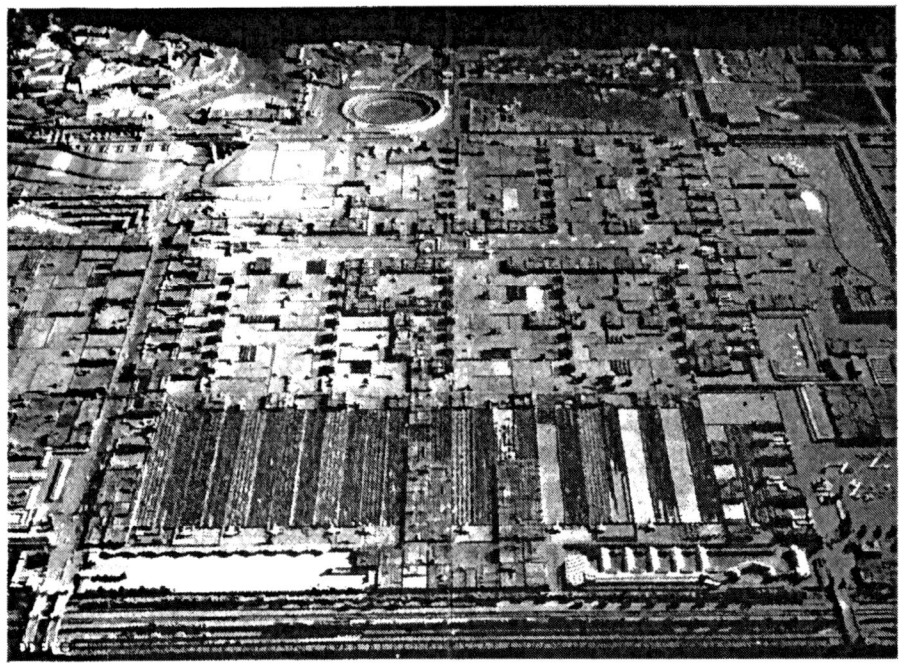

47. FRANK LLOYD WRIGHT, Broadacre City.

four square miles of typical countryside along a highway. Broadacre City provides homes for not only the families but it includes all the elements of our social structure: the correlated farm; the factory— with its smoke and gases eliminated by the use of coal at the mines; the decentralized school; the residences differing in type and size. Traffic here moves safely and swiftly. The government functions are simplified, with common interests put into coordination for all. Here are small farms, small houses for industrial workers, small schools, and a small university. Here are even small laboratories for professional men.

The minimum land allotted to a childless family is one acre. According to the number of children, the land allotments increase to five or more acres per family. The houses vary with individual choice. "There is the professional house, with its laboratory; the minimum house, with its workshop; the medium house; and the house of machine-age luxury. We speak of them as an one-car house, a two-car house, a three-car house, and a five-car house."

If Broadacre City were built it would demonstrate how city and country can be connected and become a unit. "Broadacre City would not only

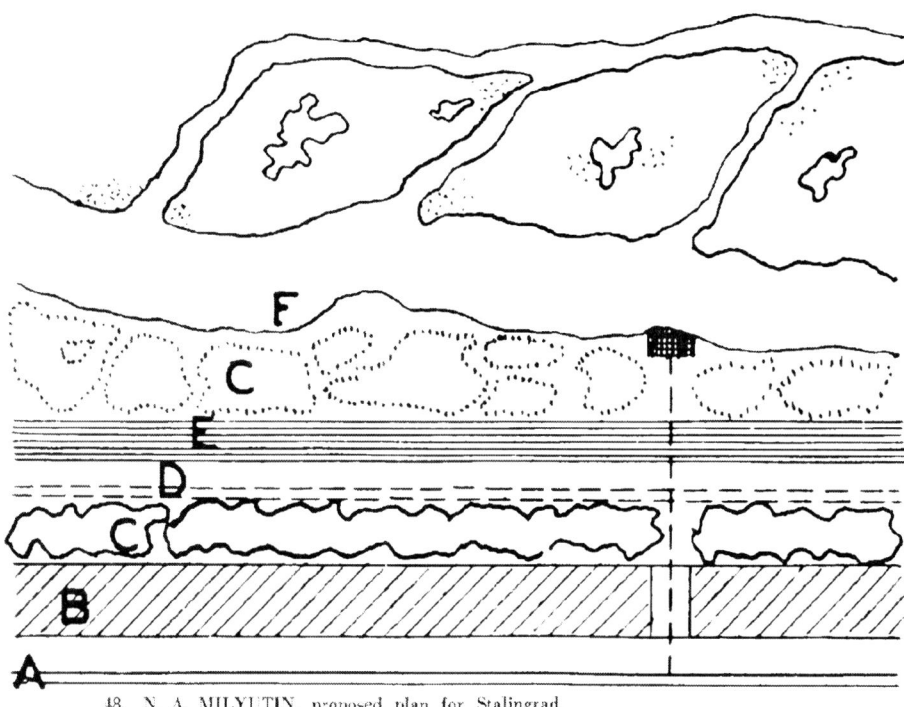

48. N. A. MILYUTIN, proposed plan for Stalingrad.
A—Railroad. B—Industry. C—Park. D—Highway. E—Residential area. F—River Volga.

preserve the integrity and beauty of the great nature-features that happen to be its site, but would add to them another beauty, considered and designed. This would come about as the natural result of a new integrity of planning and building, with appropriate systems of planning and cultivation in harmony with nature, but not naturalistic."

Milyutin's Stalingrad   N. A. Milyutin,[1] a Russian city planner, also arrived at a ribbon system for cities. In his diagram of Stalingrad *(ill. 48)* the transportation artery forms the vertebra of the settlement. He divides the city into six parallel zones: railroad; area of production (industry and industrial schools); green belt with main highway; residential area (dwellings, schools, administrative and communal buildings, theatres); recreational area with playgrounds, and agricultural area. This arrangement makes it possible to reach the industrial area quickly, to supply the population with agricultural products, and to place the industrial zone between the main arteries of railroad and highway.

[1] N. A. Milyutin, *"Sotzgorod,"* Moscow 1930.

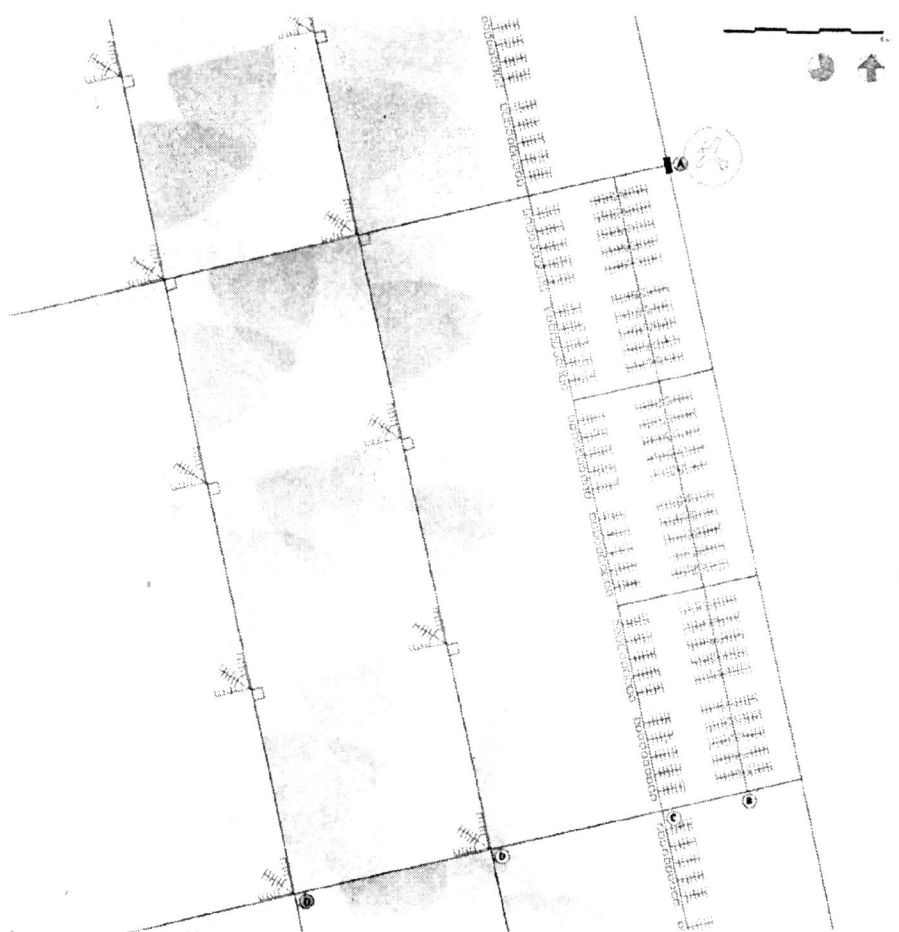

49. L. HILBERSEIMER: PLANNING SYSTEM.
A—Main traffic artery with station and airport. B—Commercial area. C—Smokeless industry. D—Smoke-producing industry.

Milyutin aims to bring industrial and agricultural production, administration, education, and housing into proper relationship. He establishes a scheme for an industrial settlement which he believes will provide for the undisturbed growth of the city.

Hilberseimer's planning system

The author of this book has himself developed a planning system *(ill. 49)* based on an independent settlement unit, limited in size and containing within itself all the necessary elements of a city segregated according to their function. In this plan, the backbone of the settlement unit is the main traffic artery. On one side of that artery are located the industrial areas; on the other side, first the buildings for commerce and administration set within a green belt, and beyond them the residential area surrounded by a park with schools, playgrounds and community buildings in it. An agricultural area adjoins this park

Settlement units of this type could be combined into groups according to requirements and could be modified as necessity arose. The settlement groups would form linear or point-formed, fanlike patterns, the exact form of the group being determined by the analysis of the settlement's function and by the conditions peculiar to each situation. Within these groups the residential areas would be within walking distance of the working area. The groups would be related to and connected with each other by a simplified traffic system. Because of the flexibility of this plan, the city in which it is used might be large or small, might increase or decrease in size, but it would always remain a working entity. Each group within the city could be extended or reduced in size without disturbing the life of the city as a whole. The settlement would decrease in density toward the open country. The open spaces between the groups could be used for gardening and farming. And such garden spaces, taken together with the adjoining agricultural areas, would achieve an integration between industry and agriculture.

Comparison of the centric and the ribbon system

To make a fair comparison between the centric system and the ribbon system and to weigh the economic merits of each, we need to consider two ideal areas of equal size and similar problems, one treated according to the centric principles, the other according to the linear. Such a comparison is afforded in two plans, one by Ludwig Sierks and the other by Peter Friedrich. Sierks worked at the problem by the centric system. Friedrich made a comparative solution by ribbon development. Let us consider these two solutions to determine which meets better, for example, the traffic problem with which both propose to deal.

The centric plan of Sierks *(ill 50)* calls for thirty-six terminals from which two trains will leave each hour. The ribbon plan of Friedrich *(ill 51)* requires only twelve terminals. From each of these six trains will leave every hour. The total number of trains is the same for both plans—seventy-two. In the centric system, however, the trains leave every half hour; in the ribbon system, every ten minutes. The average distance between center and terminal in the centric system is 3.5 miles, in the ribbon system, 4 miles. The running time in the ribbon system, therefore, is greater than in the centric system. This extra running time is offset, however, by shorter waiting time, for

50. LUDWIG SIERKS.
Centralized traffic system.

51. PETER FRIEDRICH.
Traffic system in ribbon development.

three times as many trains are running in this system as are scheduled in the centric system. In the latter system, the number of trains would increase toward the center because the different zones of influence would overlap as the center is approached. In the ribbon system, the number of trains will remain the same in all parts except in the center line where all trains meet. The accessibility to means of transportation is, therefore, practically the same throughout the entire area. The superiority of the ribbon system, as far as transportation is concerned, is evident.

The planning ideas which we have examined reveal the elements of the new city and the principles which govern the relationship of these elements. We are forced to conclude that the centric system, when it

Conclusion

exceeds the limits set by pedestrian traffic, will never solve the problems which face us today The more the city increases in size and population, the more impossible it becomes to cope with such problems Each new city block multiplies the difficulties at the city's center

All the proposals made, with the exception of those of Maechler and Le Corbusier, propose the establishment of working areas and residential areas within walking distance of each other so that local traffic may be reduced as much as possible This would lead to decentralization because it would divide the city into different and independent functional elements The linear or ribbon system, especially when it is combined with point-formed settlements which increase its usefulness and flexibility, is far superior to the centric system for the needs of our day.

Decentralization is one of the trends of the present. We are now able to concentrate what should, for human convenience, be concentrated, and to disperse over a widening area what should, for human welfare, be so dispersed As we break through unnecessary concentration and centralization, our aim is to achieve an integration between industry and agriculture to the benefit of the individual and of the community as a whole

Medical science, recognizing the dangers of too much specialization, claims that there is no disease—only diseased persons City planners likewise should understand that only the whole can be dealt with when improvement is sought—never the isolated part. It is of greatest importance that special problems be considered, not individually, but in relation to the whole Only then can the city be truly reorganized.

City planning and housing

The structure of city areas should depend upon the functions they are planned to serve The nature of their industries will determine the layout of industrial areas. The structure of commercial and administrative area must be adapted to the needs of commerce and administration. The residential area can be planned on definite basic principles, modified by geographical and topographical conditions. When we remember that these basic principles are rooted in the needs—psychological, social, physical—of the people who live in the area, it is clear that everything which affects the mode of living of these people is properly a part of the settlement plan. The plan of the houses, the distances between them, and their connection with the street system are details of city planning which we cannot overlook.

A satisfactory solution of the problems of city planning can be achieved only when plans for the whole city and plans for the houses in it are both taken into consideration. Only then will it be possible to meet the social, economic, psychological, and hygienic requirements of good human living.

We recognize certain well-defined types of houses row houses, attached houses, detached houses, and apartment houses. Any of these can be satisfactory if it is built with regard for its purpose Any of them can be unsatisfactory if purpose is neglected

Types of dwellings

The one-family house is generally regarded as the type which best fulfills the social, psychological, and hygienic requirements of life It will always be the ideal type of dwelling for families because it connects the house with a garden, a playground for children, and provides the privacy necessary for relaxation and recreation The row-house may achieve a considerable amount of privacy also if it is planned carefully and adequately It can, however, never be quite as satisfactory as the free-standing house

The apartment house is in disfavor today and the opposition to it is not unjustified Most such houses today represent only the negative aspects of this type of dwelling. The apartment house could, however, offer many advantages. It could be the ideal home for single persons and childless couples because it offers certain communal facilities impossible in other kinds of dwelling. The apartment house can be built with proper regard for its purpose. It can be free-standing so that those who live in it may enjoy the benefits of sunlight and fresh air Though the apartment dweller has no garden, he can have a view over gardens In a mixed type of settlement, where one-family houses are placed in the vicinity of apartment buildings, leaving open spaces between, such garden outlooks are easy to arrange By building such mixed settlements, it is possible to meet the requirements both of single tenants and of families *(See ill 70)*

The plan of a house must relate each room to the other rooms and to the house as a whole. It must help in the fulfillment of social, hygienic, and psychological needs of the family Let us consider what is involved in meeting those needs in planning a small house for a family of six.

Minimum requirements

The house should contain at least three bedrooms, one master bedroom and two others for the children so that there are seperate sleeping quarters for boys and girls.[1] It should have a living room with

---
[1] We considered minimal requirements, but in order to provide complete privacy and relaxation the definite goal should be to furnish a bedroom for each member of the family

75

a dining recess, a kitchen, and a bathroom. Each room should have a separate entrance from a hall, so that it will not be necessary to walk through one room to get to another. A definite place must be provided for the activities which go on within the house, and the size of the rooms must be governed by the purpose they are intended to serve. Even if the house is rather small, the living room should be larger than actual necessity dictates. A feeling of spaciousness is important. Size, fortunately, does not wholly depend on area; it is also a matter of proportion. If we want to create spaciousness in a comparatively small room, we must think of the size, shape, and arrangement of the windows; of the size and particularly the height of the furniture, and its arrangement. Light colors make small rooms seem larger, dark colors make them look smaller. A competent architect can make relatively small rooms look large.

Sunlight and housing

Planners of dwellings should never forget the importance of sunlight. In the past the importance of the proper orientation of a house was recognized. It is only in our own times that builders have flagrantly disregarded it in their construction for human dwelling, though, oddly enough, they seem to remember well the value of insolation when they build shelter for domestic animals. Poultry breeders, for instance, almost invariably take care to locate chicken houses toward the sun. It is good business for them to do so and they know it.

Socrates perception

Xenophon, in his *Memorabilia*, tells of Socrates' clear perception of value of sunlight in home planning. Socrates, he says, claimed that all dwellings should be beautiful as well as useful. Asked how such houses should be built, he resorted to his customary question method. "When one means to have the right sort of house," he queried, "must he contrive to make it as pleasant to live in and as useful as can be?" This admitted, he asked. "Is it pleasant to have it cool in summer and warm in winter?" And when this question too provoked no disagreement he was ready to expound his idea. He said "Now, in houses with a south aspect, the sun's rays penetrate into the porticoes in winter, but in summer the path of the sun is right over our heads and above the roof so that there is shade. If, then, this is the best arrangement, we should build the south side loftier, to get the winter sun, and the north side lower, to keep out the cold winds. In short, the house in which the dweller can find a pleasant retreat at all seasons, and store his belongings safely, is presumably at once the pleasantest and the most beautiful."

Socrates was not the only man of his time and nation to hold this view. He is speaking, in his inimitable manner, of a basic expression of the Greek spirit When, after the repeated destruction of Priene, that city was rebuilt in 350 B.C, its lay-out was oriented with regard to the points of the compass. The residential streets ran from east to west; the streets connecting them from north to south. The important rooms of all houses, therefore, and the porticoes and other communal buildings faced south In winter, when the sun was low in the sky, its rays could penetrate deeply into all dwellings. In summer all rooms were protected against the rays of a sun high in the sky.

As early as 1807, Bernhard Christoph Faust, a physician interested in social hygiene, advanced the theory that houses should be built with proper orientation. He was greatly influenced by Socrates, and in the settlement he planned he arranged southern orientation for all houses and placed them in rows at distances carefully calculated with due regard for the narrow angle of the solar rays in winter. B C Faust's theory

That right orientation influences the health of the people is proved by the experience of the Pueblo dwellers of San Ildefonso of which Edgar Lee Hewett writes [1] The houses of that settlement originally faced the south The sunrays could penetrate into the rooms. The people were healthy and the community prosperous Then, on wrong counsel, the settlement was moved to face north. Decline immediately set in Epidemics, famine, and consequent disaster wore the people down, until the wise men and women of the community saw that the whole Pueblo faced extinction They advised removal from the place of misfortune, and the settlement was again turned to face the south New houses were built, oriented toward the south. The improvement in the lives of the Pueblo dwellers was beyond all expectations Healthy children were born; tuberculosis slowed down; and the settlement was prosperous once more. An experience of Pueblo dwellers

In contrast to these commonsense practices of the past, a good deal of confusion clouds modern planning The therapeutic value of sunshine is of course, undisputed. But there are wide differences of opinion regarding the relative merits of various orientations of a room or a dwelling, and also regarding the effects of such orientations upon a settlement as a whole. Some planners prefer to place their rows of houses from east to west so that the rooms have southern exposure Others insist that rows of houses should run from north to south so that the rooms have eastern and western exposures. Their arguments are further complicated because a house in a row which runs from north to south may be made shorter than one located in a row Confusion of today

---

[1] Edgar Lee Hewett *Ancient Life in the American Southwest*, 1930

running from east to west. It is argued also that the distance between the rows of houses can be less when those rows run from north to south. Obviously, if it can be proved that the north-south direction is desirable, more houses can be built in a given space and certain economic advantage is secured But the fallacy of the claim is evident when one remembers that only the facades and not the rooms of such houses receive sun in winter Their insolation would then be insufficient. For it is of primary importance that the rooms should get the sun

Effects of different orientation

By actually setting up plans for a row of houses, we can make a critical analysis of these much debated questions and arrive at absolute conclusions Let us consider three different orientations one from east to west; one from north to south, and one diagonally between these two *(ill. 52)*. We shall find that the insolation of our dwellings strongly influences the structure suitable in each of these three situations.

If the row of houses runs from east to west, we can face living room and bedrooms toward the south Kitchen, bathrooms, and stairs would then face the north If the row of houses runs from north to south, we can orient the living room toward the west and the bedrooms toward the east If the row runs diagonally, we can in one case orient the living room and bedrooms toward southeast or, in the other the living room toward the southwest and the bedroom toward the northeast or vice versa If we use an L-shaped house we can utilize this diagonal direction to excellent advantage The living room can then face southwest, the bedrooms, southeast

If our comparisons are to be meaningful, we must assume that the dwellings we are considering are of equal size, each having three bedrooms, with two beds in each Let us examine first one of these bedrooms in its different orientations and consider the quantity of sunshine which would penetrate into that room under each of the three situations. Let us remember that the duration of the insolation is important as well as the size of the sun prism formed by sunrays coming through the window Both duration and sun prism depend on the size of the window, on the orientation of the room, on the time of day, and on the season of the year *(ill. 53)* As the sun changes its course throughout the year, the form and size of the sun prism is constantly changing.

Room insolation

A careful and thorough study of room insolation has been made and published by the author of this book.[1] And more extensive data

[1] L Hilberseimer, *Penetration of Sunlight Into the Room*, 1935

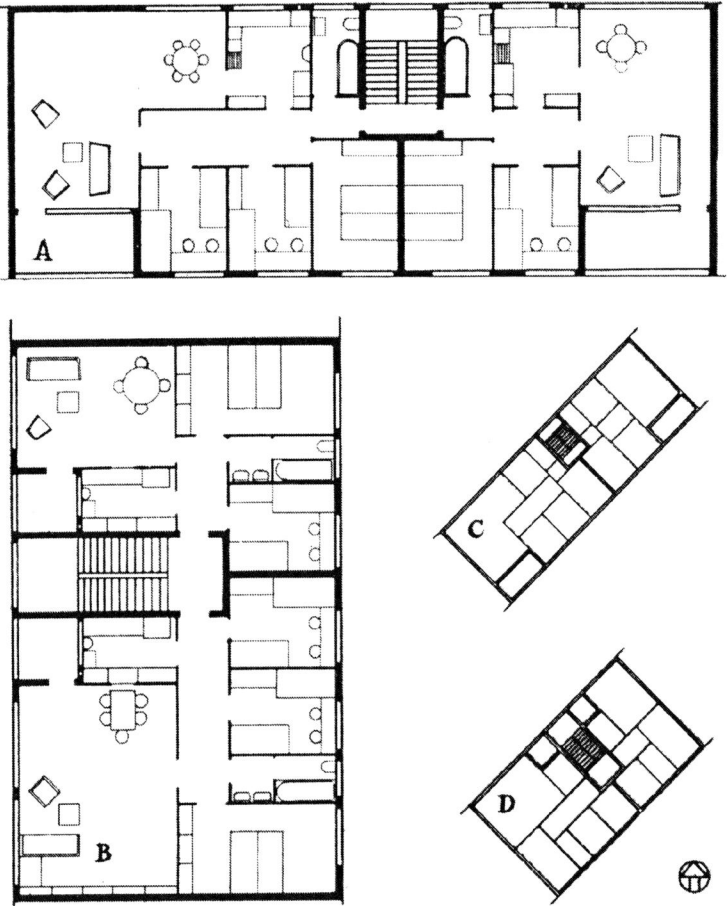

52. PLAN OF APARTMENT HOUSES.
A—South orientation. B—East and west orientation. C—and D—The same plans for south-east orientation.

on the subject under discussion may be found there. The following paragraphs and the illustrations which accompany them are intended to summarize the findings of that study.

In the illustrations which we are using here, the two sidewalls and the rear wall of the bedroom studied have been revolved around the baseboards so as to lie in the same plane as the ground plane *(See ills. 54 to 59)*. The results of this investigation can be considered absolute with respect to the amount of sunshine computed in each case. It can be varied in volume, but not in principle, by changing the plan of the room.

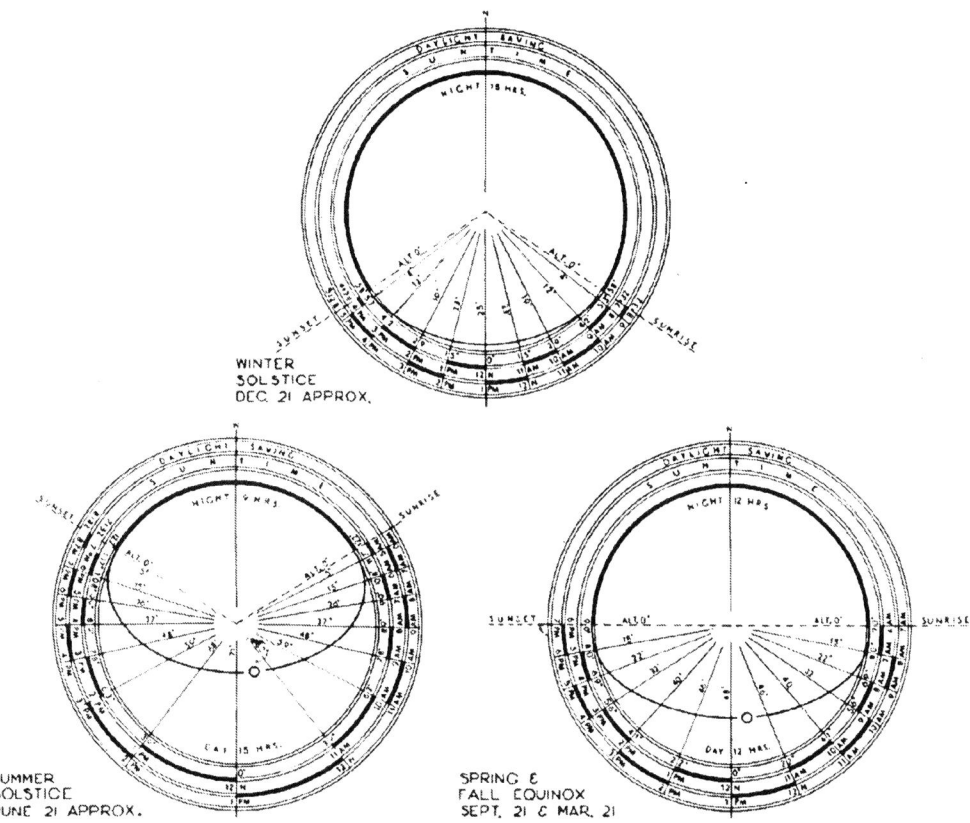

53. SUN CHARTS INDICATING THE ALTITUDE AND AZIMUTH ANGLES FOR LATITUDE 42°. After Howard T. Fisher.

Winter and summer solstice December 21 and June 21. Spring and fall Equinox March 21 and September 21. Approximately one degree of the altitude angles must be subtracted for each degree in more northerly latitudes, and added for more southerly ones.

Let us note first that the possible quantity of sunshine for the south, east, and southeast orientation of that bedroom over the entire year is almost the same for all three orientations.

This would seem to indicate that all three orientations are equally good. But we must remember that equal quantity is not the same as equal quality. When we examine also the quality of the insolation, we find important variations.

Types of sunrays and their influence

To determine the qualitative effect of insolation we must consider the different kinds of sunrays. Three kinds of solar rays are of greatest importance for our study: the light rays, the infra-red rays, and the ultra-violet rays. Their dissimilarity is due to the difference in their wave lengths. Their wave lengths depend on their location in the sun spectrum. The light-producing rays are directly perceptible, but the invisible rays can be perceived only through their effects. Infra-red rays produce heat, ultra-violet rays exert chemical influences. The effects of the various rays are modified by latitude, by altitude, by season, and by meteorological conditions.

Daylight is the result of the light-producing visible rays. It consists of both direct solar rays and indirect rays which cause diffused light. The effect of such rays is dependent on the duration of the sunshine, on the solar altitude, and on the degree of cloudiness. These factors exert much greater influence at low altitudes than at high altitudes. Remembering this, we will realize that we must use every possible means to effect insolation of rooms at low altitudes, particularly in the winter season.

Infra-red rays are believed to be especially intense in winter. In summer, when the sun reaches its highest altitude, such rays have been found to be only four per cent more intense than they are in winter when the sun is low in the sky. These infra-red rays are of great importance hygienically and therapeutically. Especially in the winter and spring, if they penetrate deeply into the body, they bring a beneficial and lasting warmth.

Ultra-violet rays exert chemical influences very important biologically. Careful study shows that such rays are especially active from May until September during the daylight hours of eight in the morning until four in the afternoon. Unfortunately, all direct rays, and particularly the ultra-violet rays, lose much of their intensity when they have to pass through the haze and smoke which hangs over our cities.[1]

Results of our investigation

Our investigation indicates that when the bedroom faces south, the insolation of that room reaches its maximum in winter and its minimum in summer. When it faces the east, the case is exactly opposite: insolation is at a minimum in winter and at a maximum in summer. The southeast orientation gives a situation midway between these two extremes *(ills. 60 to 62)* In the winter, the sun shines for only a comparatively short time, is very low in the sky, and, therefore, penetrates deeply into the room with south orientation, but hardly penetrates at all into the room facing east. In the summer, when the sun shines all day long, sunshine penetrates deeply into the room

---

[1]The National Conference Board on Sanitation states that in one year a city like New York loses 35 per cent of the sunlight that should be available. On certain days as much as 73 per cent is cut off by smoke and fog and during a certain period the loss is 50 per cent.

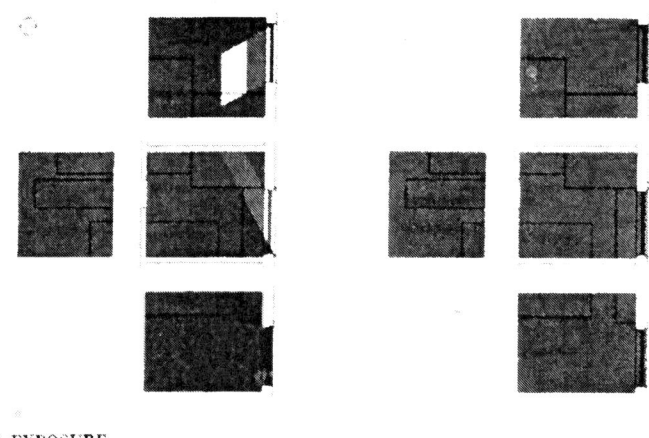

54. EAST EXPOSURE.
10 A. M.   12 Noon.

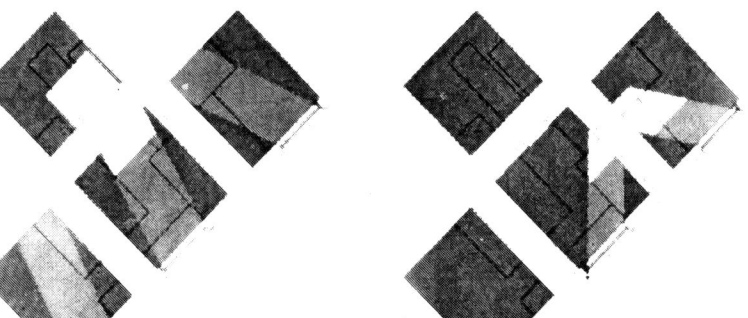

55. SOUTH-EAST EXPOSURE.
10 A. M.   12 Noon.

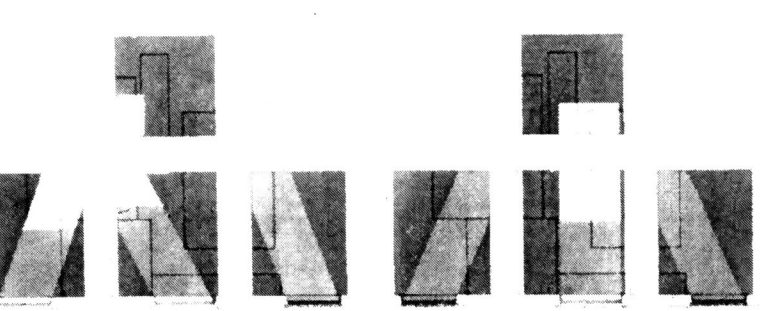

56. SOUTH EXPOSURE.
10 A. M.   12 Noon.
On December 21—the winter solstice—with due south exposure, the sunshine in a room is at a maximum; with due east exposure at a minimum.

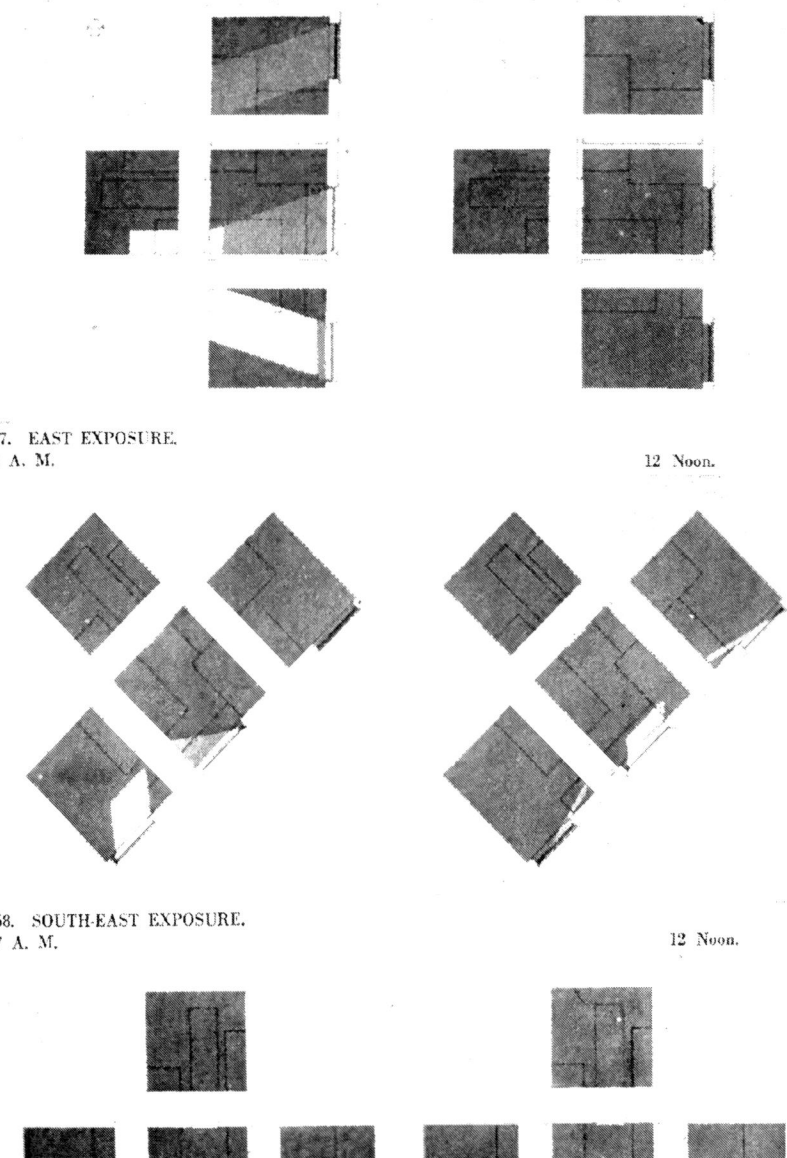

57. EAST EXPOSURE.
6 A. M.   12 Noon.

58. SOUTH-EAST EXPOSURE.
7 A. M.   12 Noon.

59. SOUTH EXPOSURE.
9 A. M.   12 Noon.
On June 21—the summer solstice—east exposure gives a maximum;—and south exposure a minimum of sunshine.

DIAGRAMS showing the maximum and minimum amounts of sunlight penetration by different orientations at different seasons.

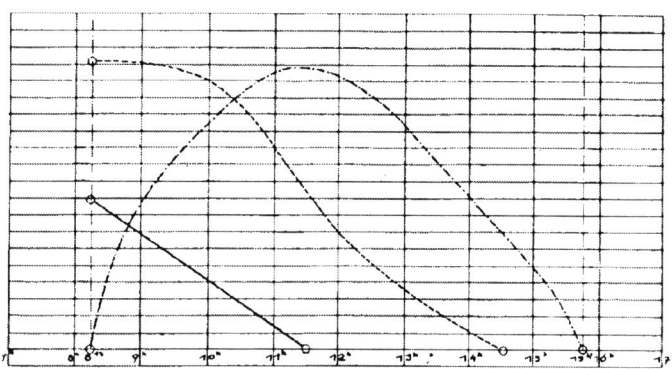

60. DECEMBER 21: East orientation——— Southeast orientation - - - - South orientation —.—.—.
South orientation—Sun Maximum. East orientation—Sun minimum.

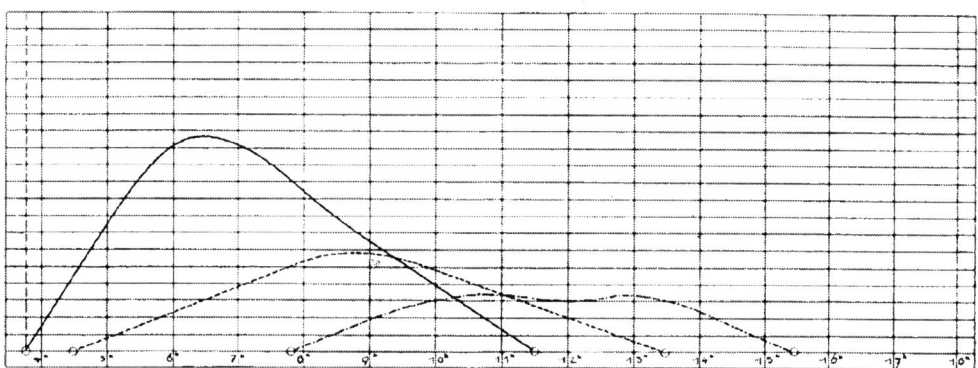

61. JUNE 21. East orientation——— Southeast orientation - - - - South orientation —.—.—.
South orientation—Sun minimum. East orientation—Sun maximum.

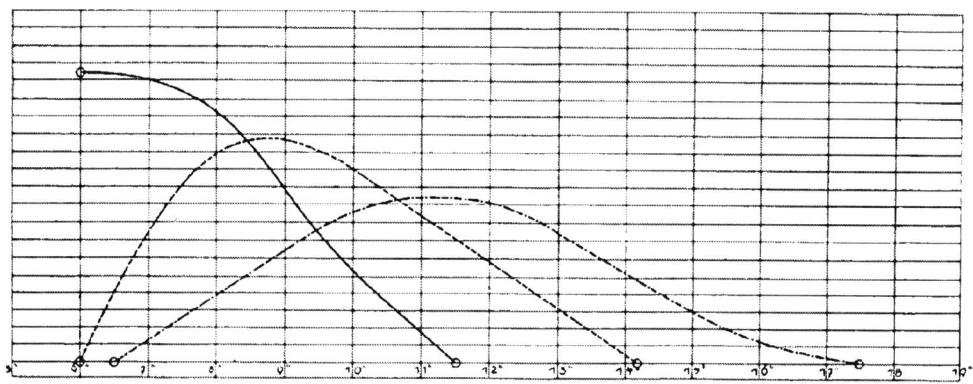

62. MARCH 21, and September 21. East orientation——— Southeast orientation ———
South orientation —.—.—. Sun penetration at all orientations approximately the same.

with east orientation in the morning and into the one with west orientation in the evening At noon, when the sun is high in the sky, little sunlight will come into the room with south orientation. During the spring and fall, the quantity of insolation lies midway between these two extremes. Then all orientation can be considered equally good

The warmth of the health-bringing infra-red rays is useful in the spring and winter only if the sun can penetrate deeply into the room at those seasons A south, southeast, or southwest orientation fulfills this condition; an east or west orientation does not

The beneficial effects of the ultra-violet rays may be obtained only when the sun can penetrate into the room at the season when they are at their maximum intensity—the season between May and September and the hours of 8 a m to 4 p m Here again the south, southeast, and southwest orientations are the most advantageous, inasmuch as the maximum sunshine, for rooms so oriented, is reached during the hours between eight and four Orientation toward the east or west is unfavorable because most of the sunshine enters those rooms earlier or later in the day.

On the basis of such study, we are justified in concluding that the east and west orientation of rooms is the least advantageous; the south most advantageous; the southeast and southwest, reasonably satisfactory. Southwest and southeast orientations are, in fact, to be preferred to due south orientation when they are combined in a single dwelling unit, so that the bedroom receives sunshine from the southeast and the living room from southeast and southwest At high population densities this arrangement is possible only with the L-shaped house. At low densities it is possible with every free-standing house

Our desire for sun in winter is matched by our need for protection against sun in summer Here again our investigation shows the merit of the south, southwest, or southeast orientations The summer sun does not penetrate deeply into rooms so oriented The sunrays do, however, strike the outer walls of the dwelling and heat them so that the temperature inside goes up To achieve maximum benefit from the orientation suggested, we must cope with this problem

Protection against sun

Cross ventilation can help to a certain extent Covering the walls with vines is also a useful device An old Chinese philosopher suggested planting trees at the south of the house The shade of these trees would protect the house in the summer, he pointed out, and in the winter, when the trees were bare, the sun could find uninterrupted access into the rooms There is much wisdom in his suggestion.

85

Structural elements, however, can afford even better protection than planting One-storey houses can be protected against the sun by eaves which prevent the sunrays from reaching the walls The same effect can be achieved for two-storey houses by cantilevering the floor slab of the second floor. A balcony can be provided in front of the bedrooms which protects the walls on the ground floor against the sun. For the protection of the walls of the second floor, eaves or awnings can be used. Apartment houses of several storeys can have tiers of balconies extending along the whole length of the house Such balconies will not only protect the walls from the sun, but will also provide an additional open-air space for each room

Population density

Population density is a social problem, housing, a building problem Yet the two problems are closely related, for population density determines the kind of housing which may advantageously be constructed The higher the density the smaller the freedom a builder enjoys; and conversely, the lower the density, the greater the scope of the construction possibilities he may consider

The main consideration in building, up to our time, has been the exploitation of the land, with little regard for the social and hygienic needs of the people who must live in the buildings constructed. Consequently, the one-family house, always generally recognized as the ideal form of dwelling for families, has been rejected in favor of constructions which seem to promise greater return on land investment. Feeble attempts to cope with the evils of too great population density have been made through zoning laws, but these laws have been altogether insufficient They have not prevented, and could not prevent, the increase of population densities in all our large cities to such an extent that social and hygienic requirements are completely forgotten.

All cities have wide variations in population densities. In their overpopulated sections, the density is often so high as to cause social, moral, and physical diseases. The alleviation of such conditions is one of the greatest problems of our time. In the sparsely settled sections of these same cities, population density decreases sharply Houses are built much farther apart in such areas The city loses its urban character and gradually assumes the aspect of the open country.

How great a degree of density is consonant with good city planning? In what ways does population density dictate structures and arrangements suitable for a good settlement plan? What factors related to density must we keep in mind as we plan?

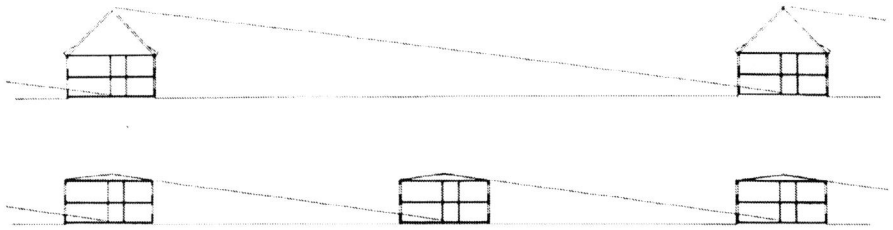

63. DIAGRAM showing the influence of the type of roof on density. Provided four hours of sunshine on December 21,—the steeper the roof the lower the density.

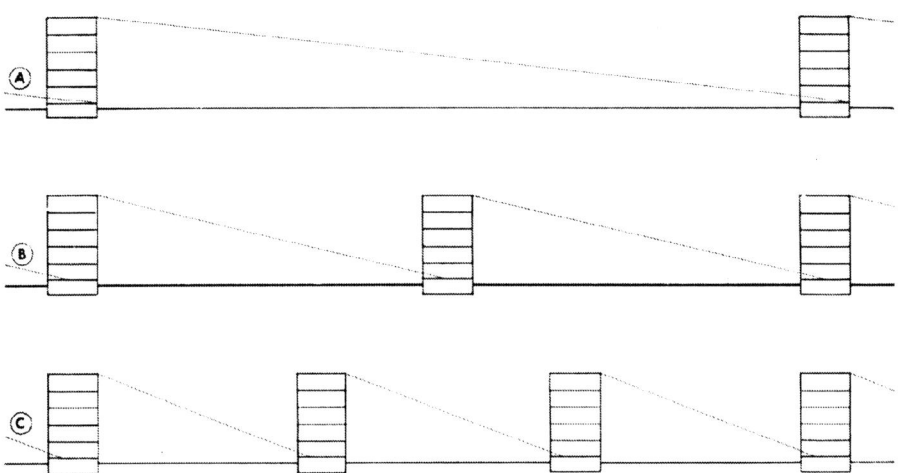

64. DIAGRAM showing the relation between latitude and population density. A—Latitude 55° Moscow. B—Latitude 48° Paris. C—Latitude 42° Chicago.

It becomes clear as we consider questions like these that the solutions we seek for the settlement as a whole must rest upon the same understanding of the importance of insolation which we sought in considering the plan of a single room in a single dwelling. Such an approach to the problem reveals new flexibility in city plans, new ways of meeting old problems which seem insoluble on any other approach.

A careful study of the effects of insolation upon the settlement as a whole and its relation to population density is available in a publication by this author, entitled: *Penetration of Sunrays and Density of Population*.[1] Only the results of that study are summarized here.

[1] L. Hilberseimer, 1936.

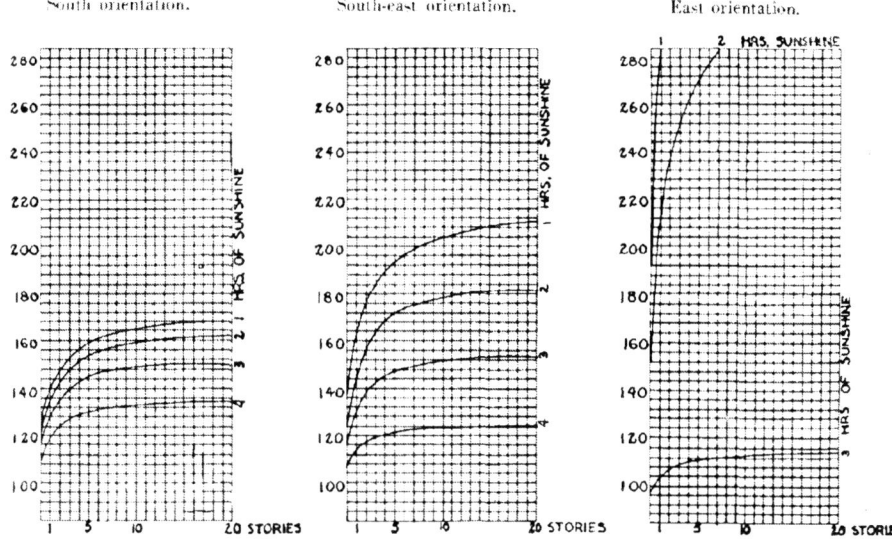

65. POPULATION DENSITY AT LATITUDE 51° 30'

For one to twenty storeys, and one to four hours of sunshine on December 21, for south, south-east and east orientation; showing that at this latitude, and by utilizing the valuable winter sun, little can be gained by increasing the number of storeys.

What does population density mean?	Population density may be defined as the number of inhabitants per acre of land. Since it is reckoned on the number of people living in a given area which includes open land as well as the buildings on that land, it is obvious that the *length* and *depth* of the house built, the distances between houses, will determine the size of the lot. If we are to arrange our buildings according to good insolation principles, the distance between the houses must be determined by the shadows cast by these houses. The length of such shadows will be governed not only by the height of the shadow-casting structure, but also by the latitude in which we build, the time of the year and the day, and the altitude and azimuth angles of the sun.
Latitude	Permissible population density—that is the density which may be attained without impairment of social and hygienic life—depends on various factors. Some are natural and unchangeable. Latitude is one of these. The correlation between latitude and population density is shown by comparing the same apartment in a five-storey building at different latitudes. The apartment in each case has south exposure and four hours' sunlight on December 21. It is apparent, however, that the desirable population density at 55 degrees latitude (Moscow) could be only half what it might be at 48 degrees (Paris) and only one-third of that possible at 42 degrees (Chicago) *(ill. 64)*. Other

conditions being equal, it is possible to achieve, without social impairment, greater population densities in southern latitudes than in northern. This is true because of the variations in the angles of the sunrays. The farther south one moves, the higher the sun is in the sky and the steeper the angle of its rays. A variation of a single degree makes a considerable difference at northern latitudes, whereas in the subtropical section the effect of such variation is negligible.

Topography is another unchangeable factor with which we must cope in our studies of population density. More people can live comfortably and healthfully in an area sloping toward the south than can live on a level area of the same size or on one sloping toward the north. The greater the southward slope, the higher will be the permissible density. That density increases with the number of storeys more in territory which slopes to the south than in level territory. On northward slopes, dwellings with southern exposure permit density of population in inverse ratio to the extent of the slope. If the angle of the slope is identical with the altitude angle of the sun, permissible density reaches the zero point. *Topography*

We cannot change latitude; we cannot change the natural contours of the terrain; but we can determine whether our buildings shall face south or east or some other direction. And our decision at this point will help determine the population density allowable in the settlements we plan. We must take into consideration also the insolation period attainable, remembering that increase of density can be achieved only by decreasing the insolation period or increasing the number of storeys in our structures. Obviously the number of storeys we may add is limited by construction considerations. *Orientation*

Orientation and duration of insolation must be considered together in relation to density. Where the insolation period is four hours on December 21, diagonal orientation will permit a lower density than southern orientation; but where the period is one, two, or three hours, the reverse situation occurs: the south orientation will permit a lower density than the diagonal. If the orientation is toward the east an insolation period of four hours on December 21 will be impossible. Three hours will be the maximum period, and therefore the density permissible under such circumstances will be much less than that allowed in the south or diagonal orientations. Such differences are much more marked in northern latitudes than in southern. The permissible density increases abruptly with an insolation period of two hours and even more so with an insolation period of one hour, as the number of storeys is increased. This is true because, as we have already seen, orientation toward the east provides insufficient insola- *Duration of insolation*

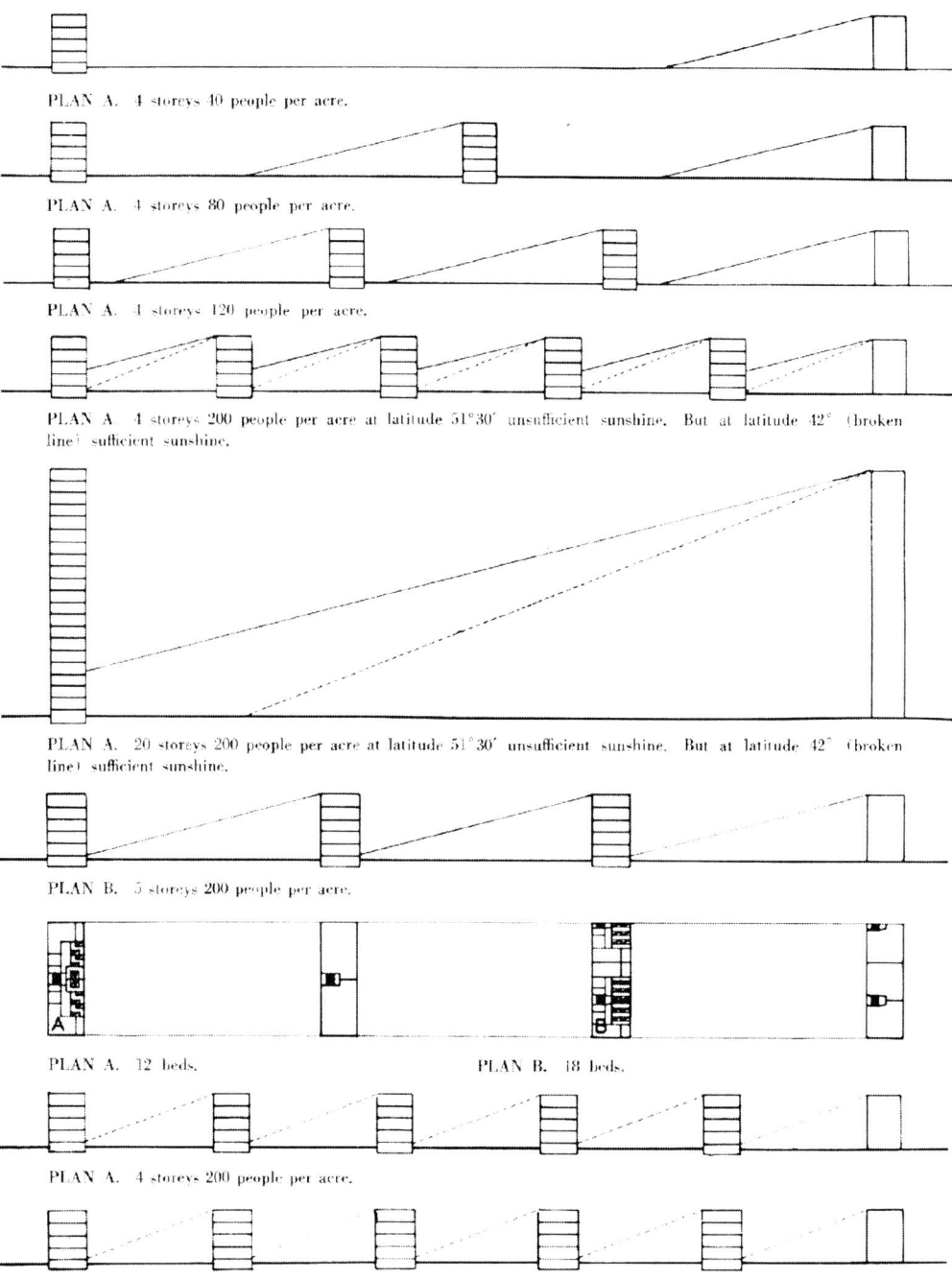

PLAN A. 4 storeys 40 people per acre.

PLAN A. 4 storeys 80 people per acre.

PLAN A. 4 storeys 120 people per acre.

PLAN A. 4 storeys 200 people per acre at latitude 51°30′ unsufficient sunshine. But at latitude 42° (broken line) sufficient sunshine.

PLAN A. 20 storeys 200 people per acre at latitude 51°30′ unsufficient sunshine. But at latitude 42° (broken line) sufficient sunshine.

PLAN B. 5 storeys 200 people per acre.

PLAN A. 12 beds.   PLAN B. 18 beds.

PLAN A. 4 storeys 200 people per acre.

PLAN B. 4 storeys 300 people per acre.

66. APARTMENT HOUSES with different densities and plans. For latitude 51°30′ and 42°. The unbroken line indicates the decisive angle at 51°30′, the broken line at 42° latitude.

tion of the rooms on December 21. At that time of year, the sun strikes only the outside of the dwellings and does not penetrate into the rooms. The high density figures which we obtain by mathematical computation, therefore, have no actual reality.

To a certain extent, permissible population density rises also with south exposure as the number of storeys increases. The ratio of this rise however, decreases in proportion to the increase in the number of storeys. At 51½ latitude (London) the permissible density increases, for dwellings with one to five storeys, by about 20 per cent. But the increase in density made possible by an increase in the number of storeys from five to twenty is only about four per-cent. This is true because the land necessary for the erection of the dwellings decreases with the increase in the number of storeys, and thus loses its influence on the density *(ill. 65)*.

Fallacy of multi-storied building

Problems of population density relate closely to the plan of a dwelling and, particularly to the relation between its depth and length. If conditions compelled us, for instance, to put 200 people on one acre at 51½ degree latitude (London) we could achieve such an increase in one of two ways. We could increase the number of storeys in the buildings of the acre in question, but we should then impair the insolation of the apartments located in the lower storeys of those buildings, or we could shorten the length of the houses and increase their depth *(ill. 66)*. All rooms would then receive sufficient insolation. They would, however, be narrow and deep, wrongly proportioned and, for that reason, very unsatisfactory.

Relation of depth to length

The population density is also related to the height of the individual storey. The greater its height the lower the population density, and vice versa. The type of roof chosen also has a bearing on our problem. At 51½ degrees latitude, a steep roof, on a two-storey house, will reduce this population density to half of that possible with a flat roof *(ill. 63)*.

Storey height

All other circumstances being equal, the difference in permissible population density between the one-family dwelling and the multi-storey building with a southern exposure and an insolation period of four hours on December 21, will decrease the farther north the settlement is located; it will increase the farther south the settlement is. At 55 degrees latitude (Moscow), for example, the difference in permissible population density between one- and ten-storey houses, will be only eight per cent. At 51½ degrees latitude (London) this difference will be 23 per cent. And at 42 degrees latitude (Chicago) the difference will be 70 per cent.

Differences between the one-family house and the multi-storey building

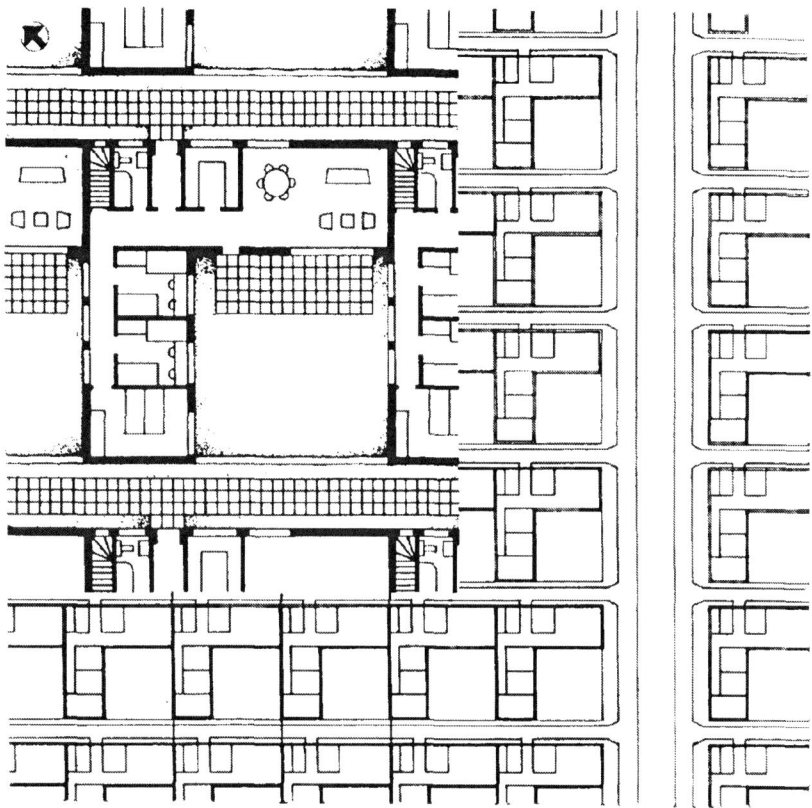

67. L-SHAPED HOUSES at a density of 120 people on one acre.

How to achieve privacy in high density

At a given population density, the greater the number of storeys the larger can be the intervals between the rows of houses. If 120 people live on one acre, the multi-storey building will usually be preferred to the one-storey, one-family house. If the settlement were at 51½ degrees latitude, the multi-storey building would not be an inevitable solution. Here the one-family house would receive sufficient insolation. But the rows of houses would have to be close together. Their residents would have little privacy and a limited view. Two-storey buildings would be even less satisfactory here. They would be too high in relation to the distance between the houses. Furthermore row upon row of such houses spread over a large settlement would create an almost unbearable monotony of aspect. The one-storey building, because of its low height, can easily be hidden behind trees and other planting. It is to be preferred, for that reason, to the more conspicuous two-storey house. If, instead of the usual rectangular shape, we choose to build our house in the shape of an L, the one-storey building loses its disadvantages at this density *(ill. 67)*. It can be isolated from the neighboring houses and achieve the privacy and quiet necessary for the relaxation and recreation of the people who live in it All its rooms would connect with a garden which, though small, would have an atmosphere of comparative spaciousness

This L-shaped form makes possible adequate insolation in every room The southeast sun will penetrate into the bedrooms and the southwest sun into the living room This L-shaped attached type of house, therefore, must be considered as a relatively perfect solution of the housing problem where population densities are as high as 120 per acre It is by no means implied that such density is necessary or desirable Our intent in this discussion has been merely to show what would have been possible if the development of our large cities had been controlled by the human needs of their inhabitants instead of by the ruthless will to exploit city land.

The lower the population density, the fewer the restrictions upon the house plan the better the degree of insolation, the higher the degree of privacy. The average density of Paris is 140, of Berlin, 120; of London, 60; and of Chicago with its suburbs, 50. The average density of city population is therefore, about 80. Where 80 people live on one acre, detached one-family L-shaped houses can be built in which the living room can receive both the southwest and southeast sun, and the bedrooms southeast insolation Here the L-shaped house offers more advantages than the rectangular house *(ill. 69)*, but the attached rectangular house, despite its disadvantages, is better than the detached rectangular house at such a density because the space between detached houses must necessarily be smaller than that between attached houses and the privacy therefore would be less.

The influence of density on the plan of a building

Not until the density drops to forty can the usual rectangular freestanding house offer all its advantages, especially that of the necessary spaciousness Where the density drops to 20, the L-shaped form of the one-family house may be reversed. Then the living-room and bedrooms would no longer need to be located along the inside of the L, but could be placed at the outside so that the dwelling, like the free-standing rectangular house, would be best exposed to the sun The houses of a settlement would not have to be built according to certain schemes. We have used several plans only to simplify the problem But an improved type always tends to be repeated. Repetition, like standardization, is undesirable only when it restricts living conditions and impairs the welfare and development of the individual *(ill 68)*

The freedom of planning houses increases, in general, as population

68 EFFECT OF DIFFERENT DENSITIES on the plan of houses A—80, B—40 and C—20 people on one acre

69. VIEW OF L-SHAPED HOUSES. 80 people on one acre.

density decreases. The lower the density, the greater the freedom in planning the house and its architectural expression. The architectural character of an entire settlement depends also on the degree of its population density. Here also, the lower the density the fewer the restrictions put upon its development. When the density sinks to very low levels, the homogeneous character of the settlement may disappear—a development which sometimes may be very desirable.

In planning four-storey houses at a density of 40 people to an acre *(ill. 66)*, we are surprised by the spaciousness possible between two rows of houses. These wide areas between the rows would be available for gardening, but they could also be used for the building of one-family, one-storey houses. The general aspect of spaciousness would be retained, for these one-storey houses would disappear, to a considerable extent, behind the trees and other plantings of their gardens. By combining both types of dwelling, we should achieve a mixed settlement, in which the population density could be increased to 80, the average density of our large cities. There would be room for even 120 people per acre, if such an increase should become necessary.

Mixed type of settlement

Spaciousness and privacy are achieved in this mixed settlement. We can have both, the one-family house with its gardens, and the apartment house with a free view over these gardens. This new type of settlement is a form of housing which meets the actual needs of man It gives him complete freedom to choose the kind of dwelling he prefers Here we may see the community of the future *(ill 70)*.

Average population density The average population density we have used in constructing these plans for a new satisfactory settlement type is, strangely enough, higher than the average population density of our cities How is it possible then that housing conditions in those cities are so inadequate? The explanation lies in two main causes. The first is the enormous density in the over-populated parts of these cities In Paris and Berlin, for instance, the density in certain areas reaches nearly 400 persons per acre The second is the division of land into unsuitable lots, so that the city is unfavorably affected even in areas of low population densities Certain advantages which cannot be gained by building on individual lots can be realized by building on a large integrated area *(ills 71 and 72)*.

Building and zoning laws If we want to meet certain social and hygienic demands in connection with population density, we must strive to influence the factors on which this density depends. Building laws and zoning laws are a means to this end, but such laws have up to now served merely to prevent the worst abuses of building; they have given no constructive aid toward real solutions

Instead of improving housing conditions, zoning laws have at times served to legalize the exhorbitant exploitation of the land. It would seem irresponsible to have made the inadequate small apartments of the lower classes more inadequate, thus tolerating ever-increasing densities Our laws have done this, however, partly because they have been concerned chiefly with individual lots instead of large integrated urban areas, even though the historical development shows an increasing preference for the erection of buildings on large land units

Minimum demands Instead of the insufficient zoning laws we now have, we shall have to establish certain minimum demands in order to have adequate buildings One of these must be that dwellings be properly insolated so that the precious winter sun may be utilized to its fullest extent. This demand for insolation should be accompanied by a law limiting population density Such a law would differ in different localities In southern latitudes, relatively high densities may be allowed, with a sufficient insolation period. High densities, likewise with a sufficient insolation period, may also be possible in northern latitudes if the relationship between the length and depth of the house is altered *(See ill. 66, Plan A and B)*. Therefore an additional law must establish a minimum area for a dwelling according to the size of the family.

Far reaching improvements can be achieved by laws based on such minimum demands These laws will permit the builder to erect dwellings according to the needs of the people No matter whether one-story or multi-story dwellings are to be erected, the builder can and must comply with the requirements of such laws But within those restrictions he can still create with absolute freedom

70 MIXED TYPE OF SETTLEMENT Apartment houses distantly separated, between them one storied single family houses

Our studies and analyses have shown us that population densities as great as those prevailing within our large cities can be handled with due regard for the minimum demands of human living Such demands could be fulfilled in all the metropolises, without enlarging the city area and without jeopardizing the economic basis of the transportation systems and the public utilities It may be that in the future. social and economic development will not necessitate urban mass concentrations with such high population densities, but no matter how small or how large may be the settlements of the future, they must be so built as to fulfill in their structure our basic minimum demands adequate insolation, a limited population density, and a minimum dwelling area

71. PARIS. View of densely built and highly populated residential areas.

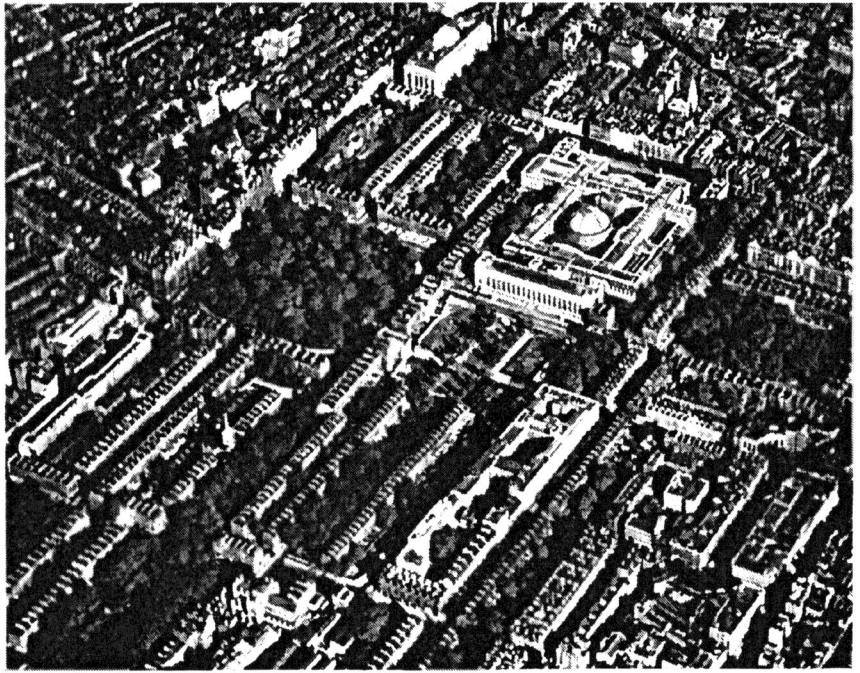
72. LONDON. View of a residential area with open and green space.

73 & 74. CITY STREETS: Past, present and future.

|Insufficiency of the present block and street system| The city today is based on a street and block system which was used in Egyptian cities four thousand years ago and which is certainly even older than Egypt. The function of the block has been the same at all times. It serves to group houses together, to connect them by means of streets, and to connect these with the entire street system. Up to our times the system functioned admirably. However our motor vehicles have rendered this once perfect system questionable and even dangerous. We are beginning to consider and try out modifications of, and even departure from, the block system. We are trying especially to solve the problem created by the speeding automobile—the dangerous intersection.

Combination of blocks

In order to avoid too many intersections, each of them not only a point of danger but also a hindrance to the speed of motor vehicles, we could put together two, four, eight, or any number of blocks. This would reduce the danger points and would also create better conditions inside the new area of combined blocks. If we put together eight blocks *(ill. 75)*, for example, we should have four intersections instead of fifteen. The combined area of the eliminated streets would be large enough to provide space for a park inside the area, in which a school and a playground for children might be placed. This park could be a green area for all the block's inhabitants. At the same time the building lots, freed from the narrowness of the usual divisions, could provide better conditions for the houses themselves. Those houses now could have the right orientation, and each room in them could get enough sunlight during the wintertime when sunlight is needed most. Each house could have a useful garden. Even though the population density remained the same, there would be far less sense of crowding. Some apartment houses could be built in addition to the prevailing single-family houses, and a housing to meet a greater variety of need would be thus afforded. Garages could be arranged as group garages. Necessary stores and shops could find their place within the area. Traffic danger would be eliminated for there would be no street-crossings within the area—only walks.

This solution of block combination is a step forward from our present community plan, but it is not a complete solution of our problems. Favorable as the conditions inside such an 8-block area would be, there would still remain the four intersections outside of it, where traffic still crossed on one level. The danger would have been reduced, but it would not have been eliminated entirely.

The super block Residential area

If we want to avoid the danger of traffic intersections altogether, we must combine a considerable number of blocks. We might plan a

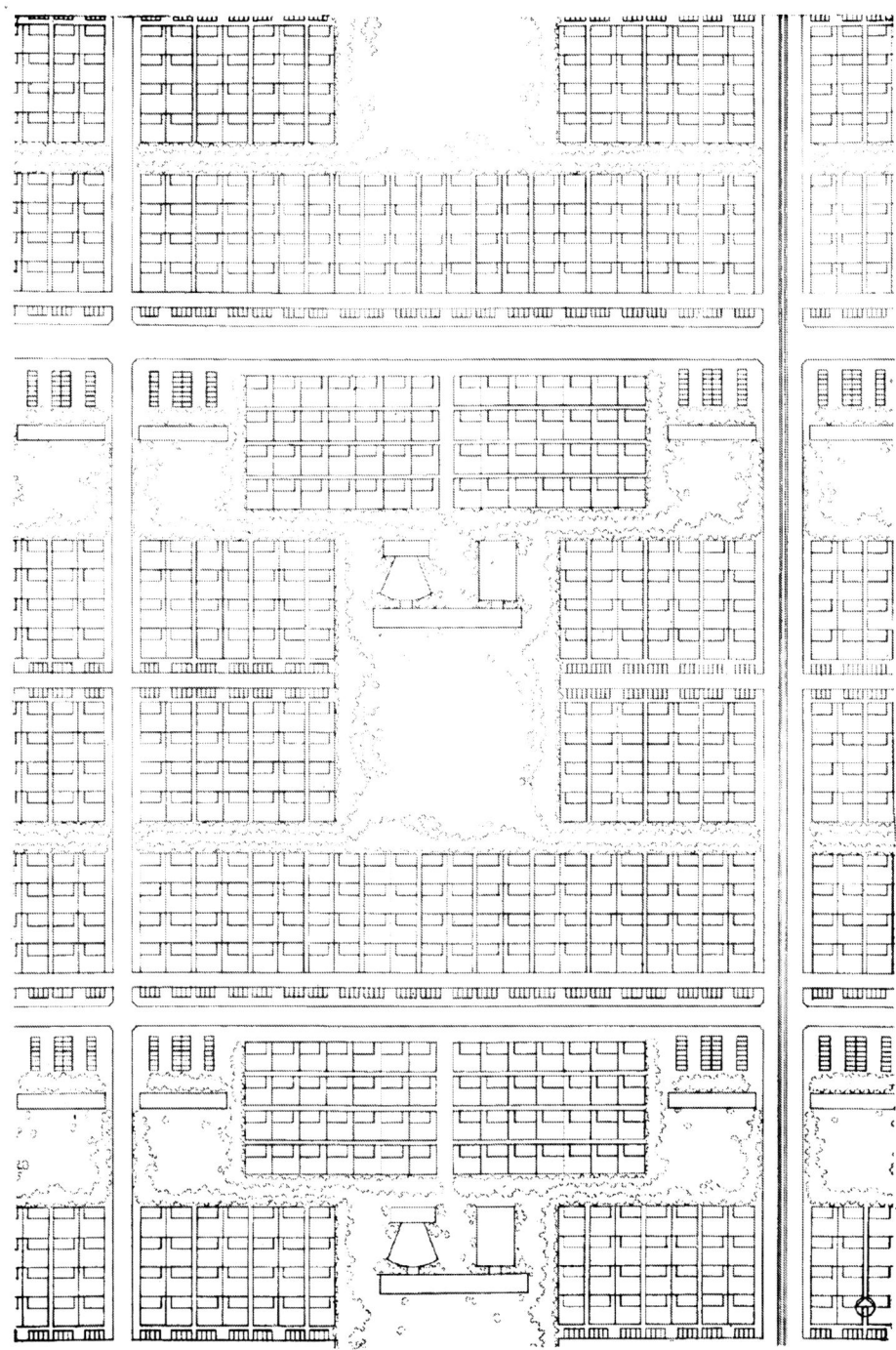

75. COMBINATION OF 8 CITY BLOCKS

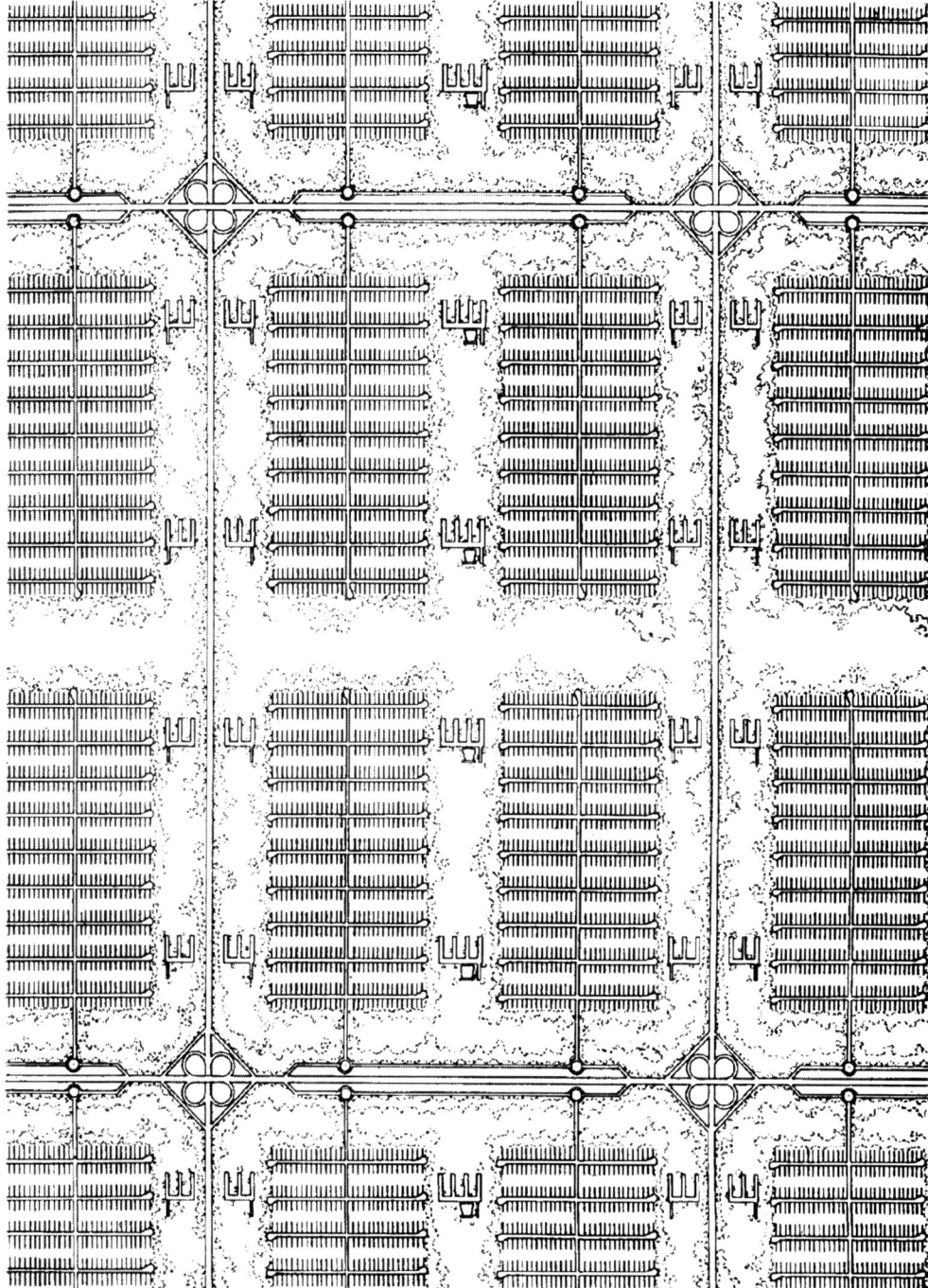

76. SUPER BLOCK: Residential area.

77. SUPER BLOCK: Commercial area.

SUPERBLOCK *(ill. 76)* of, say, an area of two square miles Ludwig Sierks first suggested such a solution. In an area of such dimension, it would be economically practical to replace the four boundary streets with highways, and to build clover leaf intersections at the four corners. This would solve the traffic problem quite satisfactorily. The new settlement units, which we shall describe immediately, within these areas would be limited in size to convenient walking distances. The park space within such an area could now be much larger. Schools and playgrounds could be located within these parks. The street system of the unit would be so planned that pedestrians would be entirely free of traffic danger. The main street would be connected with the highway. Where the size of the city would justify it, transportation could be by subway as well as by highway.

The super block Commercial area

Such a SUPERBLOCK could also be used in the commercial area of the city *(ill. 77)*. Four groups of commercial buildings, instead of four settlement units, could be placed within such a Superblock, and they could be surrounded by a park area. Each of the buildings would have two parts. In one, which would be rectangular and three to five storeys high, would be located all kinds of stores, banks, exhibition halls. In the other, which could be H-shaped and which might be a skyscraper, would be many kinds of offices. Each office room would have sufficient light. Motor vehicles could drive underneath each building and park there.

Advantages and disadvantages

Many of our worst problems could be solved with such a plan. But, as we study it, it becomes evident that it would, if the centric system is retained, leave us still faced with two important unsolved problems. There would still be a distant separation between residential and working areas, and the problems of local transportation needed to carry workers to and from their jobs would be as acute and tangled as ever. And there would still remain untouched the problem of industrial nuisances—smoke, soot, and fumes—and their ill effect upon the health of the community. These two problems can be solved only in relation to the city as a whole.

The need of a new settlement unit

We can never arrive at an organic city structure by merely multiplying city blocks. Such a procedure only increases the traffic moving toward the city center. We need a new city element to replace the archaic block or gridiron system. The structure of this new settlement unit *(ill. 80)* should permit, not only a general solution of all the different parts of the city and their relation to each other, but also free and unhindered urban growth.

The backbone of such a settlement unit would be the main traffic

78. HENRY WRIGHT AND CLARENCE STEIN, Radburn. Safety-street plan by means of closed end-streets.

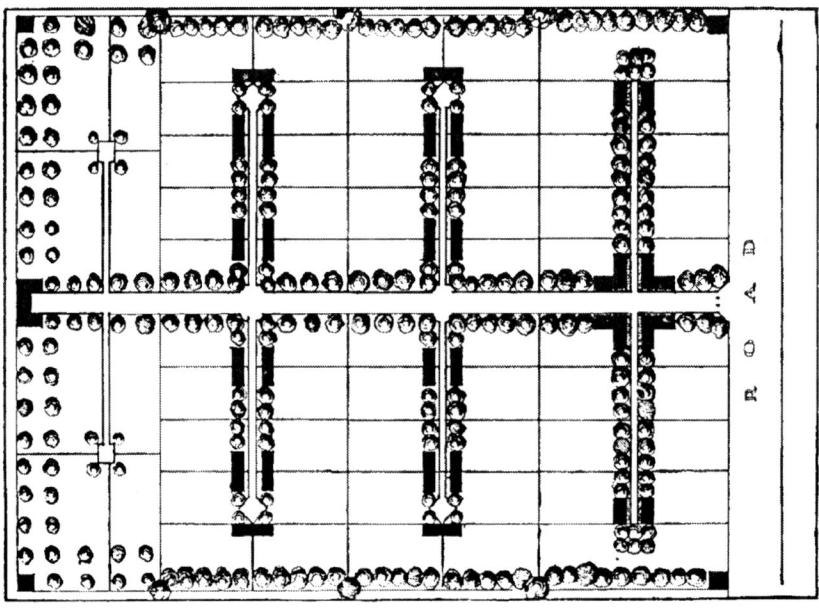

79. RAYMOND UNWIN, System of closed end-streets.

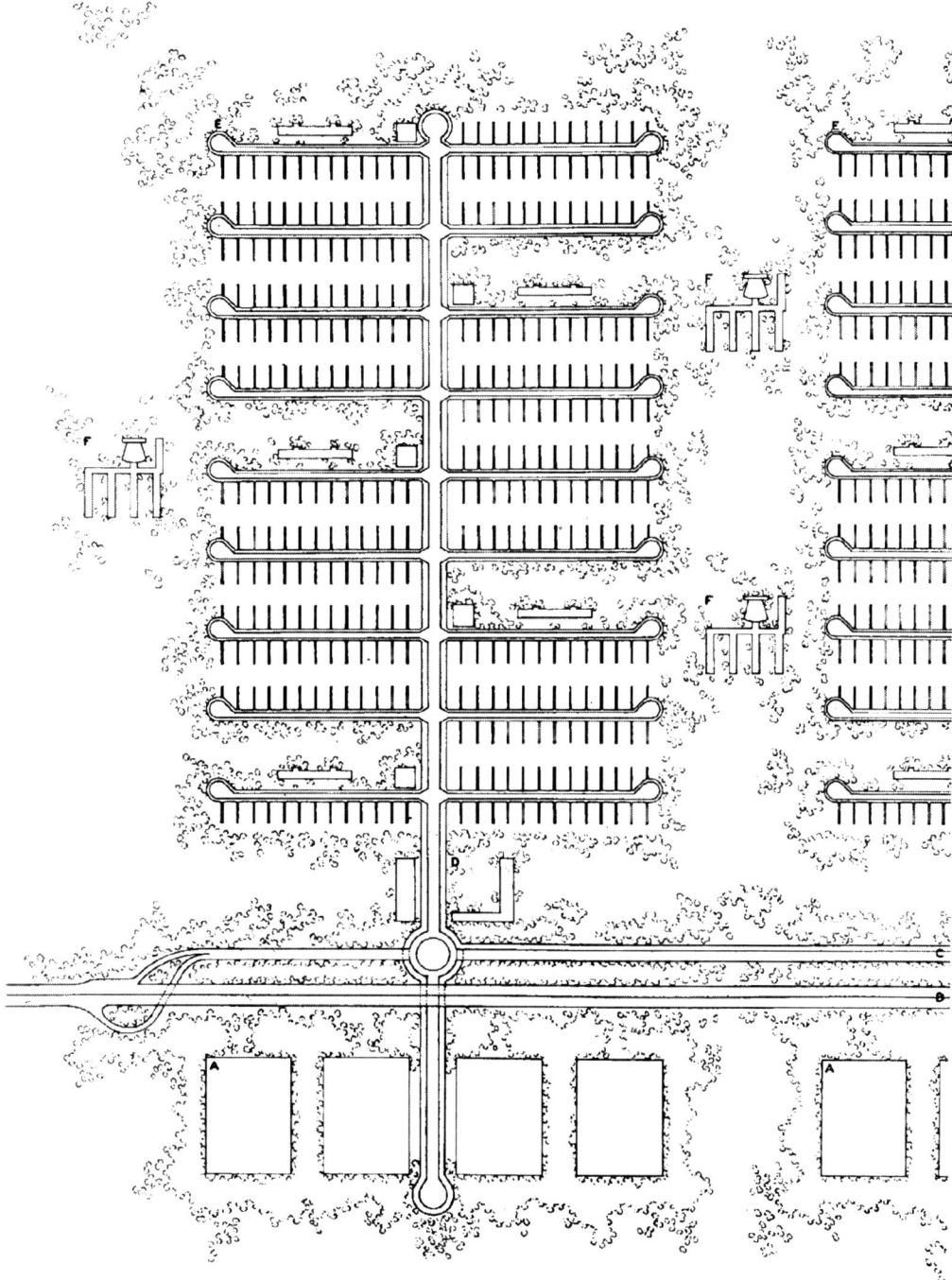

80. A NEW SETTLEMENT UNIT. A—Industry. B—Main highway. C—Local highway. D—Commercial area. E—Residential area. F—Schools in the park area.

artery On one side of it would be the industrial area: on the other, first buildings for commerce and administration located within a green belt, and then houses of the residential area surrounded by a park containing schools, playgrounds, and community buildings. This park area would make the settlement part of the landscape and create an organic relation between city and country

Theoretically the shape *(ill 81)* of such a settlement unit would be a rectangle of such proportion that it would reduce to a minimum the amount of street area required Its size would depend mainly on the number of people living within it, on the density of the population, and on the type of the buildings required The depth of these units is a consideration of utmost importance Every resident should be able to walk to and from his work. Therefore, the depth of the residential area should not exceed the distance a person can walk within the residential zone. and the functional organization of the street system would bring about a differentiation of traffic routes: from the residential lanes, intended *only* for pedestrians, to the main highways—for automobiles *only* {Structure. shape and size of the new unit}

We should have, in such a residential area, first lanes. then streets into which the lanes lead, then traffic streets into which the streets lead, and finally the traffic highways fed by the traffic streets. This traffic highway would, at convenient points, connect with the main highway

All communication roads would be planned according to their particular functions The main highway would consist of two separate roads, one for each direction of traffic This main highway might be on ground level, elevated, or below ground level Rotary or cloverleaf constructions would enable motorists to negotiate intersections and connections without difficulty The local highway would connect the main highway with the residential traffic streets at suitable points The residential traffic streets would connect the settlements with their respective business and industrial zones. The streets and lanes would be closed-end streets, so that through traffic would not enter or pass through the residential zones {Street system}

Closed-end streets are an old solution, which was suggested for the cities of our times first by Raymond Unwin *(Ill. 79)* and later by Henry Wright *(ill 78)* Only essential traffic—cars of householders, delivery cars, ambulances, and fire engines—would enter the resi-

---

[1] If anybody chooses to live farther away from his place of work, he will have the freedom to do so He would then have to use some kind of transportation, as he does today, but he would use it under greatly improved conditions

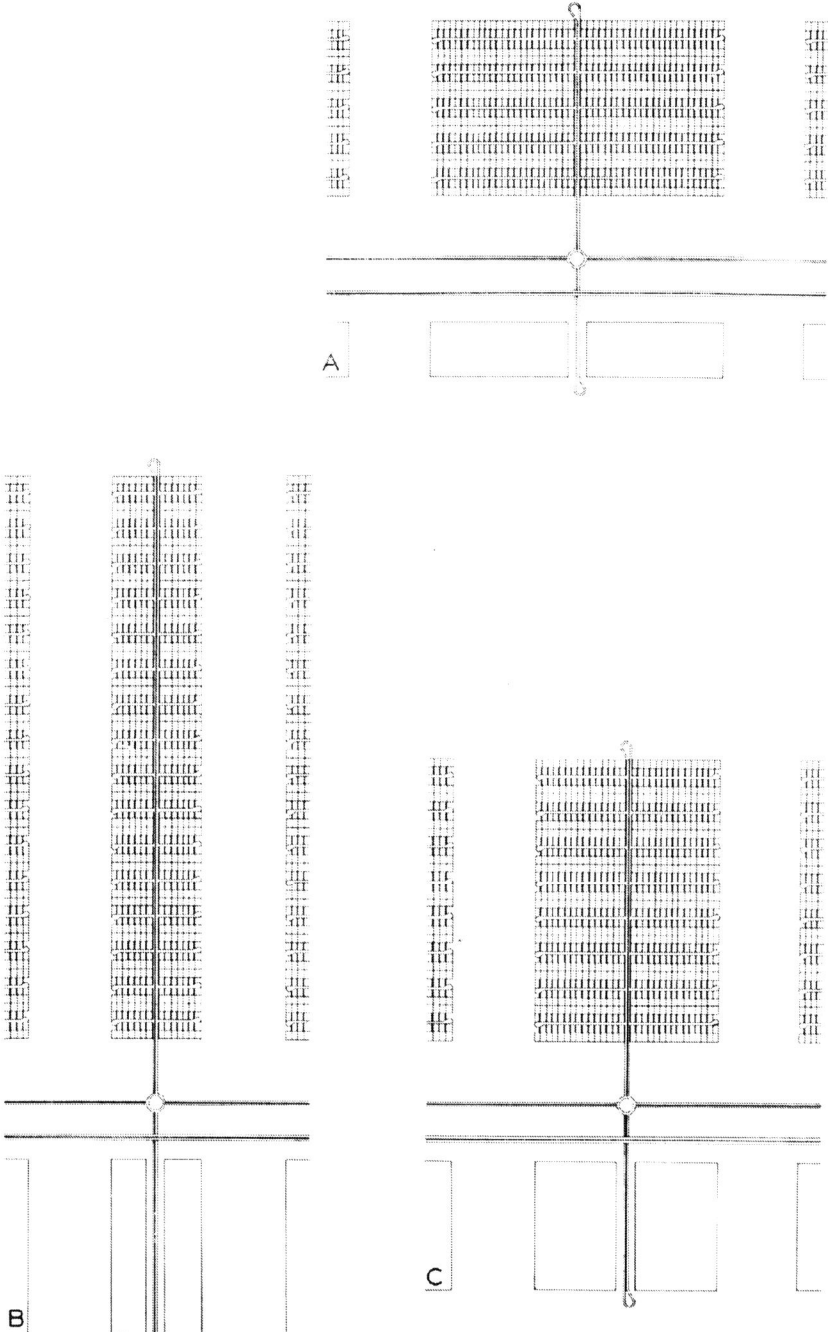

81. THEORETICAL SHAPE OF A SETTLEMENT UNIT and its requirement of street space. A needs one-fourth more than C; and B one-sixth more space than C.

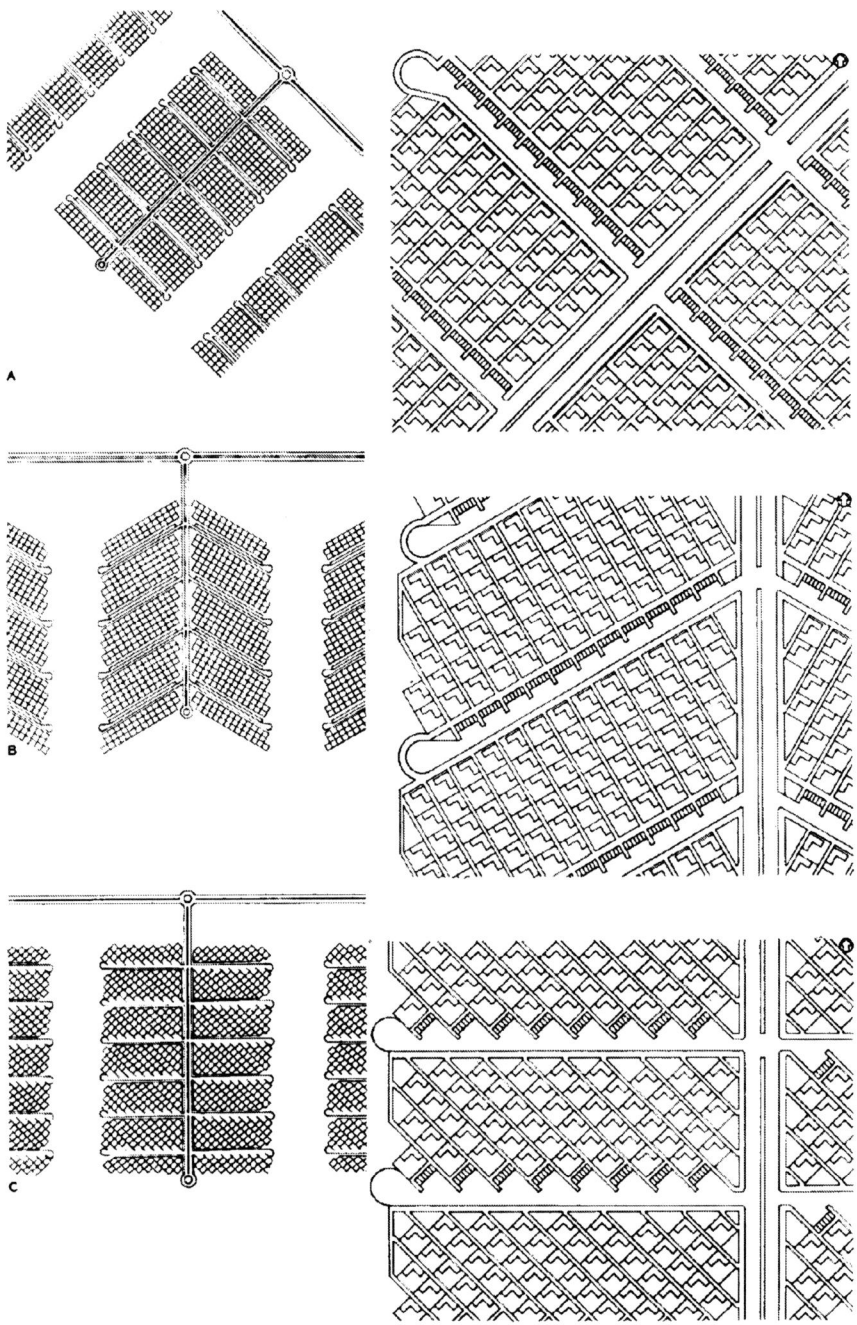

82. A NEW SETTLEMENT UNIT and the orientation of houses.

To achieve the proper orientation of the houses within the unit we can move the unit itself—A; or the street—B; or better and simpler the lanes—C.

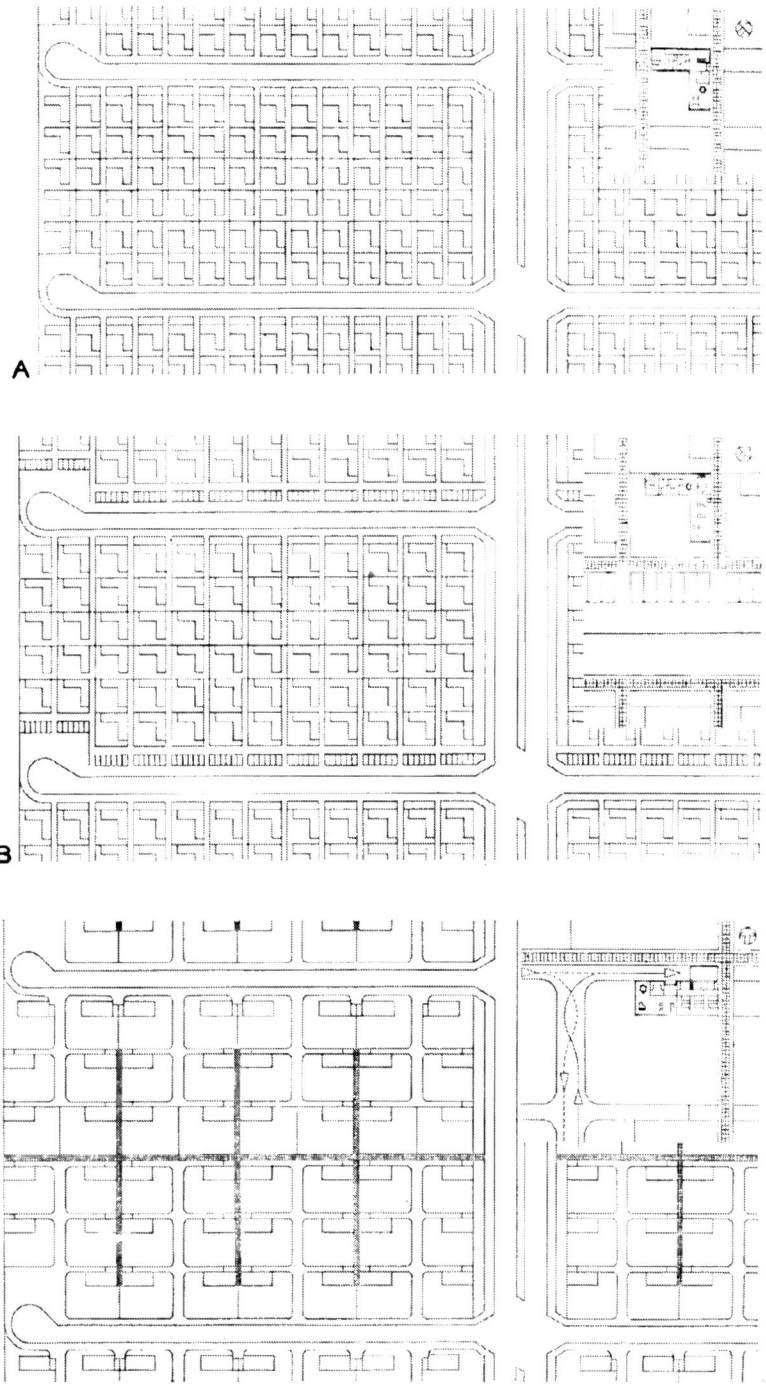

83. A NEW SETTLEMENT UNIT: Details.

A—without garages; public garages elsewhere. B—with group garages. C—with individual garages. Note the separate walks for pedestrians.

dential zones. The length of the residential lanes would depend upon the equipment of the fire department and on the calculation of the "reasonable" distance for carrying things The internal street system would also be influenced by the kind of heating system in use; whether the community received its heat through individual heating units or from a central source; the kind of fuel in use, etc.[1] To provide for emergencies, the closed-end streets could be connected with a driveway, running through the park but closed except in cases of need

The course of the main highway and the traffic highway would be determined by the settlements to be connected and, of course, by topographical conditions The course of the residential streets and lanes would be determined by the buildings and their orientations, and modified by topographical conditions.

To secure the proper orientation for the houses within this settlement unit, we could move the unit as a whole to the necessary angle, or we could move the streets within the unit, or—an even better and simpler solution—we could move the lanes leading from the houses to those streets *(ill 82)* If we followed the last plan, we could use the vacant triangles on the streets as sites for group garages.

Whether streets should be straight or curved has been a subject much debated during the last fifty years City "improvements" have been sought through the use now of the one, now of the other of these street types. We are coming to realize now, that the mere changing of a single element can never lead to an effective improvement of the whole. Only a change in the entire structure according to new demands can bring about real "improvement" for use and for beauty Incidentally, the question—straight or curved streets—is a foolish one The course of a street should obviously be determined, not by preconceived rule, but by topographical, structural, and traffic requirements.

Straight or curved streets?

The width of a street should be determined by its function. It should not be decided upon arbitrarily, but should be settled in relation to the number of vehicles the street is to serve. It should not, of course, be wider than necessary Streets and intersections of unnecessary width do not provide definite lanes for motor vehicles, and they thus increase rather than diminish confusion and traffic hazards

The width of streets

---

[1] By the ever increasing distance of transmitting electric energy it may very well be possible to heat entire cities with electricity

If we take everything into account, beginning with the installation of heating equipment to the transportation of coal through the country as well as through the cities, use of electricity for heating purposes would become less expensive and create better health conditions and cleaner surroundings

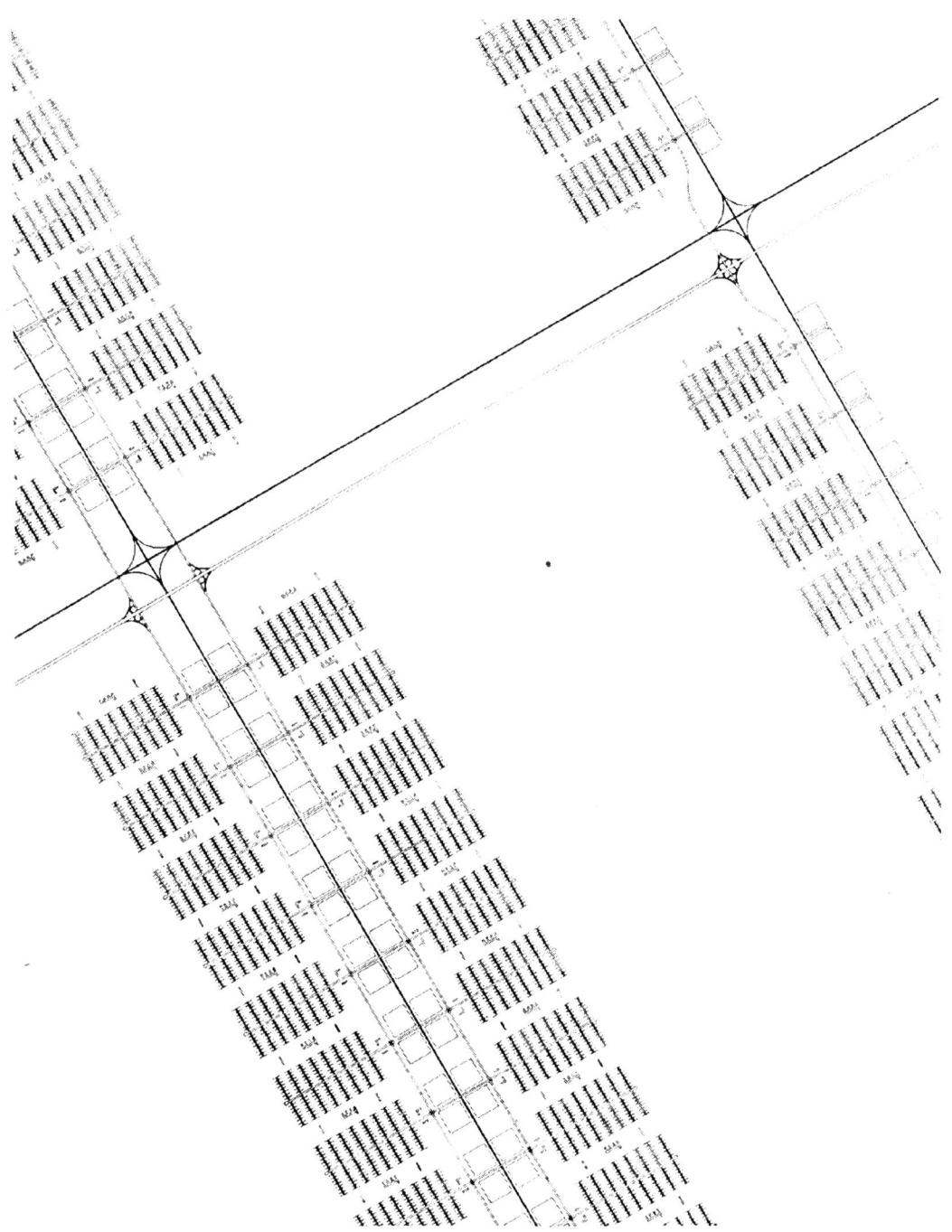

84. SETTLEMENT WITH SMOKELESS INDUSTRY.
Ribbon-formed arrangement with residential areas on one side (right), and on both sides (left).

The width of the residential lanes should depend on the number of people using them and whether those people are to walk single file or side by side. By separating highways and streets according to their different functions, by limiting their number, and planning them adequately, we could effect such savings that these new adequate highways and streets could be developed without additional cost.

Within the settlement, the buildings may be of a mixed type. They might include one-family houses and apartment houses. The dwelling types would differ according to the differences in population density in various units. But no matter how much such population density may vary, no matter how different in aspect the buildings in different settlement units may be, in each and every unit, dwellings would be surrounded by parks in which schools and playgrounds stand. Children could reach school and playground without crossing traffic streets. Even if, instead of the collective or group garages suggested, individual garages *(ill. 83)* were provided, the children could still reach school and playground without crossing traffic streets, for each "block" would have separate streets for pedestrian and automobile traffic.

Advantageous features of the new unit

Like a brick—always so typical and yet so various in use—such a settlement unit could be used for every requirement that might arise in any city of whatever type or size or topographical character. It would provide the greatest possible flexibility in itself, and the greatest possibilities for useful combination. No matter how many such units were combined, the same favorable conditions for one unit would remain in all its combinations. The use of such a unit would solve the problems involved in organizing all the city's parts. It would make a complete traffic solution truly possible. It would create an organic structure for the community life of the people.

Flexibility of use of the new unit

The simplest way to construct a settlement with industry would be to combine such units in a row along a traffic artery. A ribbon-shaped settlement would result, in which the residential area lay on one side of the traffic line, the industrial area on the other. Such an arrangement would make free industrial development possible. A second ribbon of such units could run parallel with the first and could, at convenient distances, be connected with it. If the industries produced no smoke or wind-borne nuisances, there could be residential areas on both sides of the industrial area. A denser settling would follow, but the industries could only be extended within a limited area *(ill. 84)*

Simple industrial settlements

Most industries, however, produce nuisances such as smoke, soot, gases, smell, and noise. Countless complaints have been voiced

Smoke pollution and its ill effects

113

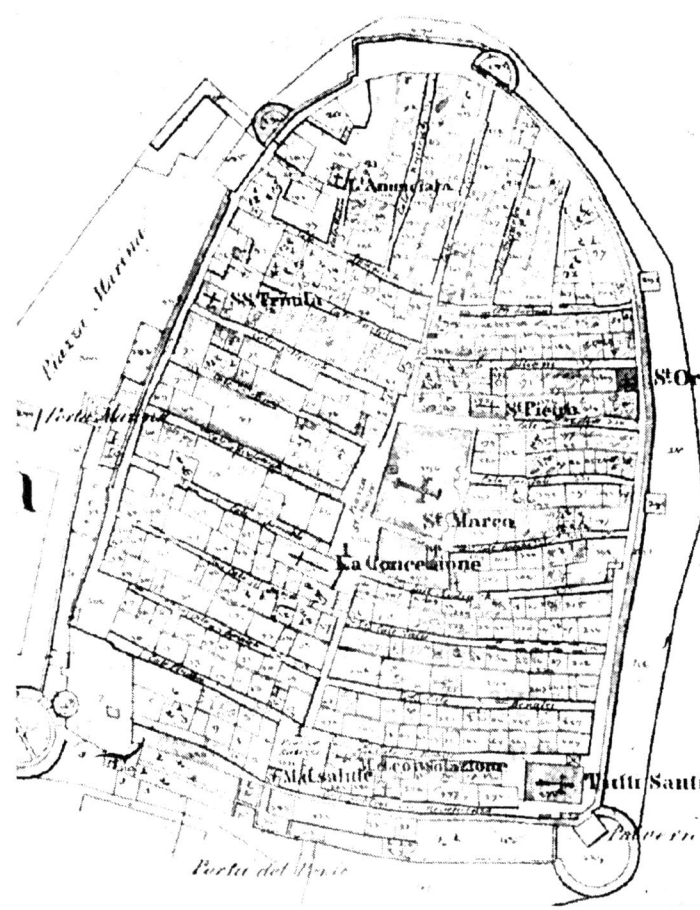

85. CORCULA, DALMATIA.
See also illustration 20.

about air pollution from smoke producing industries and much has been said about the ill effects on health[1] and property[2] of such pollu-

---

[1] During the depression, when most of the Pennsylvania factories and mines were shut down, so reducing the emission of smoke, the pneumonia death rate dropped to a low of 91.6 per 100,000 population in 1933. With the return of better times and the reopening of industrial plants, and the ensuing increase in smoke, soot, and fly ash, the death rate from pneumonia jumped from the previous low in 1933 to 167.4 per 100,000 population in 1936. The conclusion is of course obvious: an increase in the amount of smoke results in a proportionate increase in respiratory diseases.—*American City Magazine*—March, 1940.
Dr. Thomas Barlington, of the New York Health Department, has stated that in his opinion smoke is primarily responsible for a 50 percent increase in cases of cancer of the lungs. And a Health Commissioner of Chicago asserted that the death rate in his city could be reduced from 12,000 to 10,000 of population—a reduction of one-sixth—if smoke were eliminated from the atmosphere. He estimated that between 5,000 and 6,000 persons were killed each year by Chicago smoke.—Henry Obermeyer: *Stop That Smoke*. New York and London, 1933.

[2] Human beings, unfortunately, have developed no special resistance against smoke. Neither has iron or stone. Smoke defaces, corrodes, and disintegrates practically all kinds of building material. . . . This form of defacement, plus the wholesale destruction of merchandise on the shelves, is said to cause the country a net loss of five hundred millions of dollars every year. The complete total of America's smoke bill has been estimated as high as "2,400,000,000 annually or $6,850,000 every day of the year." Henry Obermeyer: *Stop That Smoke*. New York and London, 1933.

114

tion. It is as great a crime, many doctors insist, to pour poison into a man's lungs as it is to pour poison into his coffee!

What can be done to eliminate such nuisances, which all arise from our present-day industrial conditions and which harm people and property in our communities? There are two answers to that question, two methods available to us. One is techno-chemical devices, the other is planning. In other words the nuisances may be eliminated either through artificial or through natural methods. The artificial methods, however, are not wholly adequate, and they are very expensive. They cost a great deal both to install and to maintain. The only truly efficient remedy is planning—the natural means at our hand for combating the smoke and nuisance evil. It may sometimes be advisable to combine with planning some use of the techno-chemical means of smoke abatement, and certainly the possibilities and limitations of this method should be studied and fully understood.

How to abolish smoke—by techno-chemical means or by planning?

Large claims have been made for smoke abatement with techno-chemical means. Careful appraisal of results, however, make it appear that the amelioration such methods bring is too often an amelioration for the eyes but not for the lungs, the nose and ears! The only completely satisfactory method of mechanical smoke abatement would be to replace coal with electricity for energy as well as for heating. This would effectively eliminate smoke and soot, but it would not in any way change the other nuisances produced by industry. Gas and smell could be eliminated by techno-chemical means to a limited extent.[1] Noise would not be affected by such devices at all. One might go on piling up evidence to show how incompletely and inadequately we can solve our problem if we rely on such means.

Only when industrial and residential areas are brought into proper positional relationship to prevailing winds, is a true solution reached. The natural method—planning—can be fully and completely successful. Residential areas, where proper planning methods are used, may be so placed as to escape all wind-borne nuisances.

As sun and summer breezes determine the proper plan for a house, so should prevailing winds determine the shape of a settlement.

Influence of prevailing winds on industrial settlements

We are learning to use knowledge of wind patterns to shape our modern industrial cities, but prevailing winds also had in other times their effect on city planning. Obviously smoke abatement was not the end sought by these early planners, and their experience suggests that we may well consider the wind patterns and prevailing winds

---

[1] It is known that the smell of chocolate factories may carry for several miles, and that the smell from stockyards is perceptible at distances of more than ten miles.

INFLUENCE OF PREVAILING WINDS on the distribution of smoke and on the shape of settlements.

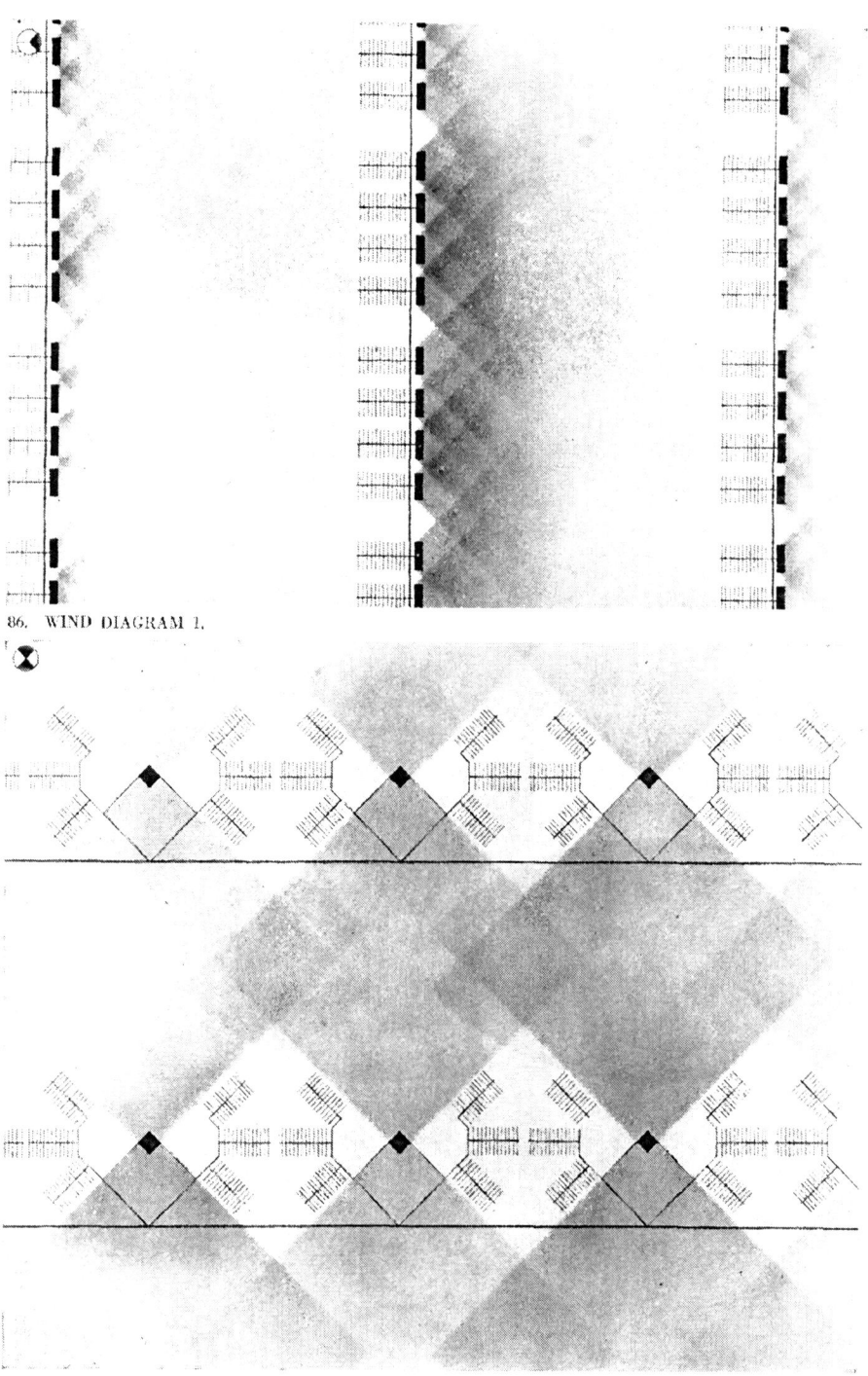

86. WIND DIAGRAM 1.

87. WIND DIAGRAM 2.

INFLUENCE OF PREVAILING WINDS on the distribution of smoke and on the shape of settlements.

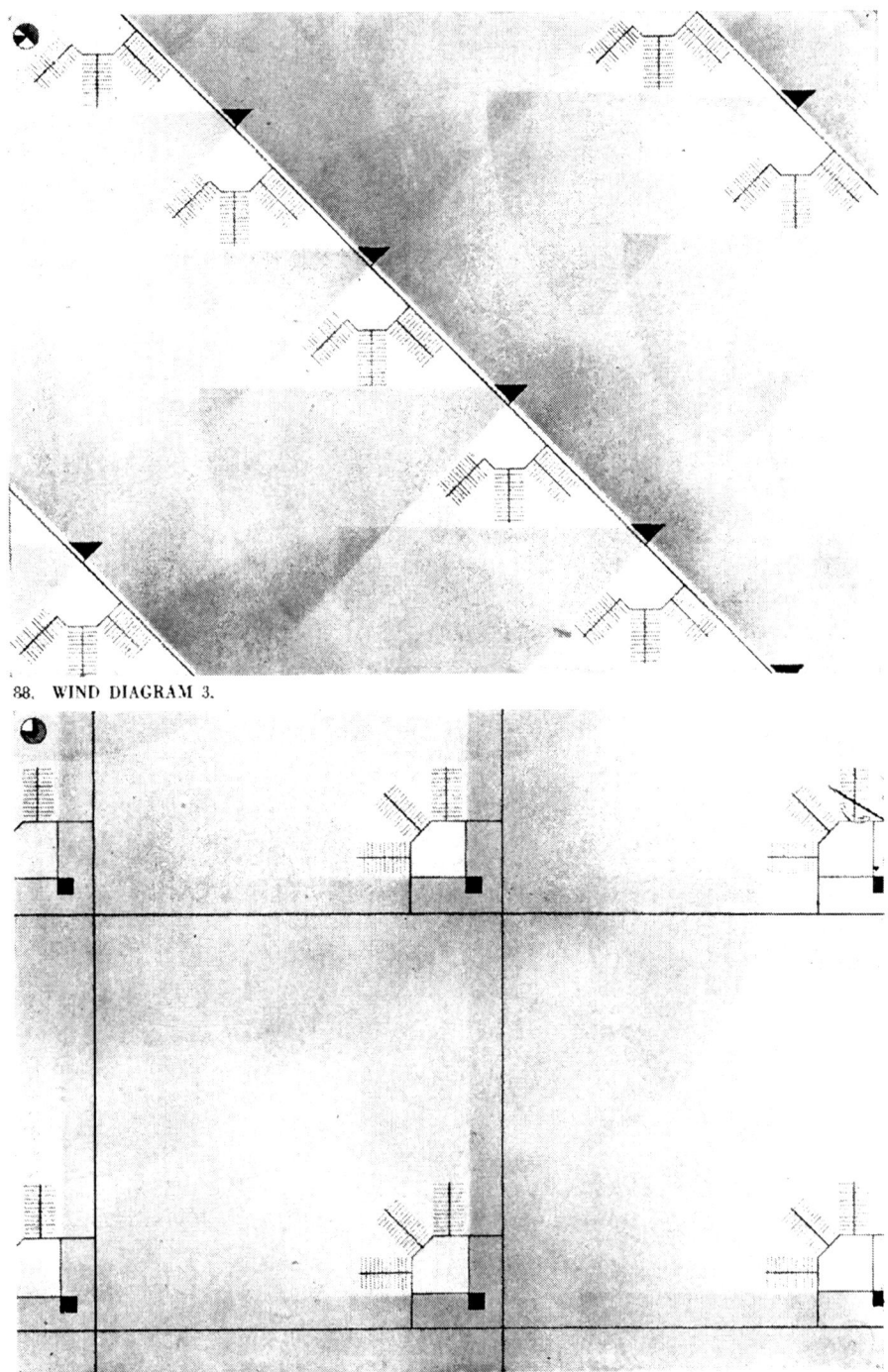

88. WIND DIAGRAM 3.

89. WIND DIAGRAM 4.

even in planning cities which have no industry and settlements where industries produce no smoke.

Corcula *(ill. 85)*, in Dalmatia, for example; is located on an island on a sound of the Adriatic Sea It faces a mountain on the mainland, the Monte Vipere. The position of this mountain influenced the location of the city; winds from its summit influenced the city's structure The streets are arranged in a herringbone pattern so that the cold mountain winds cannot penetrate them. These streets are laid out at an angle to the direction of the prevailing winds.

Four wind diagrams To protect residential areas from the atmospheric discharge from industrial areas. the layout of both areas must be determined by the prevailing winds The distribution of all wind-borne nuisances may be represented in diagram form In such a diagram, the sector of smoke is more or less extended within a circle If the residential area is to escape this smoke, it is obvious that it should be placed outside the smoke sector. As prevailing winds differ in every part of the country, no one pattern of location for residential and industrial areas can be devised. A new pattern must be worked out for each new set of circumstances.

Four diagrams show the influence of typical prevailing winds on the formation of industrial settlements. They illustrate also the great importance which wind conditions have in city planning.

In diagram 1 *(ill. 86)* we have a situation in which the prevailing winds blow from one direction only. A simple ribbon form of settlement is the result. In this arrangement, the industrial zone lies in the lee of the residential zone, in what we may call the wind shadow The distance between such a settlement and the next settlement ribbon would depend upon the area necessary for the absorption of the industrial smoke and fumes. This would, of course, vary according to the type of industry and the kind of fuel it uses

In diagram 2 *(ill. 87)* the winds blow in two opposite directions and have wind shadows of equal area and shape. Here again the settlement is a ribbon formation. The two most important elements—residential and industrial areas—are, however, no longer ribbon-like They have become squares, placed point to point, with their diagonals forming an unbroken straight line As in case of diagram 1 the next settlement ribbon can run parallel to the first at a sufficient distance

In diagram 3 *(ill 88)* the prevailing winds, blowing from two directions, do not cast equal wind-shadows One wind-shadow dominates the other, but it does not exceed half a circle. The result is again

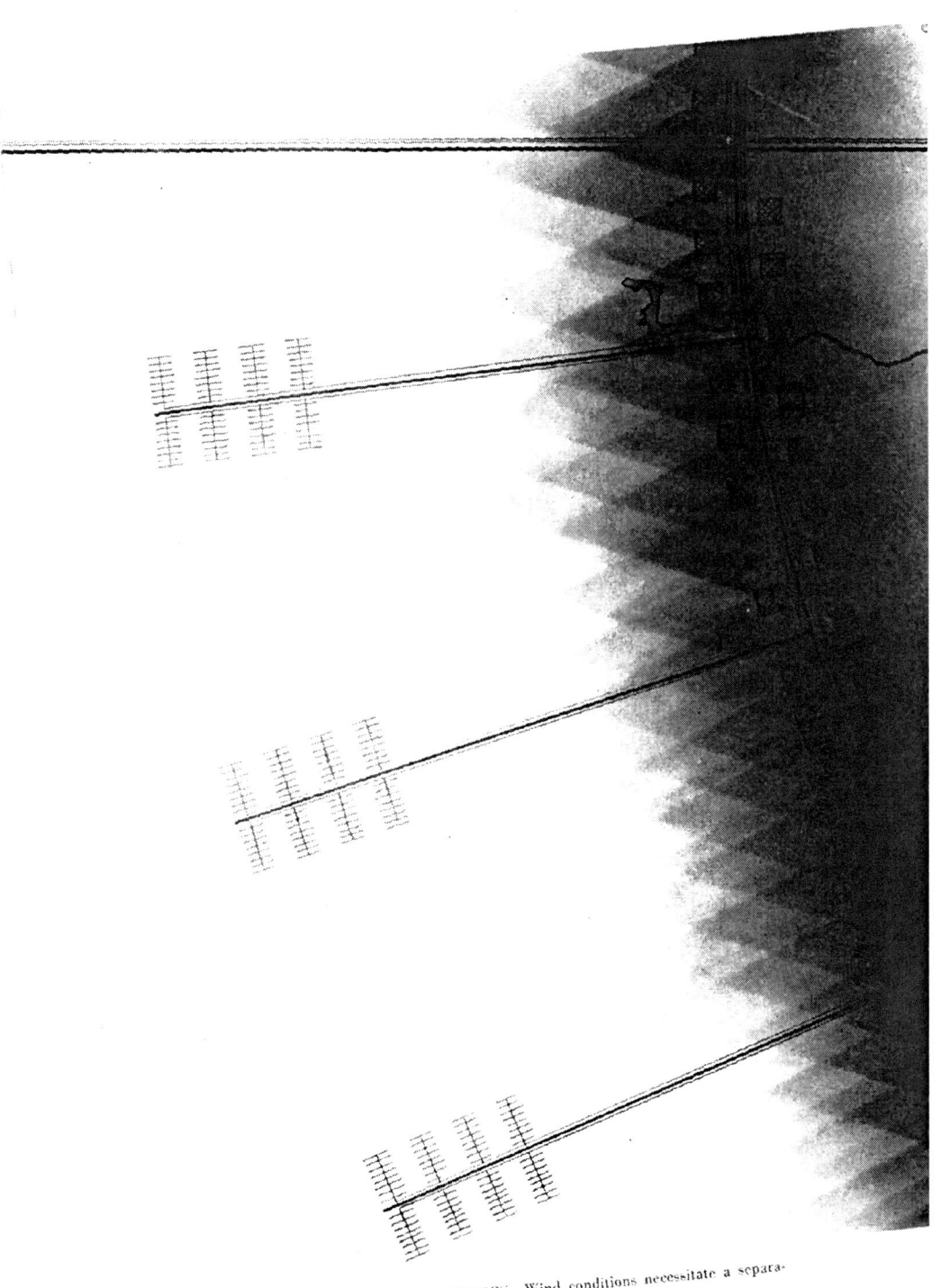

90. INTEGRATED SMOKE-PRODUCING INDUSTRIES. Wind conditions necessitate a separation of residential areas from industrial areas.

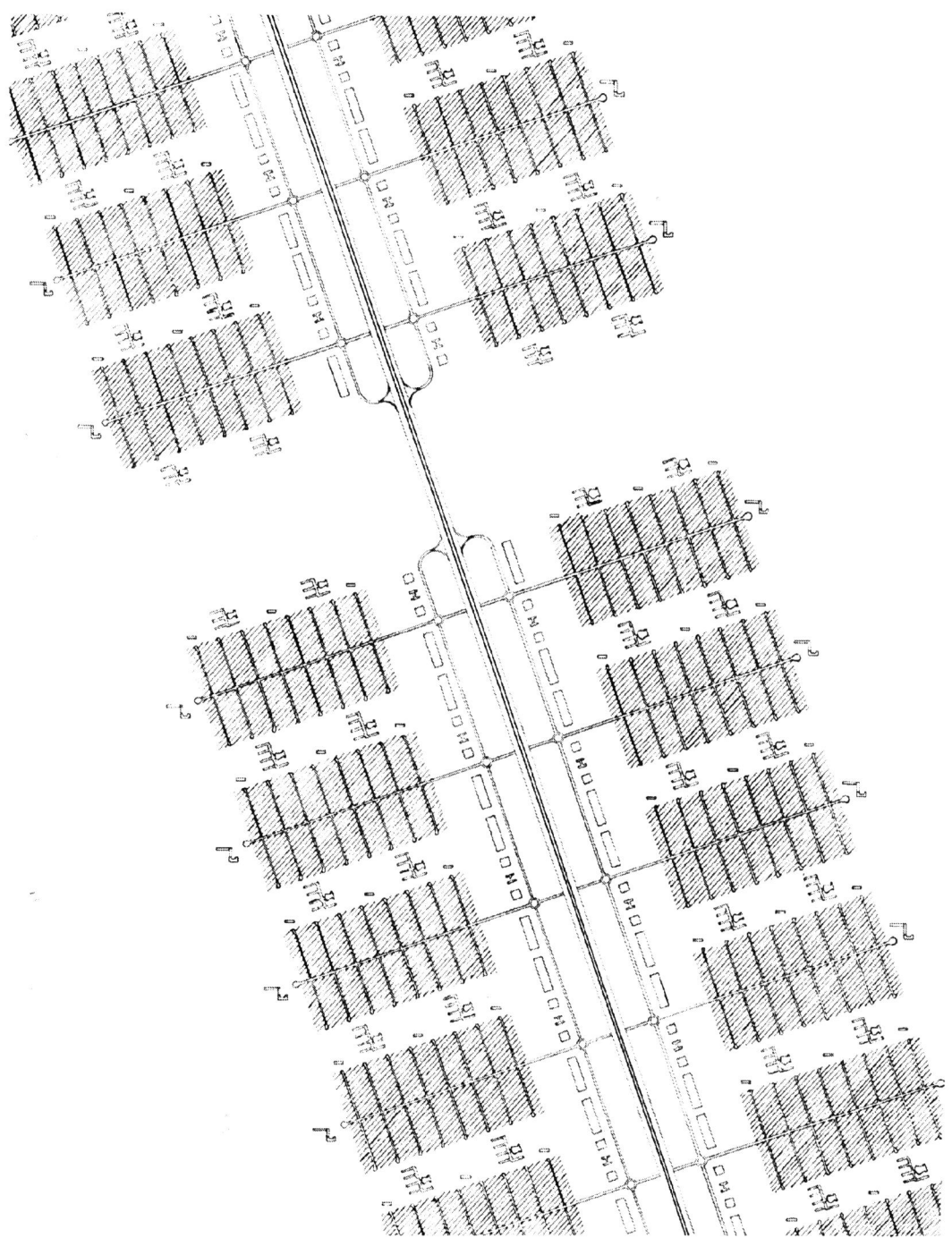

91. COMMERCIAL AREA with residential sections on both sides. See also illustration 92.

a ribbon settlement form. Here the two areas, industrial and residential, form triangles which lie opposite each other's apex. Once more, the adjacent settlement can run parallel.

In all three cases studied so far the prevailing winds have been so distributed on the wind chart that the total wind shadow has never exceeded half a circle. There are cases however, in which the wind-shadow exceeds this limit

Diagram 4 *(ill 89)* shows such a case. Here the industrial and residential areas form squares which are placed opposite one another Parallel and directly opposite ribbon-like settlements become impossible in such conditions A wind-shadow of such proportions permits only point-formed, fan-like settlements which must be built independent of one another. The spacing of these single settlement-points is, as in the other cases, dependent upon the size of the absorption area In this case, however, this absorption area is not three-, one-, or two-sided, but all-sided

These four diagrams show that, no matter how far the smoke sector may extend, a satisfactory solution can always be found and our settlement unit can always be used. That unit may not always retain its rectangular shape, for it may be modified according to conditions

Integrated industries When integrated industries must be located where prevailing winds result in point-formed settlements, then industries would be divided into several parts at considerable distances from each other Such a division would disintegrate the industries, and the solution would, therefore, probably be unsatisfactory It would be better in such a case, to abandon our principle that the distance between residential and industrial areas should not exceed that which a man can conveniently walk. We would remove the residential area beyond the reach of the smoke—that is, to a distance from the industries identical with the radius of smoke absorption The industrial and residential areas would then need to be connected by highways and railroads *(ill 90)*.

The commercial area For commercial areas too a proper relationship can be established Because these areas are free of smoke, we need not consider that problem in their planning Residential areas may be on either side of a traffic artery which passes through a park-strip amidst the commercial area If necessary, this traffic artery may consist of a railroad as well as a highway. Motorists can drive and park underneath each building in the commercial area—a solution for the tremendous parking problem in the commercial areas of our present cities There would be no pedestrian hazard, no traffic congestion It would be

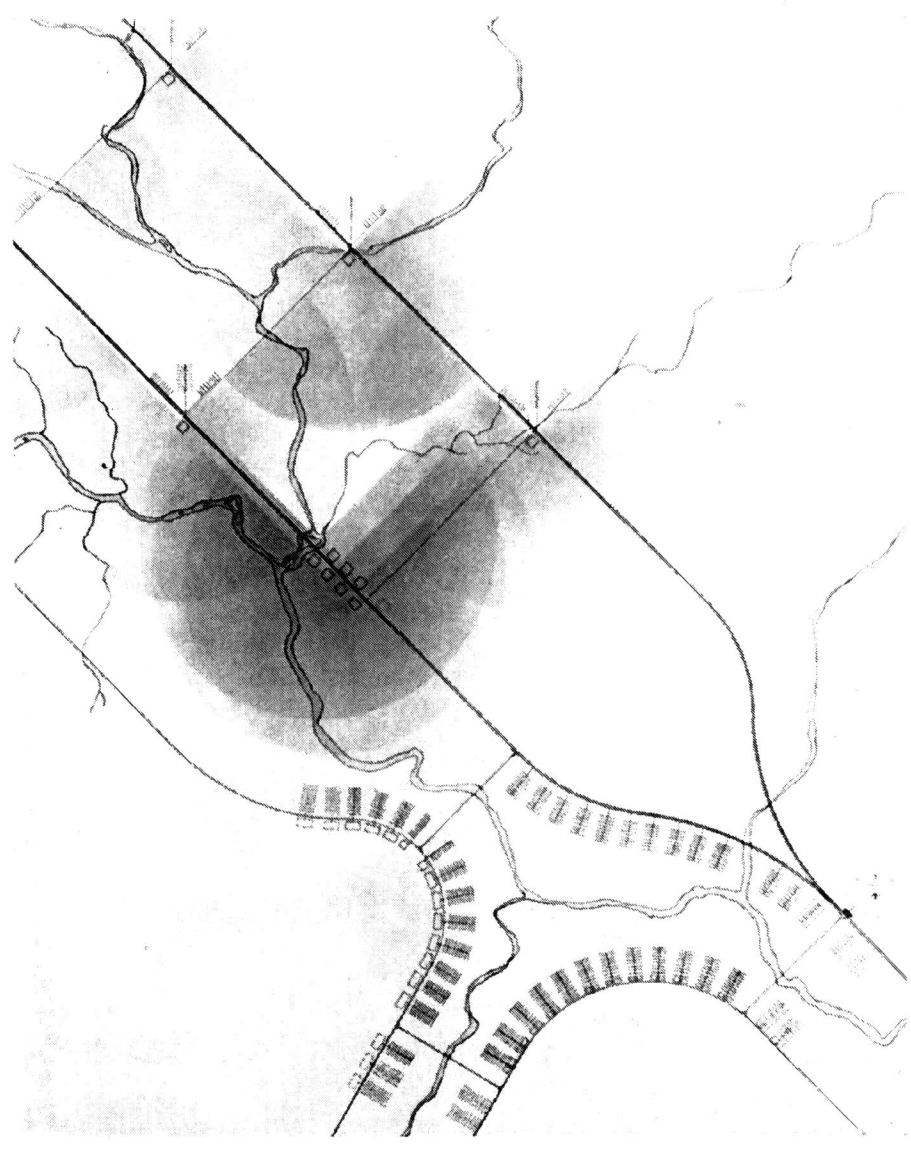

93. PLAN OF AN INDUSTRIAL CITY. Showing how natural features—in this case the river—can be included in the planning. The river together with a park form an ideal recreation area.

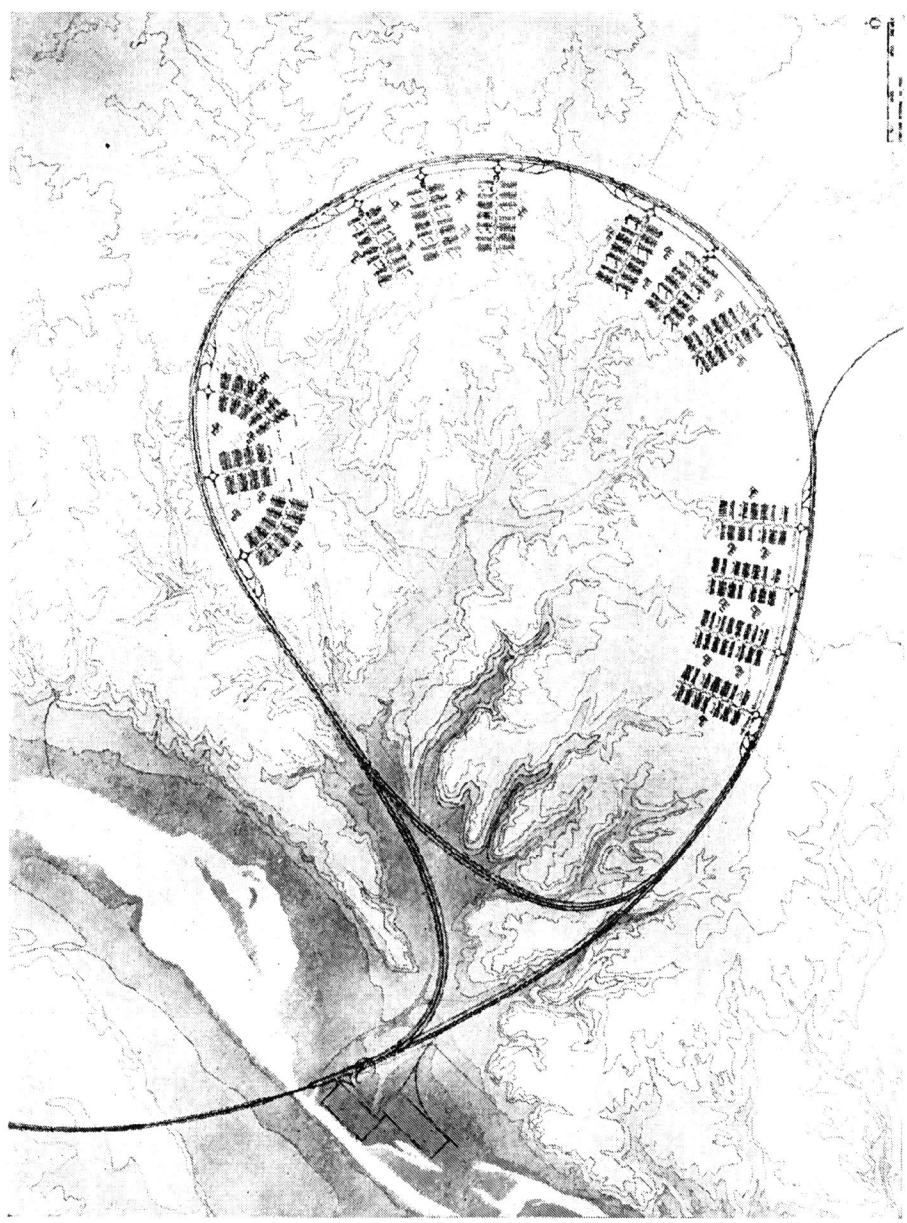

94. PART OF A REPLANNED CITY ON HILLY GROUNDS. Showing the flexibility and adaptability of the settlement units to any kind of terrain.

possible to walk from the residential area to every building in the commercial area Each building in the commercial area could be reached from two sides. from one by car *only*; from the other on foot *only* The pedestrian, freed from the dangers of traffic, could shop as leisurely as if he were in a park *(ills 91 and 92)*.

To simplify the problems under discussion, we have considered, in making our diagrams, only level ground But the flexibility of our settlement unit as well as of our planning system makes it entirely possible to use these units on any kind of terrain whether flat or hilly *(ills. 93 and 94)*. Sometimes the units may be used without modification Sometimes they must be modified according to topographical conditions They can be so modified and yet retain all their essential advantages.

Adaptability of the unit to any kind of terrain

As settlement units in every part of the city would be surrounded by parks, and the parks connected with the open country, a wide-spread recreational area would exist within easy reach of every dwelling.

Only in residential areas with a comparatively low population density will it be expedient to connect vegetable gardens directly with the houses Where population is dense such gardens might be located in the adjoining open area, though a small garden plot would still be available near each home Such a plan would make it possible to keep at a minimum the length of the streets, the conduits for water, gas, etc., and so keep the cost of settling the area low

Increase of the number of units by decreasing density

Our diagram *(ill. 95)* shows how large gardens directly connected with the houses would increase the size of a settlement To settle a population of 25,000, at a population density of 80 people per acre, we should require four units If the density were to be 50 seven units would be needed. And if the density were decreased to 30, ten units would be required to settle the 25,000 people.

The location of the vegetable gardens in the open area instead of beside the homes has certain advantages other than economy Such an arrangement would create a productive park system. The recreational area would thus be increased and the cost of its maintenance considerably decreased

The city in the landscape— its natural recreation area

The free space between the settlements could be used for farming The extension of this agricultural area would depend on two factors first, the open space necessary for the absorption of smoke. which, of course, would vary; and second, the number of people which the area has to supply. The farm area should be large enough to feed the whole population of the adjoining settlements. Where areas are

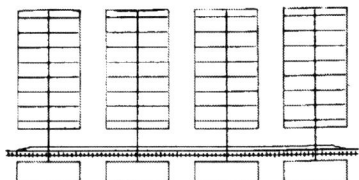

80 people on one acre.

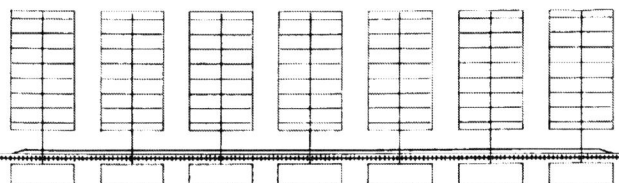

50 people on one acre.

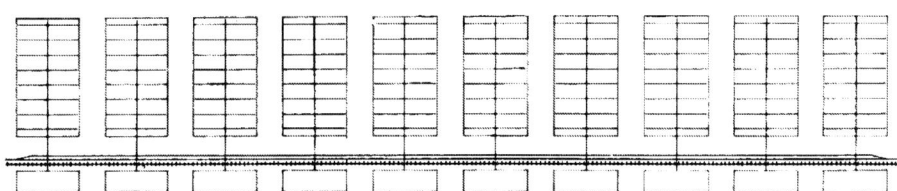

30 people on one acre.

95. DIAGRAM showing how the number of units increases by decreasing population density.

densely populated, it would be necessary, therefore, to have additional agricultural areas in connection with the settlements. This will be true also at points of central and regional concentration. Such points of concentration would have to receive their food supply from other agricultural areas.

Settlement units such as we have been considering, with their gardens and surrounding parks and the adjoining agricultural areas, bring the city into close relation with the landscape—its natural recreation area. The city, in fact, becomes part of the landscape. The one-storey house in the settlement unit disappears among trees and behind shrubs and a natural camouflage results *(ill. 96)*. The city will be within the landscape and the landscape within the city *(ills. 70, 92. 105)*.

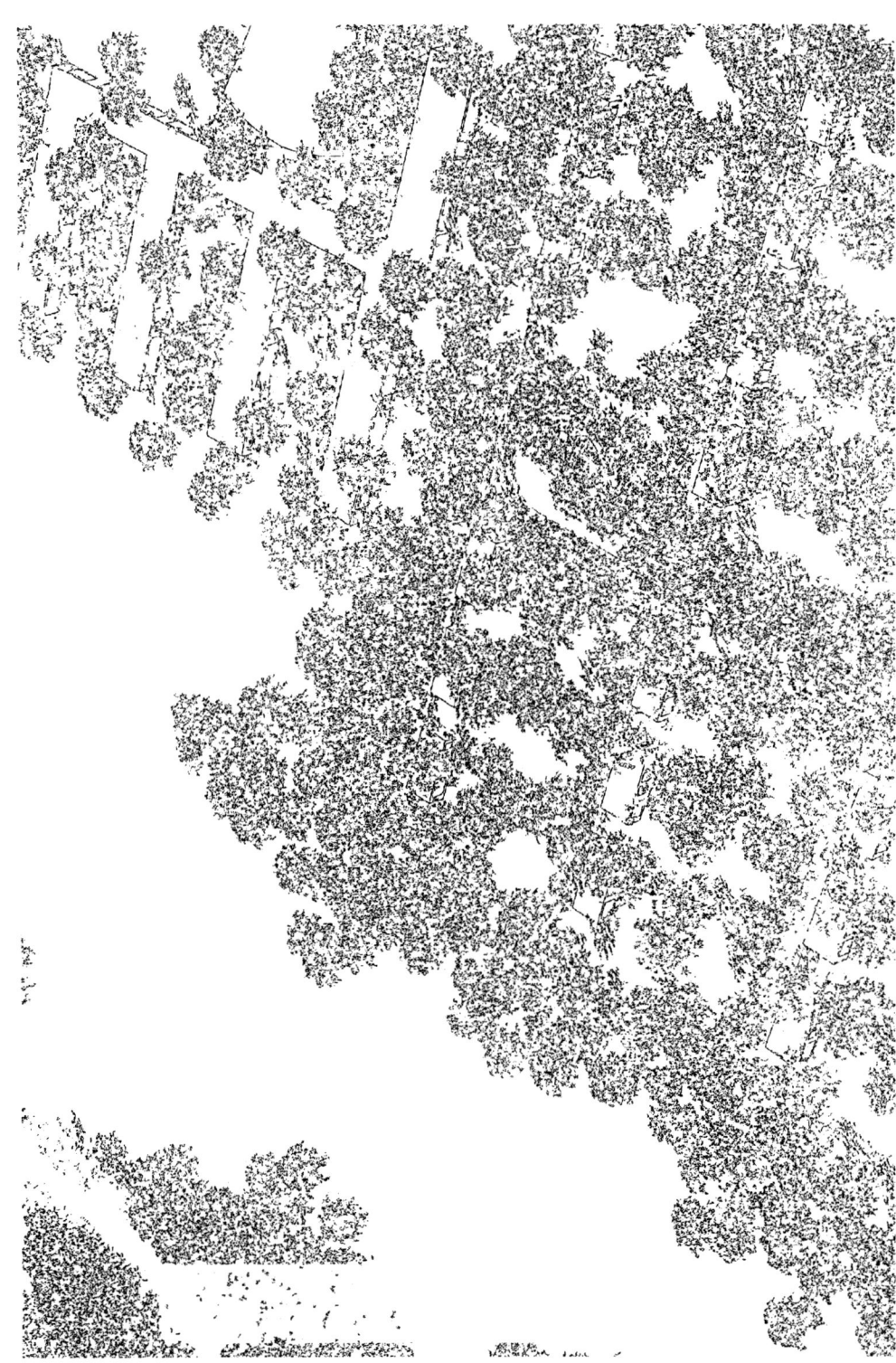

Theory and reality

The proposed combinations of settlement units to form cities constitute neither definite plans, nor suggestions for standardization. They are abstractions. Absolute cities do not exist. Cities are individuals. Their physiognomy depends on the character of the landscape, on the people who live in them, and on their function in the nation's life. Therefore, these elements which we have described, and their manifold possibilities of combination, must remain in the realm of theory. We need such theory as a starting point for the discovery of our methods of work. But when we undertake the actual work of planning, our methods must always be modified by reality. For city planning is not an abstract task. It is the fulfillment of human needs; the realization of human aims.

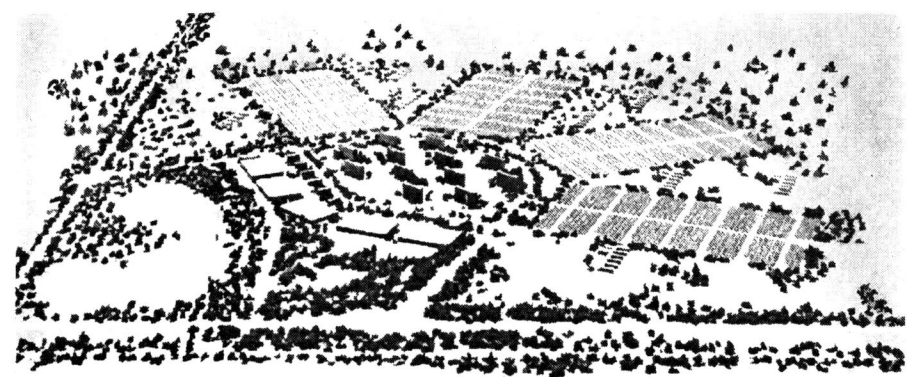

97. AMERICAN INDUSTRIAL CITY Replanned. See also illustration 102.

PART THREE

REPLANNING OF CITIES

To replan an existing city seems even more difficult and, therefore, more utopian, than to plan a new city. *Obstacles of replanning cities*

Great obstacles stand in the way of intelligent replanning. A considerable part of the national wealth is invested in the buildings of our cities. And even when the material values represented in these buildings no longer serve the interests of man, man still clings to them, not realizing that he has become their slave. Because of this paradoxical situation, many of the recognized evils of our cities are not being eliminated, even though their elimination is known to be absolutely necessary for the welfare of the whole community. Where material values are allowed to overshadow human beings planners are allowed to attempt only partial solutions. They have been consistently and constantly blocked from adopting plans which would involve changing the structure of the city. But the chaos within our cities can never be eliminated by individual partial solutions. Such solutions, in fact, only serve to perpetuate the chaos. And much of the money spent for "improving" the city is, for this reason, sheer waste.

How can we—and how must we—change our cities? How can we eliminate their defects and transform them so that they meet our present-day requirements of health and safety? *Old methods*

We must remember at the outset of our discussion that the old methods of replanning were costly and only temporarily successful They reached only partial solutions and were mainly concerned with the alleviation of traffic conditions They usually consisted of expensive reconstruction of old streets and equally expensive construction of new highways and subways Such measures improved specific conditions for a time, but did not touch the causes of the evils they sought to remedy The old conditions soon began to reappear as traffic continued to increase The "improvers" failed completely to recognize that traffic in itself does not cause the difficulties Those difficulties have a far more fundamental cause, and it is essential to find and deal with that cause if we are to effect a permanent and complete solution.

The ever changing city

The city is in a constant process of change. A comparison of our present-day cities with those of fifty or one hundred years ago shows how tremendous are the changes which have occurred *(ill 98)*. Will not similar changes also occur in the next fifty or a hundred years? Is it not obvious, therefore, that the only satisfactory plan must be one which takes account of this element of change? Would it not seem obvious also that expediency and economy alike dictate the basing of all necessary reconstruction on a comprehensive plan instead of perpetuating the present chaos by planlessly building new houses. streets, highways, and subways? Only when all reconstruction is based on such a plan can a new and organic city structure develop.

The city's environment

The process of change is as typical of the city's zone of influence as it is of the city itself As conditions within the city become increasingly unhealthy, prospective home owners choose to built outside the city limits. New settlements develop rapidly in the environs of the city. Such settlements exert a negative influence upon the city, even though the city continues to be the basis of their existence

Industry, as well as individuals, is in flight from the city, though the reasons for that flight are somewhat different An industry, for example, is compelled to enlarge its factory Land inside the city is expensive An investment in city property sufficient to allow the enlargement of the plant there would, if used outside the city limits, provide perhaps. for the purchase of a new site and the building of a new factory. The new factory in its new location could be built to incorporate more economical productions methods More favorable production conditions could be achieved. whereas those in the city are becoming increasingly unsatisfactory. Quite naturally the move to the country seems attractive Yet the relief secured by the move is temporary Within a relatively short time, the conditions typical of our present-day city. will prevail in the new location, since the

98. NEW YORK'S BROADWAY. 100 years ago, 50 years ago, and today. Tomorrow. . . ?

development of these new settlements is proceeding as planlessly as did that of the city itself. A sound plan for a city must reach beyond the city borders to its environs and its zone of influence. We must always realize that city planning involves regional planning.

Application of our planning principles

In order to demonstrate how our principles of city planning can be applied to the replanning of existing urban communities, let us consider three cities and make diagrams of their replanning. These diagrams do not pretend to be final solutions. They are general suggestions only, intended to offer planning ideas. City planning will always depend upon specific conditions and upon the tasks demanded of each particular city. No two cities have identical problems. Yet by dealing with typical problems generally and abstractly, we may clarify certain recurring urban problems and simplify the theoretical possibilities of reconstructing the city.

Let us examine first two small industrial cities and follow their development and their possible replanning. We have chosen these particular cities because they have defects characteristic of many of our cities and because they present varied problems due to the differences in their prevailing winds. Later we shall examine a metropolis and show how our principles could be applied in the replanning of a city of several millions.

An European industrial city

The first of our small cities was founded during the twelfth century, at the time of the colonization of Eastern Europe. The original settlement was protected by its location on a height within a flood area of a large river. Situated on an old highway, the city was, like most colonial cities of its time. peopled first by peasants and craftsmen. During the 14th century it became the residence of a prince and the center of a territorial state. Gaining in importance during the 18th century, it became the administrative seat of a small state, and parks and palaces typical of such cities appeared within it. It was so favorably located near a region rich in natural resources, that it developed during the 19th and 20th centuries into an industrial city. Its population has increased steadily and is still increasing. Today it numbers 80.000.

The city's chaotic structure

As the city gradually developed into an industrial one, its structure was completely disorganized. Residential areas are located in the wind shadow of the industrial plants which rose along the railroad lines. The defects of such a city are only too apparent. The entire residential area suffers from the smoke, fumes. soot, noise, and odors from the industries. Conditions within the residential area vary considerably. Large parts of the city are desolate, other parts are situated in the flood area. The replanning of such areas is essential for social and hygienic reasons. The railroad is located on street level, causing traffic disruptions which will have to be eliminated by elevating the tracks. The main highway cuts irregularly through the residential area and traffic accidents are therefore numerous *(ill 99)*.

Three schemes

These structural defects can be rectified only by reorganizing the city. Such reorganization must be based on the correlation of the city areas. It must pay special attention to the expedient location of industrial and residential areas in relation to prevailing winds. Once such fundamental reorganization is effected, traffic disturbances and dangers can be easily eliminated.

A simplified scheme shows the principal defects of the present city and, particularly, the faulty location of the residential area in relation to the industrial area.

A second scheme demonstrates how, if the industrial area is retained and concentrated, suitable location of the residential areas will eliminate the nuisances caused by the industries. This solution is not completely satisfactory. It still has faults which a more efficient reconstruction could eradicate. Should the city expand, the distance between residential and industrial areas, which should not exceed the limits set by pedestrian traffic, would increase to such an extent that mechanical means of transportation would become necessary.

A third scheme proposes a ribbon-like arrangement of the existing industrial area along the railroad. Here too the residential area must be re-located opposite to the wind direction. All traffic disturbances are eliminated in such a plan. The railroad and the main highway are located within a green belt between the residential and industrial areas. The workers live opposite their places of work and they can walk to work since the maximum distance between residential and industrial areas is kept within the limit of convenient pedestrian travel. Future expansion of the city can proceed organically, along the traffic belt, with no impairment of favorable traffic conditions. Congestion, such as might arise if the second scheme of reconstruction were used, will be avoided. Considered from every point, the superiority of the ribbon system is evident *(ill 100)*.

The replanned city

The final scheme shows how the replanning of this city should be carried out. The ribbon of the city is divided into three groups; each group subdivided into four settlement units. Each unit contains those community institutions necessary for it. Each unit shares with its neighboring unit those social and cultural institutions which are necessary for two units in close proximity. All four units together maintain those community institutions and services which can best be main-

133

99. EUROPEAN INDUSTRIAL CITY. Diagram of present state and condition. In lower left corner the historical development during six centuries — at 1200, 1400 and 1800 A. D.

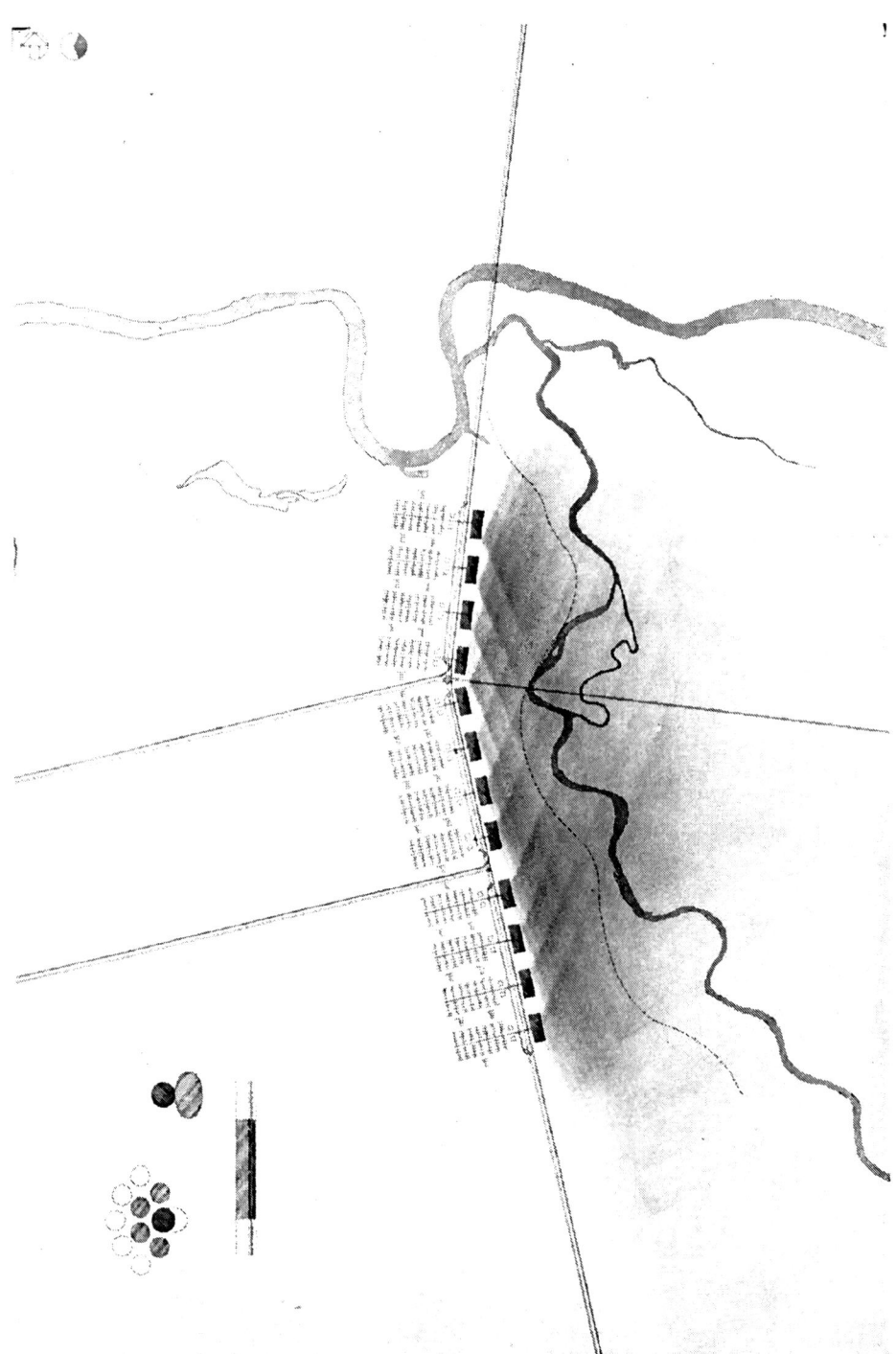

100. EUROPEAN INDUSTRIAL CITY. Diagram of its proposed replanning, 1933. In the lower left corner three schemes; the upper showing present state; the left a replanning around the existing industrial area; the right as a ribbon development.

tained by the entire group. The institutions of the business and administrative zones can be distributed in the same way. Adjacent to the units are kitchen gardens, situated in parks surrounding these units. Though separated by these parks all these units of the three groups comprising the settlement together form an urban organism. Each of the three main groups of the city has a railroad station for local traffic with the other groups of the settlement and for long-distance traffic. The highway connects the different groups with the main highway. Communication among neighboring groups could be also achieved by buses, or streetcars.

The actual reconstruction

The actual reconstruction of the city, in accordance with this scheme, would be very simple. The existing industrial plants along the railroad could form the basis for it, and later industrial developments could be added in accordance with the plan. All new dwellings could be built according to this scheme. The large desolate areas of the old city could be gradually rebuilt in new locations. Their necessary reconstruction might be the beginning of a rebuilt city.

An industrial city in the Middle West

The other small industrial city we have chosen for study was founded with the settling of the American Middle West. It is located on one of the Great Lakes, between two large cities, one of which has developed into a metropolis during the last hundred years. These two large cities have influenced the development of their smaller neighbor. Geographical location has also been a determining influence upon its development. In 1835 a few families founded this settlement at the mouth of a river, in the midst of a rich farming region. It soon became the trading center and port for the surrounding countryside. Rather early in its history, it concerned itself, not only with trade, but also with the processing of agricultural products and the manufacture of farm machinery. In 1850, when the settlement was incorporated as a town, its population was 3,500.

The coming of the railroad made the town's port location less strategic. Gradually, like many another small trading center, it lost its importance as a port. Changes in agricultural production, as the cultivation of corn and grain was replaced by the raising of cattle and the production of dairy products for city consumption, also contributed to the change in the character of the town. Such new conditions spelled disaster for many similar communities. For this city, however, they marked the beginning of a period of new growth. Because it was situated between two large settlements, of which one became a transcontinental railroad center, land prices were low there and skilled labor plentiful, the town gradually developed into a manufacturing city with a population of 50,000.

This change from a small agricultural trading center to an industrial city provided a new basis of existence. But it weakened the structure of the city. Two railroad lines traversed it and were connected by a third. Industrial plants developed along these railroad lines and an H-shaped industrial area arose within the city. This arrangement of the industrial area was favorable economically, but it had unsatisfactory effects upon the entire city area. All the residential areas are now located within the smoke zone. Motor highways cut through the city area, with consequent hazard and confusion. Conditions in the residential districts vary. A considerable number of the dwellings should be rebuilt, particularly in the old parts of the city and around the industrial plants *(ill. 101)*.

Any permanent solution for this city's problems must include the elimination of all its defects. As soon as a suitable location of the different areas in relation to the prevailing winds has been found, unsatisfactory traffic conditions can be easily rectified. Wind conditions are such in this city as to require the type of layout where residential and industrial areas form squares lying opposite to each other. The wind shadow exceeds half of the area of a circle, and therefore, a point-formed, fan-like arrangement of the single settlements built independently of each other is indicated. The square of the industrial area can be expanded according to its requirements. All plants producing smoke, fumes, and noise must be located within this square. The residential area, also theoretically a square, can likewise be expanded as necessary. The entire population of the city could be placed within one such square. But if this were done, the distance between residential and industrial areas would be so great that mechanical means of transportation would become necessary. This would be in contradiction to our basic principle that the distance between such areas should not exceed the limits set by pedestrian traffic. If it seemed desirable or necessary to concentrate the entire population in one such square, however, a solution could be found by increasing the population density. This would avoid the use of mechanical transportation, but it would mean the sacrifice of another of our basic principles—the desirability of housing the entire population in one-family houses. We should have to provide only apartment houses. A better solution would be to plan two settlements. At a population density of 80 people to an acre, 25,000 could be housed conveniently in each settlement. The distance between the two settlements would be determined by the extent of the smoke zone.

Each residential square is divided into four converging units. In the sectors between these units are parks which connect the settlement

The replanned city; wind condition result in fan-like arrangement

101. AMERICAN INDUSTRIAL CITY. Diagram of present state and condition.

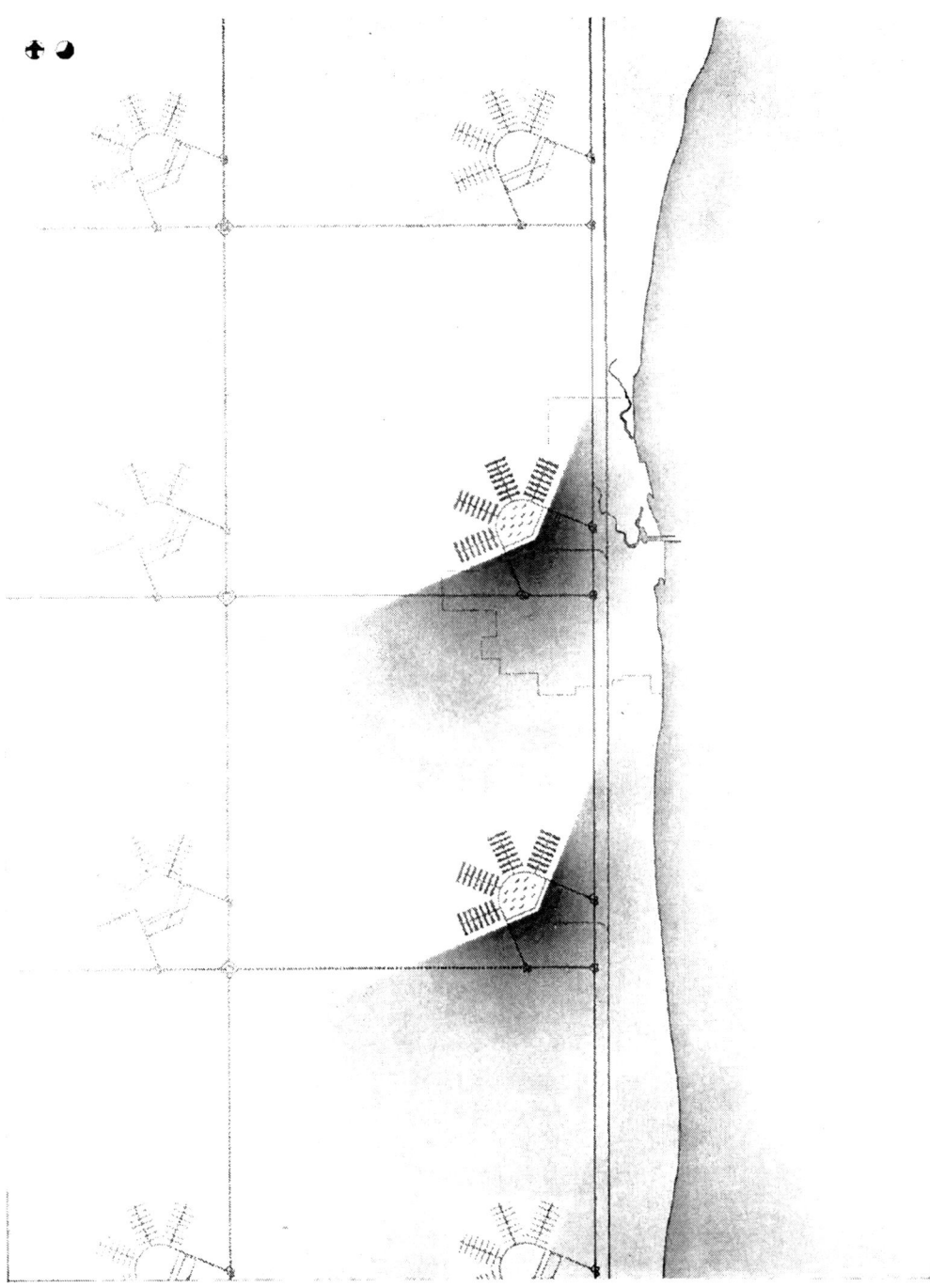

102. AMERICAN INDUSTRIAL CITY. Diagram of its proposed replanning, 1938. See also illustration 97.

with the landscape. Schools, playgrounds, and kitchen gardens are located within the parks. To compensate for the different location of their units, we have chosen one-family houses which differ in their shape but which have the right orientation. In front of these units within a park area are located apartment houses where single persons and childless families may live. Between these apartment houses and the industrial area are the commercial and administrative buildings *(ills 97 and 102).*

Future expansion

Future expansion will be accomplished by the erection of new settlements either in a north-south or an east-west direction. While railroads and motor highways connect the settlements with one another and with other cities, the settlements themselves will be free of through traffic.

Procedure of reconstruction

The actual reconstruction of this city could begin in connection with the existing principal industrial plants. All building of new residential dwellings could then be carried out in accordance with our diagram. Buildings in the slum area could be replaced in the same way. A reconstruction of the city could thus take place gradually without disturbing its life.

Chicago Its planless and rapid growth

Now let us apply our principles of city planning to a metropolis. The diagram we use is, of course, simplified. This metropolis, Chicago, was founded in the beginning of the nineteenth century. It is located on Lake Michigan where an old trade route crossed the intercontinental river system of the Mississippi and the St. Lawrence River. The city early achieved prominence as an inland harbor, as well as an overseas port. With the development of the railroad, it became the center of a continental railroad system and the most important commercial and industrial center of the Middle West. Today its population—suburbs included—is almost 4,000,000. Due to its rapid and unprecedented growth, a considerable part of the city still has an aspect of incompleteness. It shows all the symptoms typical of our present-day cities. Industrial plants are scattered over the entire city area, so that all parts of the city suffer from the noxious fumes those plants produce. The residential districts are very uneven in quality. Large parts are in such desolate condition that their removal is one of the main and pressing problems of the city. The large commercial district, though it is also to some extent dispersed over the whole area, is mainly concentrated in the city's center. Here too is little uniformity of quality. Many of the buildings have become obsolete, and even the good buildings have decreased in value because they have been built too close together and therefore deprive each other of light and air. The divergence between city plan and its buildings is particularly evident here The existing block and street system has no organic relationship to the skyscraper.

Traffic constitutes the principal problem here Industry and, to some extent, business, is dispersed over the whole city There is no natural relationship between these districts and their residential areas Therefore, traffic has had to develop beyond reasonable requirements, with the result that today communication by means of motor vehicles has become extremely difficult and slow Many costly attempts have been made to improve traffic conditions, but the problem, which is caused by the disorganization of the city structure, and that of the suburbs, has not been solved We have here clear evidence of the way in which the disorganization of the city affects the suburbs We have indicated in our diagram the zone of influence of the smoke and gases from the industries dispersed over the whole area If we observe the steady growth of the suburbs and their industries, we can see that soon we shall have the same unfavorable conditions outside the city as now prevail within the city limits *(ill 103)*

"The growth of the city," wrote Daniel H. Burnham[1] in the introduction to his famous Plan of Chicago, in 1909, "has been so rapid that it has been impossible to plan for the economical disposition of the great influx of people, surging like a human tide to spread itself wherever opportunity for profitable labor offered place Though few people are appalled at the results of the progress, at the waste in time, strength, and money which congestion in the city streets begets; at the toll of lives taken by disease when sanitary precautions are neglected, and at the frequent outbreaks against law and order which result from narrow and pleasureless living The people in Chicago have ceased to be impressed by rapid growth or the great size of the city What they insist upon asking now is, How are we living? Are we in reality prosperous? Is the city a convenient place for business? Is it a good labor market in the sense that labor is sufficiently comfortable to be efficient and content? Will the coming generation be able to stand the nervous strain of city life? When competence has been accumulated must we go elsewhere to enjoy the fruits of independence? If the city does not become better as it becomes bigger, shall not the defect be remedied? These are questions that cannot be brushed aside They are the most pressing questions of our day, and everywhere men are anxiously seeking the answers."

Daniel H. Burnham's opinion

Today, one generation later, these questions are still unanswered

---
[1] Daniel H Burnham and Edward H Bennet *Plan of Chicago* Edited by Charles Moore, Chicago, 1909

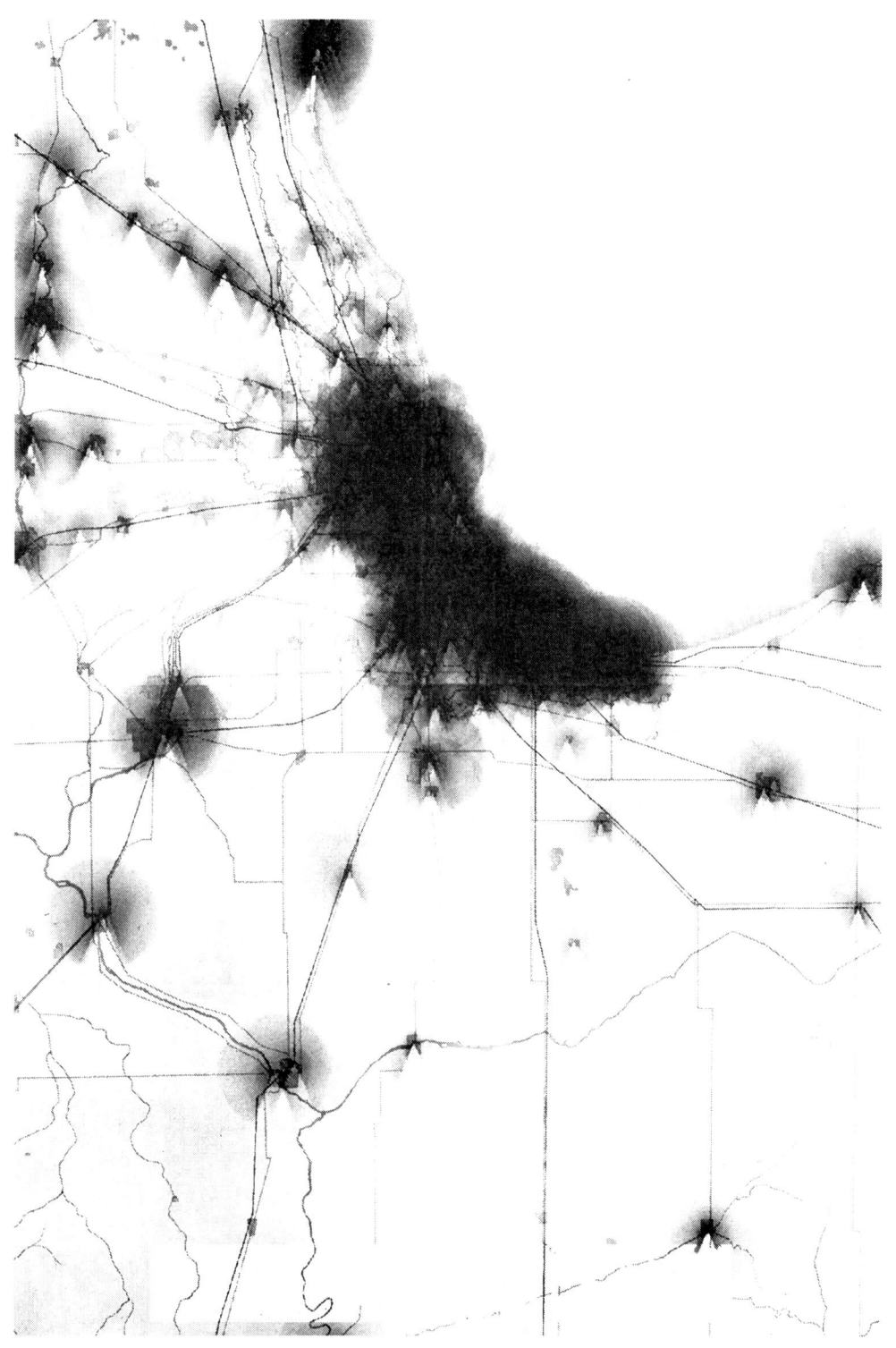

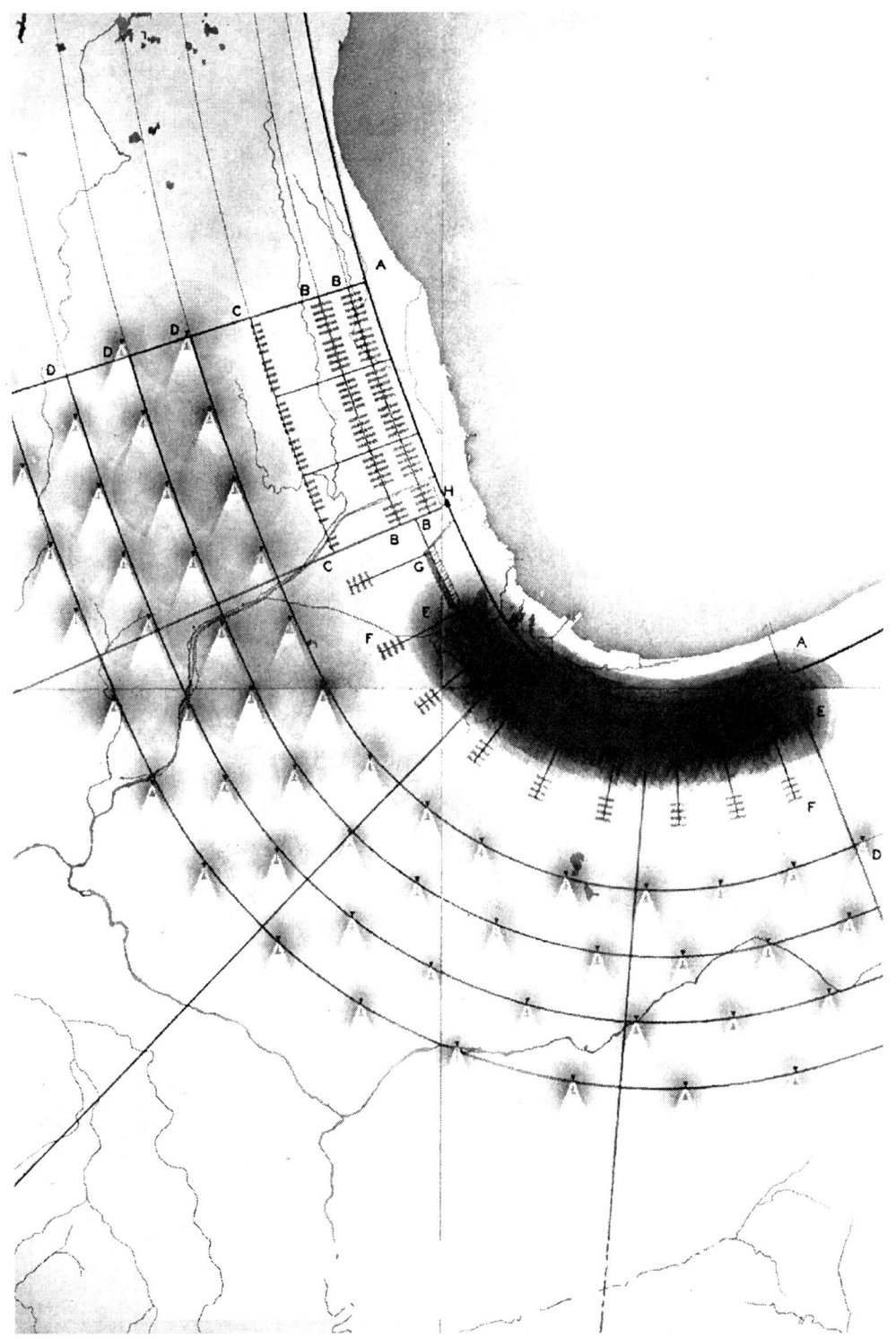

	The problems remain the same. Chicago has become bigger and more populated. Its difficulties have increased in even greater proportion.
The reorganization of the city	The reorganization of the city areas is essential here. To effect this we must distinguish between two main parts of our city plan: The commercial area and the industrial area. The industrial area may be subdivided into two parts; heavy and light manufacturing industries. These parts, together with their respective residential districts, form the city. The suburbs, and also the areas containing country residences, are parts of this whole. A replanning of the city must begin with the reorganization

A VOICE FROM THE PEOPLE.
From the column of "Here is Chicago": Chicago Daily News.

of these areas. It must establish a proper relationship between them and provide for their connection with one another by adequate means of transportation.

Heavy industry	The large area of the heavy industries lies along the lake to the south. This location provides access to direct water transportation as well as to railroads. In our reorganization, the heavy industries could remain where they are, for the time being, but they should ultimately be removed from the lake front and situated along a canal. The residential districts related to these areas will have to be changed, for their present location, within the zone of especially heavy fumes and gases, is extremely unsatisfactory. If the entire area of the heavy industries were rearranged according to the prevailing winds, it would have to be divided into various parts, at a considerable distance from one another. A better solution would be not to sub-divide these industries but to place the residential area at an adequate distance from the industrial area, and to use railroads and highways to connect the two *(ill. 90)*.

101. CITY OF CHICAGO. A diagram of its proposed replanning, 1940. A—Park. B—Commercial area. C—Smokeless industry. D—Smoke-producing light industry. E—Heavy industry. F—Residential areas for heavy industry. G—Airport and central station. H—Harbor, freight yard and warehouses. Turn to

Unlike the fairly concentrated heavy industries, manufacturing plants of light industries are scattered over the whole city. Some are located on the river which connects the lake with the Mississippi. This river will in part determine the future location of the manufacturing industry. By a system of canals connected with it, adequate water transportation as well as adequate railroad transportation would be available These light industries can easily be divided into smaller units without impairing the production process. Some of them are producers of smoke and fumes. but some are free of such disturbing by-products In the former case, the prevailing winds will determine the theoretical shape of the settlement, in the latter the settlement can be laid out without regard to the winds New plants of the smoke-producing industries should be spread over a wider area, but their residential and industrial areas can still be located within the limits set by pedestrian traffic The different settlements form a quasi-ribbon to which, at adequate distances, other settlement ribbons run parallel All settlements, as well as the settlement ribbons. are connected with one another by a railroad and highway system

Manufacturing industries with smoke and without

Proper relationship can also be established between the residential and commercial areas The size of the residential area here must be kept within the limits set by pedestrian traffic, so that transportation is unnecessary in the commercial area Since commercial areas are not smoke-producers, residential districts can be erected on both sides of them.

The commercial area

The efficient reconstruction of the commercial area presents very difficult problems. The main consideration which has guided their building hitherto has been. not actual requirements, but the exploitation of land. An ever-increasing number of storeys was the unsatisfactory result of this policy One building, therefore, deprives the next one of light in the lower storeys The over-valuation of one building causes the depreciation of the next Technical progress in the construction of office buildings has steadily advanced, but little or no attention has been given to the problems of city planning which arise with that construction As a result of this one-sided development, the office building has never attained the utility of which it is capable.

In order to determine at least approximately the amount of office space actually needed, we shall base our calculations on one of the settlement units of the residential area About 12,500 people can be housed in such a unit, at a population density of 80 people to an acre Approximately one third of these people—about 4.000—are employed Each one of these employed persons will need 100 square feet

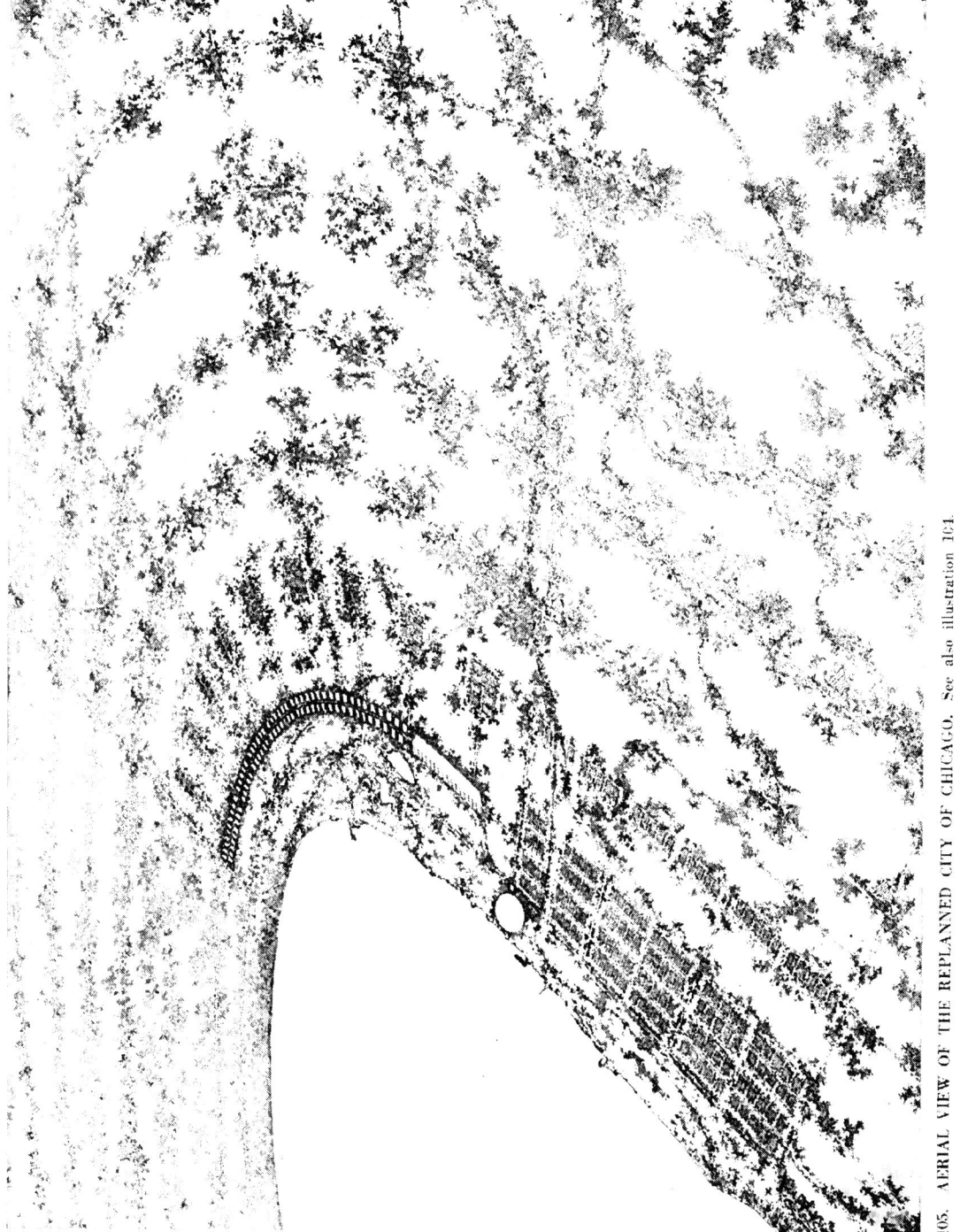

165. AERIAL VIEW OF THE REPLANNED CITY OF CHICAGO. See also illustration 164.

of office space, a total of some 400,000 square feet for our commercial unit This area could be provided by one twenty-storey office building. having a floor space of 20,000 square feet per storey. Since the settlement unit, with its adjacent park area will be approximately 2500 feet wide, the length of the related commercial unit would therefore be 2500 feet. The width of the commercial unit would be determined by local conditions An office building such as we have described. if an H-shaped plan is used in its construction, would require an area of only 200 feet by 200 feet Enough space would thus be left for the other buildings required by the unit, such as administration buildings, stores, restaurants, theatres. Even when all these buildings are erected, ample space will be left to give the entire commercial area a park-like aspect *(ills 91 and 92)*.

In our diagram we show how the various parts of the city might be arranged *(ills 104 and 105)*. The entire lake front becomes a park In this large wooded area are spacious residences, apartment houses, hotels, gardens, farms. playgrounds and camps. When the heavy industries have been moved to a canal inland. this park will stretch unbroken along the entire lake shore Inland, behind this park area, are the heavy industries to the south and the commercial area to the north, both with their residential districts

Diagram of the reorganized city

The commercial area as well as that occupied by heavy industry is shifted somewhat from its present site The beginnings of such development could, therefore, be made in unoccupied land where new buildings could be erected to replace those which have become obsolete.

Parallel to the commercial area, but separated from it by another park strip, lie the light industries which do not produce noxious fumes. Beyond these and the residential settlements of the heavy industries, the other light industries are so arranged that each settlement is free of the smoke and fumes produced by its own or neighboring factories. The land between these scattered settlements could be used for farms and woods A system of highways and railroads connects all parts of the city. All heavy industries and, where necessary, light industries as well. will be served by canals The center of this transportation system—the main station—lies between the heavy industry and the business area Here are the airport, the warehouses. the freight yards, and the docks.

Any of the areas of the city could be easily expanded by the addition of new units. A new railroad running from north to south. parallel to the lake shore. will unite all existing railroad lines and connect the areas of the new city Communication with the remotest parts of the

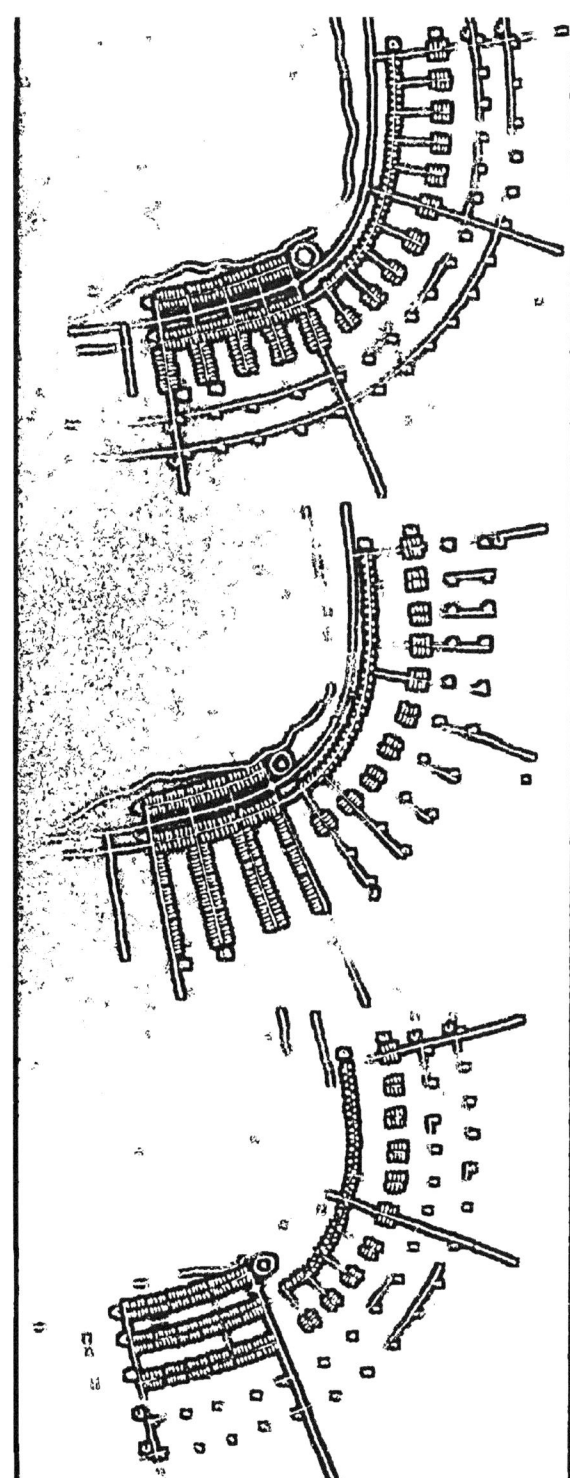

106. CITY OF CHICAGO. Three sketches showing arrangement of the different parts of the city determined by the ratio between the smoke producing and smokeless industries. A—Commercial area B—Smokeless industry C—Smoke producing light industry D—Heavy industry E—Residential areas for heavy industry

whole city area will be possible by means of the network of railroad lines. Another network of highways provides additional means of communication. The enormous traffic problem of the metropolis which today seems to defy solution will disappear. Citizens will be able to reach all parts of the city by automobile, not only quickly but safely.

All the residential areas in this plan are based in their structure on our settlement unit. The buildings in these units can, however, be varied according to particular requirements. And, no matter how much the units may differ, they will all be free of through-traffic, because only necessary traffic will enter them. The size of the units is limited always by pedestrian traffic. In all parts of the city, except the area of the heavy industries, the residential areas are opposite the places where their people work, and traffic, therefore, is greatly reduced. All residential districts of the industrial areas are located according to the prevailing winds and are therefore free from the nuisances of industry. Good hygienic conditions can prevail everywhere. Sunshine will penetrate into each room of every house and every apartment. Each house can have its garden. Since the settlement units are surrounded by parks, recreational areas are in the immediate vicinity of the houses. Schools and playgrounds are in these parks and can be reached from the houses of the settlement units without crossing a traffic street.

"Urbs in Horta"

If we meet these requirements, we shall have, not only a city built according to the needs and demands of today, but also a city rather well protected against aerial warfare. It will tend to be decentralized, and it can thus combine the advantages of the small town with those of the large city. The metropolis, too, can be merged with the landscape; it can, in fact, with its parks and gardens, become a part of it. "Urbs in horta"—the city set in a garden—Chicago's old motto, could become reality again.

It is claimed that such reconstruction of the metropolis is impossible, but the objections raised do not stand the test of reason. Naturally a reconstruction cannot be effected by tearing down the existing city. But if all future building were to be carried on according to a comprehensive plan, the desired end could be reached with comparative ease. If we understand clearly the necessity of the task, if we visualize with imagination the steps toward its accomplishment, the means and possibilities to carry through the work can surely be found.

Is reconstruction possible?

Reconstruction could begin with the construction of a main highway and the connection and consolidation of the railroads. Such reconstruction is badly needed, not only for the city's development of the future, but also to meet pressing needs of today Because there is little space available for expansion, many industries are being compelled to move their plants outside the city limits. If the building of such new plants is carried out systematically, the beginnings of actual reconstruction will already be made. Thousands of new dwellings are needed each year, as old structures become obsolete. They also could be built in relation to a comprehensive plan

The slum problem   The rebuilding of large slum areas and the removal of their insufficient and unsanitary buildings is a task we know to be imperative We should undertake that task, but not without understanding and recognition of the causes of the conditions we seek to remedy Slum clearance as a project independent of an over-all plan can never hope to accomplish its purpose A brief survey of the making of slums will show that this is true

What has created our slum areas? Certainly not the impoverished slum dwellers who must live here because here alone are rents within their reach Why are rents low in such areas? There are three principal reasons In the first place, the houses and flats are old, overcrowded, in disrepair, and without modern conveniences In the second place, the owners are holding their property in the hope that the spread of the commercial administrative center of the city may bring that property into demand as a skyscraper site While they wait for their property valuation to be thus suddenly increased, they are content to make from the obsolete structures on their land just enough to pay the taxes This hopeful waiting is, of course, useless, for as the modern office building tends to increase in height the area required for commerce and administration tends to decrease, and the possibility of increased valuations in the slum area becomes more and more remote. In the third place, as warehouses and factories with their smoke and fumes encroach upon these once desirable residential districts. their tenants leave in search of more pleasant surroundings.

It is possible to approach slum clearance by the simple expedient of replacing obsolete apartments and houses with modern dwelling units But such an approach is futile. The factories would still remain, and therefore the new buildings would be far less attractive than dwellings in the suburban districts with their better air and more favorable surroundings.

If we undertake to clear these slums then, we must ask ourselves: Who will occupy the new dwellings built to replace obsolete structures? Will the tenants of the old slum tenement move into the newer better homes, or will new tenants who can pay higher rentals take their place? If old tenants are driven out, where will these old tenants find homes?

It has been argued that people now living in the suburbs would move back into such new dwellings in order to be nearer their places of work. It does not seem quite plausible, however, that such suburbanites would exchange their more favorable living conditions for those of a congested city center, even though that center were greatly improved. It is much more probable that families living within the city in old dwellings where they pay substantial rentals would move into the new houses. Former slum dwellers might then fill the vacancies these families left, but they would not be able to pay as high rentals as their more prosperous predecessors had paid. The landlords might balance their reduced income on these houses by neglecting upkeep, or they might subdivide the property so that they could take more tenants into the same space and thus increase their returns. In either case, a higher population density would result and another slum be produced. The disease would have moved from one part of the city to another, but it would still exist. Investments in land and building in these rebuilt districts would soon depreciate. Slum clearing can be effective only when based on an adequate city structure.

How reconstruction can be achieved

During the next generation an estimated half a million new houses will have to be built in Chicago. This means rehousing half the city's population. Such a vast housing program would make it possible to change the whole city.

All these new buildings could be built according to a comprehensive plan. Gradually, without forcing a change, those parts of the city which are becoming obsolescent would be reconstructed according to the plan without impairing the life of the city. The best of plans, however, is inadequate unless there is behind it a determined will to execute structural changes according to its provisions. Only where there is a will to do so can permanent values be created. The aims of city planning are not determined by present needs alone, but also by the needs of the future.

"Master plan for London"

In June 1942, the M A R S. group published the *Master Plan For London (ill 107)*[1] If we venture to compare that plan with the diagrammatic sketch for a future London which this author worked out in 1941, we do so only because planning is an all-comprehensive subject. Comparison of two solutions, discussion of the relative merits of the two plans, helps to clarify the problems of planning. Every opportunity for such comparison and discussion should be fully utilized.

[1]*Architectural Review* London June, 1942

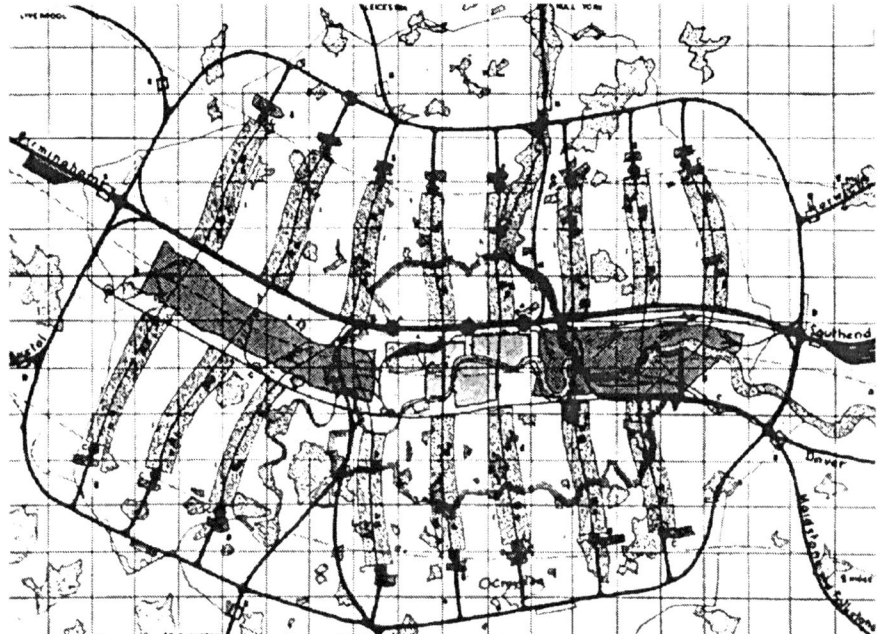

107. THE M. A. R. S. PLAN FOR LONDON. 1—Residential area. 2—Commercial administration. 3—Political administration. 4—Shopping center. 5—Cultural center and park. 6—Western industries. 7—Eastern industries and Port of London. 8—Local industries.
A—Main passenger station. B—Main goods station. C—Secondary goods station. D—Market halls.

Analysis   The M.A.R.S. plan reveals its merits at first glance. Its great freshness of conception is apparent. It does not indeed, err on the side of the academic and the conventional.

The "herringbone" arrangement is evidence of structural thinking which renders the plan most convincing. The "vertebra" of this herringbone comprises the areas of administrative and commercial buildings, with the docks and industries at its ends. The "bones" are the residential areas with the local industries at their ends. Between the residential ribbons are parks and recreation grounds where schools and playing fields are located. All parts of the city are connected by an interurban railroad system, whose stations are within walking distance even from the remote parts of the residential area. The long-distance lines are connected by means of a belt which forms a traffic ring to the north and south, meeting in a central line where the main passenger stations are located.

Traffic   Interesting as the plan is, however, it does seem to fail in its solution of certain fundamental problems.

One of these is the problem of transportation and traffic.

Since Ebenezer Howard, repeated discussions have centered on the

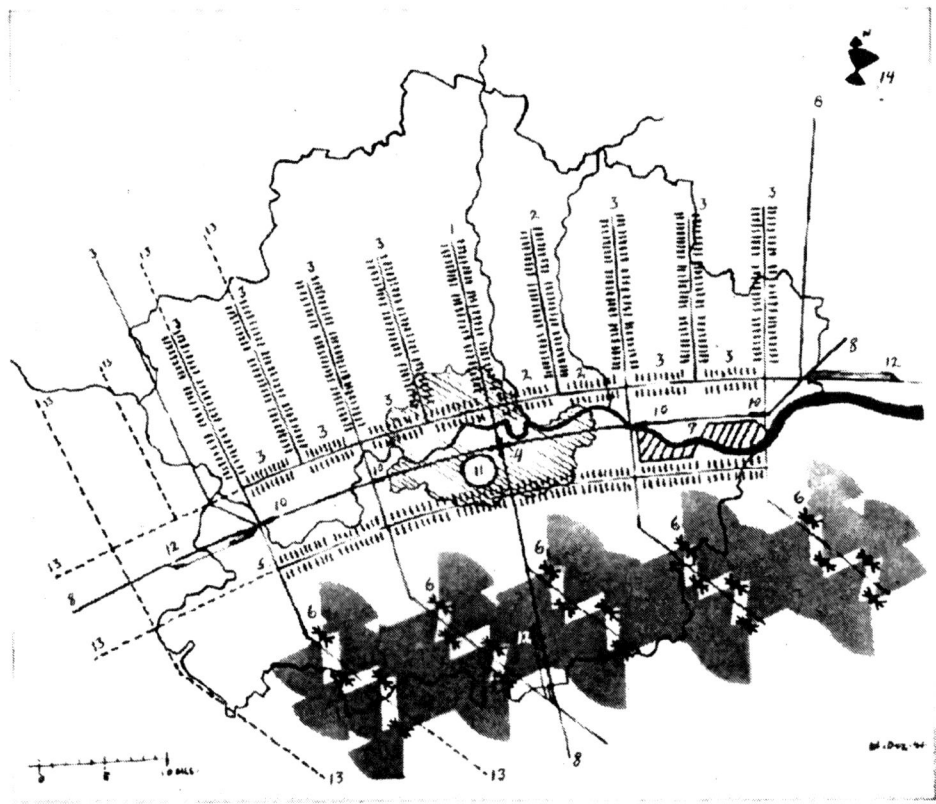

108. A DIAGRAMMATIC SKETCH FOR LONDON, 1941. 1—Political administration with residential areas. 2.—Financial administration with residential areas. 3—Commercial administration with residential areas. 4—Central station. 5—Smokeless industry with residential areas. 6—Smoke-producing industry with residential areas. 7—Port of London. 8—Long distance railroad. 10—Main railway station. 11—Airport. 12—Railroad yards. 13—Possible extensions. 14—Wind diagram.

best means of establishing a more satisfactory relation between working and residential areas. Special thought has been given to limiting the distance between such areas to a reasonable walking time. The end sought was the elimination of transportation between areas and the consequent saving of time, effort, and money.

The M.A.R.S. Plan does not establish such a relationship between working and residential areas. The two areas are separated so that much traffic will be necessary and traffic congestion within the working area will be inevitable. The nucleus of the city remains crowded and hazardous. It is still exposed to the same dangers the old city experienced in air raids. Only the residential areas have been decentralized. Why not go a step further and decentralize also the working areas, bringing them into direct relation to the residential ones?

Another point where the M.A.R.S. Plan is weak is in its handling of the smoke nuisance. The adverse effects of smoke upon the health

Industry

of the city population have always been considered a failure of our industrial cities. An official report issued in London in 1940 states "One of the Medical Officers of Health went so far as to state that the lack of success in controlling smoke was the great failure of modern public health. It is true that smoke pollution still persists to a harmful extent in many large towns, and the adverse effects of smoke are not confined to health. It is unquestionable that smoke costs the country many millions of pounds a year."[1] Much has been achieved in the field of smoke abatement. The use of power, for example, has eliminated many sources of smoke. However, this step toward healthy living has achieved success only in certain industries, whereas others have not been affected favorably. Even if the smoke nuisance could be completely abated, other nuisances, such as gases and noise, would remain. A complete solution of this nuisance problem can be reached only when those who plan cities divide industries into two classes: those which cause nuisances, and those which do not, and provide for the location of industries of the first class according to wind directions. The M.A.R.S. Plan locates industries without regard to wind conditions and the subsequent effects of industrial nuisances upon the city. To dissipate these nuisances, an absorption area is required. Industrial areas should, therefore, be farther from each other and from commercial and administrative areas than this plan provides.

Railroads   A third weakness in the M A R S plan has to do with the position of transportation lines and their connections. The terminals of the first railroads were always located at the periphery of the old city. As cities developed and expanded, this arrangement created great obstacles to the free movement of goods and passengers. To connect the different lines within the city itself was proposed, but it would have been extremely costly. Therefore, the lines were connected by means of a belt line outside of the city.

The M A R S Plan seems to apply the same method, fencing the city in, as it were. This is obviously a fault in the plan, and perhaps a fault which could be simply avoided. For instance, lines leading to different cities could branch from a main line without destroying the structural shape of the city.

Housing   Finally the M.A.R.S Plan appears limited in the kind of housing facilities it proposes.

Different forms of dwellings have both advantages and disadvantages. The one-family house is the ideal dwelling for families with children, because it has the obvious advantages of privacy and a garden space

---

[1] Royal Commission on the Distribution of the Industrial Population Report London 1940

for children to play in. The apartment house is the ideal form of dwelling for childless couples and single persons. A combination of these two forms would, therefore, best serve the needs of a community including both groups.

The M A R.S. Plan appears to favor apartment houses. It does not, therefore, provide for all kinds of people. The use of the apartment type is not conditioned by lack of space. The average population density is 75 persons to one acre. It would be quite possible to build free-standing family dwellings of varied types as well as apartment houses.

Our own diagramatic sketch *(ill. 108)* divides the city into two parts. To the north of the River Thames are the areas for administrative and commercial buildings, with their residential areas located in parks. South of the river are the industrial areas, with their residential parts likewise in parks. The two parts of the city are separated by a large park area, through which flows the Thames. In this park area are located the main highway, the main railroad line with its central station; the airport, and, at the east end, the docks. All parts of the city are connected by an interurban highway and railroad system. The ribbons of the administrative and commercial areas could also be connected with each other by a bus line leading over a highway through the park areas between the ribbons. The main highway and main railroad lines run from east to west and connect with all long-distance lines. These long-distance lines branch off in any convenient direction without interfering with the city structure.

^{Our diagrammatic sketch for London}

The basic principle would be to connect all working areas with their respective residential areas and place these areas within walking distance of each other. Thus the bulk of the traffic would be eliminated. Both areas would, moreover, be decentralized.

The administrative and commercial districts are arranged in a manner like that shown in *ills. 91 and 92*. On both sides of the highway and railroad system are office buildings, department stores, shops and all the buildings necessary in this zone. Separated from the structures by a park strip are the residential parts of this area.

^{Administrative and commercial districts}

Each building in the administrative areas, as well as each settlement in the residential areas, can be reached by automobile on traffic streets which connect with the highway at suitable points. Cars can be driven and parked underneath each building in the administrative areas, thus solving the parking problem. Each building in the administrative area can also be reached on foot from the residential area.

| The industrial area | The industrial area is divided into two parts. One contains those industries which produce smoke and fumes, the other those which do not. The latter are arranged in a manner similar to that illustrated in *ill 84, left* The layout of the industries producing smoke and fumes is determined by prevailing winds Those winds in London—(See wind diagram)—blow north-northeast and south-southwest, influencing settlements in a manner somewhat comparable to the arrangement illustrated in No 2 of our wind diagrams *(ill 87)* To provide the necessary absorption area for smoke and fumes, these industries and their settlements have to be spread over a large area. All residential districts are divided into units, similar to those shown in *ill. 80* Their streets are so arranged that the surrounding parks with their schools and playgrounds, can be safely reached without crossing a traffic street |

The park areas between the two parts of the city, and between the settlements and ribbons, include vegetable gardens, woods, and farms They are, therefore, productive parks.

| Possibilities of expansion | The city could be expanded in either of two ways The city as a whole might grow (as indicated); or any one part of it might be expanded It is interesting to speculate, however, whether the city, especially the metropolis, will be as necessary in the future as we now believe it to be. Decentralization will influence our cities, as concentration once did, possibly much more than we know or can imagine City planning would then become regional planning, or national planning. Its aspects and its significance would be greatly changed |

Our diagrammatic sketch is a mere outline of the problem involved Much more data, more maps and statistics not now available, would have to be analyzed before the details of that sketch were filled in. Topography and local conditions will modify the scheme However in a planning system as flexible as this one, such change is easy and adaptable to any conditions or size.

The city changes constantly Houses, streets, bridges, transportation lines become obsolete and have to be rebuilt and replaced. In London, dwellings for four million people were built during the last twenty years Just think what could have been done if these new houses and the schools, streets, and transportation lines built in the same years had been built and placed according to a comprehensive plan of London!

| New York. Manhattan | The commercial area of New York—Manhattan—is one of the over-congested Metropolitan areas It presents the most difficult planning problems, and these problems seem to defy any solution Approach by

technical means have failed, because the central problem is not merely a technical but basically a structural one Only if the right structure has been found, can technical means be employed successfully The recent suggestion by Herman Herrey[1] still fails to meet this test He proposes a super-structure, a Highway belt some 80 feet high consisting of six separate levels for truck. bus, passenger and express traffic, and two levels for parking. His suggestion is technically admirable but it would not change very much basically, and would not create a new structure. This proposal is reminiscent of the attempted skyscraper solution, which did not eliminate the then existing problems, but rather added immeasurably to the difficulties which are prevalent to this day Planning is more than the use of technical means Its main purpose will always be to provide a framework for life One wonders how life in all its ways can be maintained in such an overcongested area as Manhattan has become

Every new highway leading out of a city has a concentrating as well as dispersing effect and will unavoidably increase traffic in its center. Only when working areas are connected with their residential areas in walking distance can traffic be reduced and more of it eliminated. In a diagrammatic sketch, *Ill 109*, we applied our planning principles to the commercial area of New York *Ills 91 and 92* show how we developed another commercial area, a scheme which modified according to local features could also be applied to Manhattan.

Our suggestion is based on a simplified traffic system A traffic belt is suggested consisting of two highways, one local which connects all units of the residential area, and one for express traffic These highways can be connected with each other at convenient points Subways or cut-in drives could, wherever convenient or necessary, connect both traffic belts and also any other part of the city Outside of this traffic belt is located a strip of buildings needed for commerce. offices stores, and so on. Then, separated by a green belt. follow the units of the residential area Residential units and commercial buildings are everywhere within walking distance of each other Between traffic belts is a huge park area; an extension of Central Park North and South. Within this park area are hotels and apartment houses in very spacious arrangement It will be possible to drive and park underneath each building in the commercial area as well as under hotels and apartment houses The parking problem which appears to defy any solution so far would then be eliminated.

About 80% of Manhattan's buildings are overaged and obsolete and

---

[1]*Time*—February, 1944

will have to be replaced before long. Here is a great oportunity for a planned rebuilding After a comprehensive plan, Manhattan could be changed gradually All good buildings could be used until they are obsolete. Rockefeller Center, for example, would be located in the park and would remain there during its useful lifetime

We have limited our suggestion to the commercial area To replan the metropolitan area of New York is a problem of regional planning Regional planning however makes the city an integrated part of the region so that "the ruralizing of the stony wastes of our cities" as Lewis Mumford puts it, become possible. Our suggestion is an attempt to ruralize the stony wastes of the city Manhattan could become a park and garden city and still maintain its importance

Two schools of thought in city planning

There are two schools of thought in city planning. One takes into consideration only parts of a city, without connecting these with the whole "Little" things are thought about, and little parts are changed. Everything is done on a "sound basis." This is the school of the practical man Paradoxically, this practical work, which considers economy first, eventually reveals itself as impractical and unsound The expense it entails is futile expense The city so tinkered with remains essentially the same

The second school thinks about the city as a whole. its zone of influence. its function in the region, and in the nation. It takes everything into consideration and tries to conceive of the needs and function of the city as an entity

This school is often regarded as impractical and theoretical It is indeed accused of being destructive, eager to tear everything down. Its real purpose, however, is to reconstruct the city, according to a plan, building everything in its proper place

Such a plan should be completely flexible. It should provide for future growth or future shrinkage in the city without disintegration of its unity It should plan to use buildings as long as they are useful and to replace them when they become obsolete. Provision should, of course, be made for the preservation of certain historical landmarks. The city could be changed step-by-step by the careful and patient following of such a plan And the expense incurred at each step would be sound constructive investment

Procedure of rebuilding a city

Four diagrams show the steps in rebuilding a city. The city represented is an industrial one which has all the disadvantages of our existing cities. Four diagrams show, in a synoptical way, how its dis-

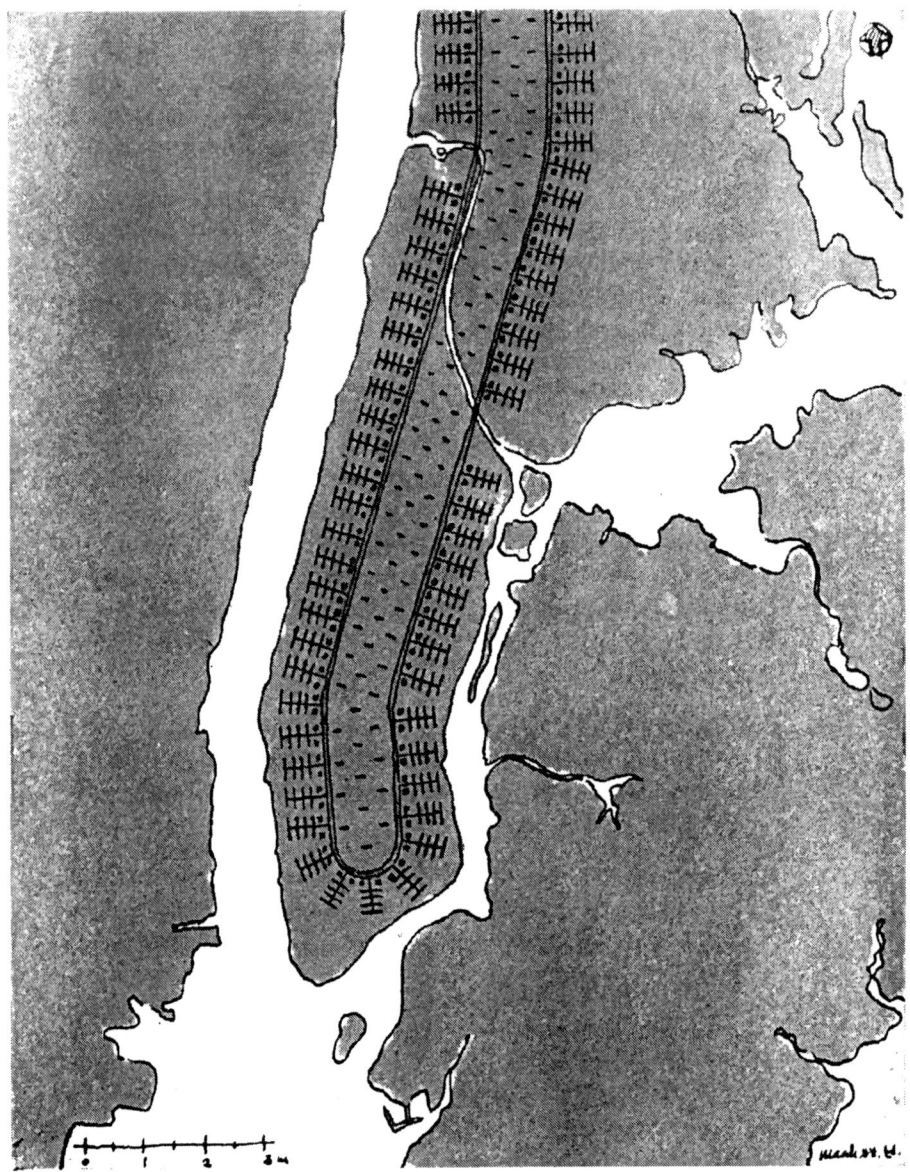

109. MANHATTAN. A diagrammatic sketch of its replanning.

order could gradually give place to constructive order, without interference of the city's life during the reconstruction.

Diagram A *(ill. 110)* shows the present city; its disorganization, the disorder of its parts, and the lack of relation between residential and working area. It also illustrates the all-pervasive nuisance of smoke and fumes from the scattered industries. Highways and railroads radiate from the center of the city, cutting it into disjointed parts.

Diagram B *(ill. 111)* shows the first step in rebuilding. A new railroad and highway system has been constructed, and some of the smoke-producing industries have been moved to new locations according to plan. Workers employed in these factories can, for the time being, live in their old houses and reach their places of work by the newly built railroads and highways.

In Diagram C *(ill. 112)* the removal of most of the factories of smoke producing industries has been accomplished. Some of the other industries and parts of the commercial areas and their respective residential areas have been established also in new planned locations.

Diagram D *(ill. 113)* shows the completed reorganization of the city with everything in its proper place. The change could be accomplished gradually within one or two generations. The new city would be not only a better working "organism" economically, but also a better and a more pleasant place to live.

The same method could be applied to large as well as to small cities. It would work a transformation, but it would in no way disrupt the life of the city in the process.

The purpose of our city diagrams

The diagrams presented here make no claim to be complete solutions of the problems involved. They are rather a framework for solutions. Their main purpose is to encourage discussion about the traffic and planning problems which we have to face.

Administration and legislation

All communities, especially the larger ones, are today confronted with the necessity of replanning and rebuilding themselves. It is the task of the present and of the future to eliminate existing defects by productive reconstruction. Only by the creation of an adequate city structure can the rebuilding of the city be effective. Prerequisite to such reconstruction are a comprehensive city plan which takes everything into consideration, and a new kind of zoning which determines where what may be built.

The rebuilding of a city has its important influence on administration and legislation—local, state, and national. Our modern metropolis, because of the rapidity of its technological development, has become too small for effective administration and for some essential services —such as water, power, sewage disposal, and transportation, which the city provides and controls. The suburbs, meanwhile, cling to a theory of administrative independence which, in fact, no longer exists They have become part of the larger city upon which they are dependent for their livelihood. But the old habit persists and suburbanites vigorously refuse to recognize that dependence They want to have all the advantages they can derive from the large city without assuming any responsibility for its maintenance The trend, however, is strongly toward an integration of city and suburbs Such unification is prerequisite for effective city development

The cost of city rebuilding makes many officials shake their heads when plans for such rebuilding are proposed. It has been the regrettable tendency of our time' to regard money, not as a means to an end, but as the end in itself We recognize that an individual is concerned with quick financial return on his investments We forget that a community is not bound by the same necessity. In time of war, we somehow see these facts more clearly. Adolph A Berle, Assistant Secretary of State, says: "Too often the opportunities for improvement of our social structure have been lost, not because we did not know how, but because no one really wanted to make them effective. In finance, for example, there are techniques which are as able to rebuild and to rehouse the United States as they are to equip an army They have not been used primarily because there was no compelling desire to use them " *Finance problems*

In planning and building cities, the best solution is also the most economical solution But we must remember that temporary economy quite often proves to be a burden in the future, and that the fortuitous gain for an individual frequently becomes community loss Real economy in the building of dwellings and cities cannot be effected by saving money through reduction of space It can be achieved only by perfect planning and construction, and by reducing the costs of production. *Economy of planning*

The automobile is no longer a luxury Mass production methods have made it available to all Mass production could also decrease the costs of houses and put well-built structures within the reach of all. The late Edsel Ford, president of the Ford Motor Company, told the Federal Monopoly Committee on April 10, 1940. that the cost of a popular priced automobile, then selling for about $700, would be more than $17,000 if it were manufactured by hand labor instead of by huge labor-saving machines At $17,000, probably not more than 50 cars a year could be sold, and few of the 125,000 men employed at Ford's plants would have their jobs Houses as well as motor cars could be mass-fabricated. Their parts could be produced in quantity and assembled into different types of dwellings without making the houses stereotyped *The pre-fabricated house*

PROCEDURE OF REBUILDING A CITY

110. A. EXISTING STATE AND CONDITIONS. Disorder and no relation between the various areas.

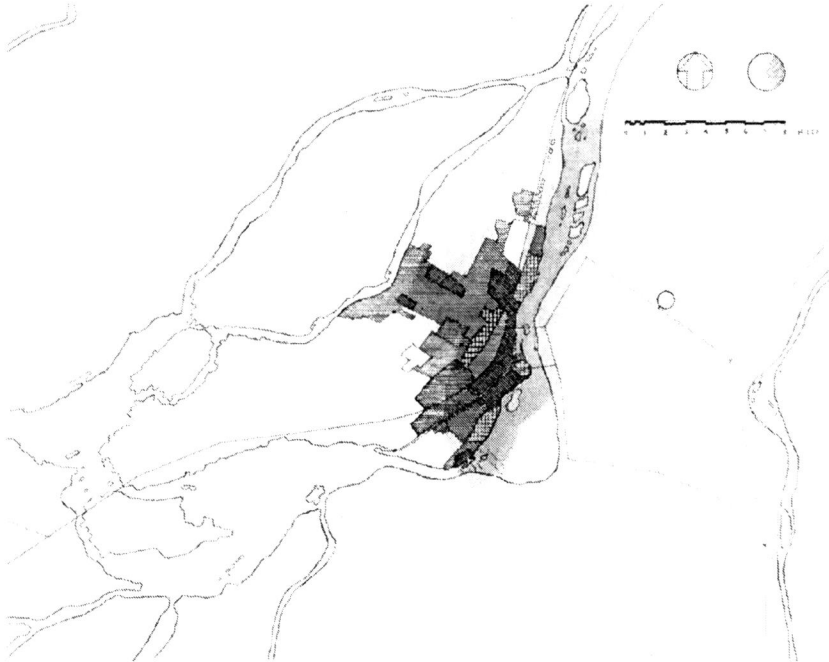

111. B. FIRST STEP. Relocation of railroads and highways. Parts of smoke-producing in-

PROCEDURE OF REBUILDING A CITY

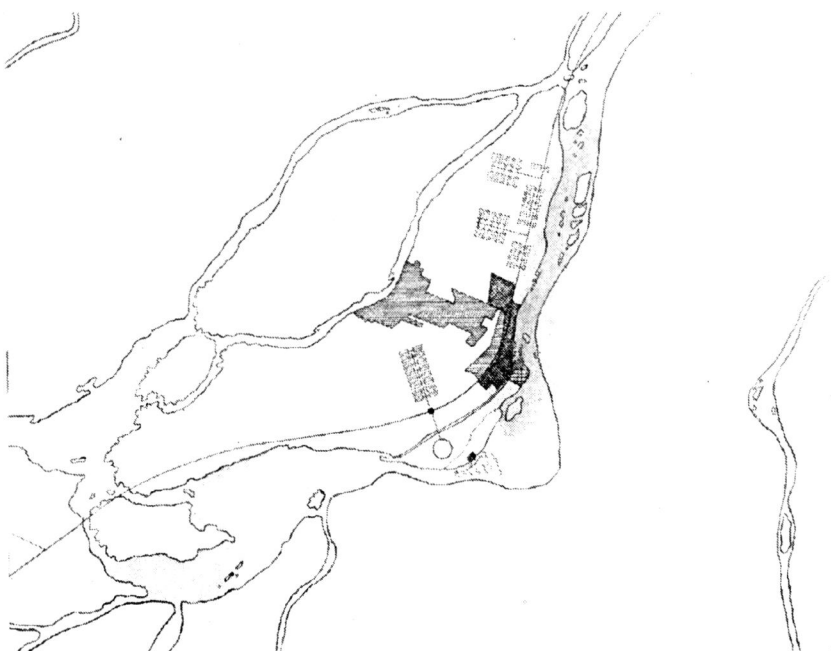

112. C. SECOND STEP. Most of the smoke-producing and parts of the smokeless industries, the commercial areas, as well as their respective residential sections removed.

113. D. THIRD STEP. Within two generations an entirely new city can be gradually built. A—Central station and airport, B—Civic center, C—Commercial area, D—Smokeless industry, E

The prefabricated house, which has seemed until recently merely an interesting theory, is now becoming a reality. Some companies are working out production methods for such houses, but Henry Kaiser has gone ahead of plans to concrete proposals. He proposes to produce a six-room house, prefabricated and completely outfitted, at the cost of $1500

Charles Breesey's proposal

Sir Charles Breesey and Sir Edwin Lutyens have made interesting suggestions for practical economy in the reconstruction of London. Sir Charles Breesey proposes planning new traffic routes instead of widening existing streets. He believes that the cost of improving traffic conditions in city districts where buildings have high value is out of proportion to the advantages gained. It would be more expedient, in his opinion, to use funds available for the improvement of traffic conditions for the planning of necessary traffic routes through obsolete city districts

Pooling of ownership

Sir Gwilyn Gibbon suggests a plan to avoid the complications which ensue when individual owners must be dealt with separately.[1] He proposes the compulsory pooling of ownership, each owner to be reimbursed according the value of his property. Freed from the obstacles of property boundaries and rights, the reconstruction of some city districts, and the creation of new traffic routes, could thus be more easily effected

Mortgages and their amortization

Banks and insurance companies are also exponents of united action in the reconstruction of obsolete areas. Some of them have proposed the elimination of private ownership where obsolete dwellings must be torn down and replaced by new buildings. They have hoped to increase the value of these buildings sufficiently to pay off the old mortgages with the earnings gained in the new construction.

Rebuilding without loss of national wealth

A better method of financing the rebuilding of city areas is to free the houses from their liabilities by amortizing their mortgages gradually. Such amortization, which would have to be regulated by appropriate laws, would permit reconstruction on a large scale without loss in national wealth

Passive observation or creative action?

We have traced certain forces which have brought about the concentration of cities, and we have considered other forces which today are tending toward disurbanization and decentralization. It is not enough merely to observe passively this tendency of our times. Creative action is vitally necessary. Decentralization, as we now see it, affects not only the locality and the surroundings of the city itself.

---

[1] Sir Gwilyn Gibbon *Problems of Town and Country Planning*

but also a whole state, a region, even a whole nation This broad field must now be included in our planning. Local, state, or regional planning can be adequate only if it is related to national planning

National planning must develop according to comprehensive principles, in which local and regional planning are interrelated parts Such national planning has to do with agriculture and forestry, with industry, mining, and manufacture, and their relationship to each other. It must deal also with power systems and transportation lines A broad concept of our task would enable us to find, not only the right location for the decentralized industries, their settlements and their related agricultural areas, but also the best routes for power lines and transportation systems, we could discover new and better ways for the use of land and water; for the development and conservation of local, regional, and national resources.

National planning

Every city has its zone of influence the area where live people who work within its boundaries The larger the city, the more its zone of influence expands Interurban tracks at first, and later the automobile, have provided the means of transportation within this zone As transportation has advanced, settlement of such areas has increased The tendency toward decentralization, the exodus from the city, is manifest here.

Planless decentralization and its consequences

Because the growth of these suburban areas has been planless, however, a disorganized and chaotic suburbanization has resulted, uneconomic and unsatisfactory to the population

As people leave the city because conditions become unfavorable for good living there, so also do industries seek more convenient locations for their plants outside the city limits. Their movement, like the movement of the population, is proceeding without plan or foresight This planless decentralization of industry is even more dangerous than the random flight of residents to outlying areas In a very short time, it will produce outside the city the same unfavorable conditions of smoke, soot, and fumes which now prevail within it.

Such a planless suburbanization must unquestionably be put under control The zone of influence of the city as well as the city itself must be replanned Even the replanning of this influence zone may not be enough. It becomes evident, as we study into our problem more deeply, that adequate solutions can be reached only when planning extends to the entire region, of which the city and its zone of influence is only a part.

The region and a balanced economy

Our diagram of Chicago shows that local or areal planning is no longer sufficient. The area shown in this diagram extends far beyond the limits of the existing metropolis and its suburbs. It comprises, and must comprise, the whole area related to Chicago. This area reaches beyond the borderline of Illinois. The area of Chicago, in fact, spreads out into several states. Chicago affects these states, and is affected by them, for better or for worse.

It becomes evident here that state planning, like areal planning, may sometimes be too limited in scope. An adequate plan must be a plan for an entire region. But what is a region? It may be defined as an interrelated part of a nation, a natural unit, self-contained by reason of its geographical characteristics, its natural resources, the conditions of its soil, the natural and artificial transportation routes used and developed by its people. Such a region should constitute an interrelated community, in which individuals and groups of individuals all bear their share in working toward the good of all. It should be an organic unity, an economic, social and cultural region with a homogeneity of living conditions. The creation of such organic and self-contained regions would enable us to divide the nation into her natural geographic and economic parts. The organic interrelationship of such regions would bring about an harmonious and balanced economy not only within the regions, but also in the nation as a whole.

Harmony between the parts and the whole

The city by itself cannot solve the great national economic problems, nor can the country alone master them. The nation needs its urban industrial centers and its agricultural areas, both working together. To render such cooperation possible and efficient, we need national planning, superior to the planning of city and country, state and region. National planning can link together the different functions of different areas and relate them to their respective importance.

Such co-related planning would usefully develop and conserve national resources to the advantages of the population. It would also establish real harmony within the parts, and between the parts and the whole.

Man—the object of all planning

Plan we must, not only economically, but always and primarily for the benefit of man. We should always bear in mind that at the center of all things is man—man who creates everything and for whom everything is created. Our real problem is life itself. Agriculture, industry, and transportation are important only as they contribute to the richness and fullness of life. We should plan to make this earth a better place to live in. Life has cultural as well as material aims. Planning can be one of the means for their realization.

114. GREEK TEMPLE in the landscape.

PART FOUR

THE ART OF CITY PLANNING

The objective in the art of city planning is the creative use of the city's elements. Its basis is spatial feeling, expressed according to its era. The city planner has but limited means of expressing artistic aims. The more clearly these means are recognized, the more effectively can they be related to particular tasks; and the more completely they are mastered, the more constructively can they be employed to achieve satisfying results.

The object in the art of city planning and its means

The means, however, remain always the means. Their mere application does not insure fruitful results. Artistic ability cannot be acquired: it is innate and intangible. The only tangible factors in city planning are the social and practical requirements which can and must be fulfilled. Since there is an inner relationship, an enigmatic correlation between art and utility, the meeting of utilitarian aims is prerequisite to creative city building. Artistic expression will vary according to the particular task and according to the creative aims of the planner. That which is designed primarily to serve utilitarian ends can, without sacrifice of utility, gradually ascend into the realm of art.

Principles of the "organic" and the "geometric"

At the outset of this book, we distinguished between two diametrically opposite city types the organic and the geometric We saw that they were expressions of two distinct forms of society We noted that these two types are just as much an expression of different social structures as they are the outcome of different structural conceptions. Rectilinearity and rectangularity have usually been regarded as the distinguishing characteristics of planning, but this is not necessarily true. The organic city may be just as much an expression of planning as the geometric city.

It is true that the plans of the organic cities of the past were not drawn as we should draw them today. The plan was a helpful, but not a dominant factor in the building of such cities The decisive factor there was the spatial concept influenced by conditions and topography in fulfillment of definite needs and particular demands of the community The builders considered, for example. the kind of fortifications needed for defense; the relation of the entrance of the city to those fortifications; the connection of the city with a stronghold or a cloister; the streets necessary within the city, the roads for communication between the city and its environs, and the most useful arrangement of churches and other communal buildings They often achieved great harmony between natural conditions and practical requirements In the organic cities all parts. developing according to their own laws, were correlated into a harmonious whole

It should be remembered that rectilinearity and rectangularity can be used as organic means without forcing upon a city the character of the geometric. The city of Ragusa in Dalmatia *(ill. 25)* shows this, and so do our own suggestions for organic city planning

Organic city formations are, as we have seen, intrinsically the result of conditions and requirements Geometric cities, in contrast, are based upon an abstract idea which dominates the entire city area The development of the parts and of the whole according to their own laws is usually impossible in such cities because of the dominating force of the axial geometric system The abstract preconceived planning idea is, generally speaking. contrary to functional demands Utility tends to decrease in direct proportion to the increase of emphasis upon axial monumental expression. pomp and display

Two examples

The plans of Jueterbog and Karlsruhe *(ills 115 and 116)* illustrate this point. Jueterbog is a small city, structurally unchanged since its founding in the Middle Ages Its structure was determined primarily by its need for defense and by the location of its church and city hall The thought of defense led the planners of the city to arrange the city gates so that they did not give immediate access to the center of the settlement. The main streets in the city itself can be entered only through winding narrow streets. Streets crossing the main streets lead to the defense towers. Behind the city wall is a circular walk. The main street is slightly bent, giving an impression of spatial limitation. The church and city hall are placed behind the main street on squares removed from traffic. The church towers high above the houses and dominates the view of the winding streets. The city shows what may be achieved with very simple means.

Karlsruhe, in contrast, is typical of cities founded during the territorial state system. At the time of its building the reigning prince was considered almost a god, and the social structure of the day is symbolically expressed in the structure of the city. The palace of the prince stands at the head of the city, which spreads in a fan-like formation before it. All nine radial streets are oriented toward the palace tower which, in its prominent position, symbolizes the omnipresence of the prince. This tower is also the center of a circle, one quarter of which comprises the palace, the palace grounds, and the city, and the other three quarters, the park. Radial roads oriented toward the tower cut through this park as the streets do through the city itself. The city structure has a geometric axial design. Striking effects have been achieved here, but they are in no proportion to the extraordinary architectural means employed. It may even be said that no more has been achieved artistically here than was achieved in Jueterbog where the very simplest architectural means were used.

At the beginning of the nineteenth century, Karlsruhe was expanded according to a plan by Weinbrenner. The plan of the old city was retained. The center axis was made particularly impressive by means of a series of contrasting architectural squares connected to the axis. The largest of these squares was the marketplace, which was surrounded by imposing edifices. If we compare this marketplace with that of Jueterbog, we see at once that the essential difference between the geometric and the organic city lies not only in the city formation itself but also in its contributing parts. The market place of Jueterbog, like the city itself, is simple yet adequate. It is free of through traffic and is connected with the main street by small streets. The market place of Karlsruhe has by no means the same functional value. It is surrounded and even crossed by traffic streets and is, therefore, quite inadequate for its intended purpose. No link has been forged between architectural expression and utility. To achieve a monumental effect, the functional purpose of the market has been neglected. Architectural display and utility can be combined only by a mutual diminution of their respective values.

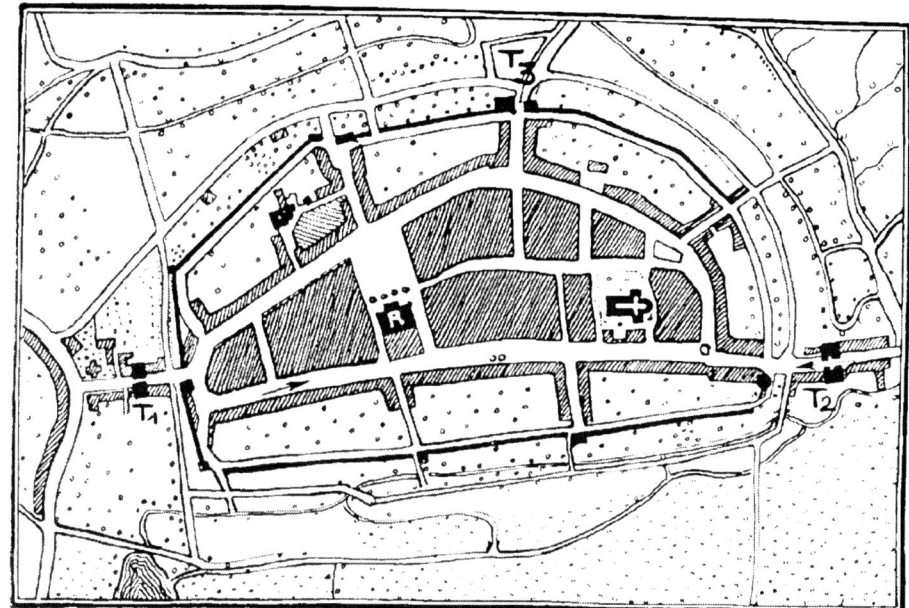

115. PLAN OF JUETERBOG: An organic city.

The ancients had a better understanding of the difference between the functional and the monumental than did the builders and planners of Karlsruhe. The market of Priene, for example, was located at one side of the main street. The forums of Imperial Rome—the prototypes of monumental squares—and its many other monumental squares were invariably set at one side of the street, and, therefore, free of through traffic. They could serve adequately their important functional purpose in a day when much civic life centered around the public square.

Structure and art

The idea of planning is at the base of all art. It is basic to organic cities and to geometric cities. We have not always recognized this. We have believed, for example, that aesthetic values undeniably found in certain organic cities of the past were achieved accidentally. Today we see that the structural difference between organic and geometric types of city is of no importance aesthetically. Cities of either type may be built artistically or inartistically. Art is not dependent upon type. Each type can offer its own possibilities of expression. This remains true whether we plan a city or a building within a city. Buildings with bearing walls, for example, offer certain possibilities of expression; skeleton buildings quite other possibilities. No matter how the possibilities of expression may vary, the structures of well

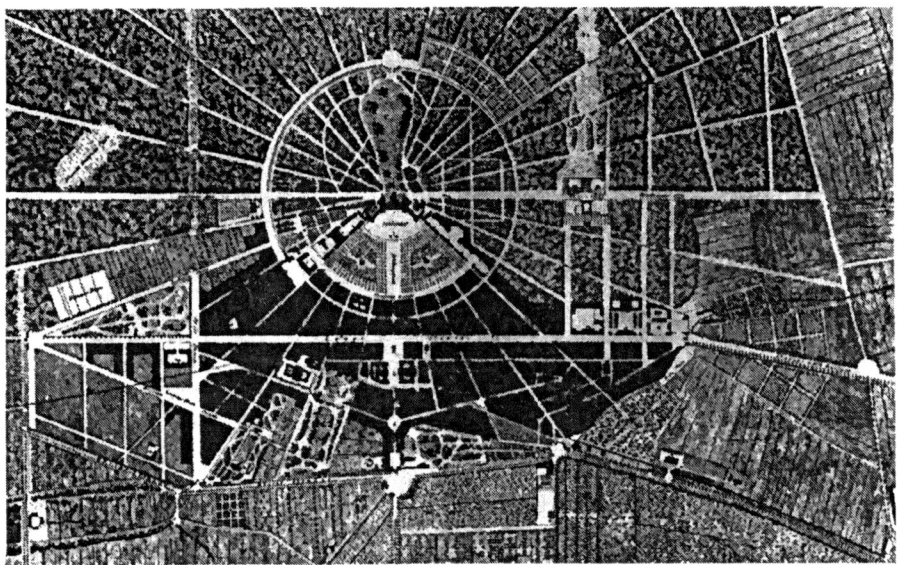
116. PLAN OF KARLSRUHE: A geometric-axial city.

planned cities can have artistic values—values which may overshadow the material structure.

The material of the art of city planning is the city area and its topography, its buildings and its free space. The artistic means the planner uses are proportion, contrast, and perspective. We can consider and analyze these means separately, but we should not forget that in reality they are so closely interrelated as to be inseparable.

Material and artistic means

Proportion is the relation of the parts to the whole, and of the whole to the parts. In city planning, the whole is the city area; the parts its buildings and its free spaces. We can study proportion in city planning effectively only when we link it with the other means at the planner's command. We must recognize that, inasmuch as all these means arise from one source, the planned effect we seek can be achieved only by the close interworking of them all. By skilful use of proportion, for example, we can make buildings appear solemn and grave, or graceful and spirited. Deliberate contrast of small and large, of high and low, can increase visual dimensions. With the means of perspective, proportion can become the predominant spatial factor. It can make large objects appear small, and small objects large. It can make distant objects appear near, and near ones far away.

Proportion

Contrast between small and large is also a means of increasing visual

117. MANSION.

118. FRAUEN-KIRCHE, DRESDEN.

dimensions A small mansion *(ill. 117)* may have its dimensions visually increased because a smaller building, having different proportions, stands next to it. The same effect of visually increased dimensions can be achieved even when the buildings which surround the first edifice are comparatively high. This may be accomplished by replacing relative proportion by absolute proportion

By relative proportion we mean a system in which the relations of parts and whole remain constant regardless of scale In absolute proportion, these relationships vary with variations in scale. Relative and absolute proportion

The Frauenkirche in Dresden *(ill 118)* illustrates how the use of absolute proportion can achieve interesting contrasting effects. Certain parts of this edifice, such as the high windows, the slender dome which rises high above the towers, are disproportionate in the sense of relative proportion. For this very reason, they effect an extraordinary increase in dimension which increases the visual size of the building

In the Church of Saint Peter in Rome *(ills 119 and 120)* application of relative proportion achieves the opposite effect—an optical decrease of actual dimensions—despite its contrast to the colonnades which surround the square. The difference between actual and apparent size is even more striking in the interior of Saint Peter's There the dimensions of the tremendous dome above the crossing are visually decreased so that it seems incredible that this dome is actually higher than that of the Pantheon

The effect of contrast between small and large is particularly impressive when it is also a contrast between high and low Cathedrals of the Middle Ages *(ill 125)* were usually surrounded by small low buildings. The contrast between the familiar scale of the houses and the unusual scale of the cathedral increased the visual size of the cathedral beyond its actual dimensions This optical illusion is further enhanced by the use of absolute proportions—a characteristic of medieval architecture In this absolute measure, parts and sections of a building are not proportionate to a relative scale, as they are in the architecture of antiquity, but they appear in their absolute dimensions. Contrast

An entire town may be in contrast to a single predominant edifice or group of edifices. Medieval strongholds dominated the cities in which they stood, visually as well as functionally. Such visual contrast is reduced if the structure of the stronghold is divided The stronghold of the city of Sebenico in Dalmatia *(ill 121)* illustrates how the effect of contrast may be lost through segmentation. The towers of this

119. ST. PETER'S, ROME.

120. ST. PETER'S SQUARE, ROME.

stronghold visually decrease the bulk of the unit It takes on a structural resemblance to the rest of the city and there is no real contrast Melk on the Danube *(ill 123)* presents a quite different aspect. Here the large massive structure of the cloister on the hill above the city forms a real contrast to the city, and that contrast is enhanced by the formation of the landscape

Even large cities can be dominated optically by a group of buildings In Prague, *(ill. 122)* the widespread horizontal edifice of the Hradschin, with the Cathedral of St Viet as its vertical accent, is situated on a hill Its homogeneous structure forms a strong contrast with the conglomeration of buildings in the city and therefore dominates the entire settlement

Compact and homogeneous buildings on hills are an important element in planning, not merely because they provide contrast, but also because they introduce an organizing principle which brings visual unity into the city area. A comparison between Stuttgart and Bath *(ills 141 and 142)* shows this clearly

Cities on hills and in plains

In Stuttgart many small detached houses have been built on the heights surrounding the city. The result is that the city appears disconnected and insignificant In Bath large buildings on the city heights create a very different effect. The crescent-shaped apartment houses on the hill embody a new principle of city planning Not only do they bring visual order into the city area, but they also broaden the view and connect the city with the landscape.

When a city is located on a plain, the city area can also be brought into visual order by large individual buildings In Stralsund *(ill 124)*, for example, this order is achieved by the location of the churches. These churches are varied in structure but, being all oriented alike, and far apart from each other they achieve the effect of spaciousness They create an impression of expanse within the narrowness of the city They give it a large scale in contrast to its inner dimensions and the narrowness of its streets Here is a creative possibility which can be applied to the cities of our time, and which can be carried out in the mixed type of building which we advocate

The temples of Aesculapius in Priene *(ill 128)* and of Zeus in Magnesia *(ill 127)* are approximately of the same dimensions, but the effects which they create upon the observer are widely different The temple of Aesculapius stands in a small court and is built against a building which forms the rear wall of that court The temple of Zeus stands free in the Agora. The porticoes surrounding the Agora and those of the court in which the temple of Aesculapius stands are of

Perspective

121. SEBENICO, Dalmatia.

122. PRAGUE, the Hradschin.

123. MELK, on the Danube.

the same height. Because of the relatively great distance between the temple of Zeus and the porticoes of the Agora, and also because the temple is interposed between those porticoes and the observer, the porticoes seem reduced in scale and the temple appears disproportionately large. The top of a distant hill can be seen far beyond the porticoes and this contributes further to the perspective effect. The temple, the porticoes, and the landscape, connected in perspective, form a visual unity. The distant is connected with the near and, through such connection, contributes to an increase of the temple's apparent size.

In the temple of Zeus in Olympia *(ill 126)*, perspective has been employed conversely. The dimensional difference between the relatively small temple of Zeus and the relatively high hill of Cronos, which rises behind it, is here visually neutralized and balanced by means of perspective.

A noteworthy example of the effectiveness of perspective spatial devices is afforded by the squares bordering on the Cathedral of Saint Mark's in Venice *(ills. 129 and 130)* The piazza in front of the cathedral, as viewed from the church, becomes narrower toward the rear because the walls of the palaces enclosing the sides slant inward The feeling of depth is thereby increased because the converging horizontal sidewalls reinforce the perspective effect and make the square appear deeper than it actually is.

<small>Saint Mark's Square</small>

One might expect that, looking toward the cathedral from the far end of the piazza, the opposite effect would be apparent, that the square would seem shorter than it actually is. But the free-standing Campanile has been so placed that this foreshortening effect has been neutralized and an impression of greater depth attained. The tower seems to make the space in front of St Mark's contract and, therefore, appear deeper. It enhances this effect of depth to an extraordinary extent by interposing itself between the observer and the church so that the church is forced back visually. The illusion of depth is still more increased because the tower is well removed from the church, and is of considerable height

The piazza of St Mark's is enclosed on all sides. The piazzetta adjoining it at right angles is open The contrast between the two squares increases the feeling of confinement of the piazza and emphasizes the openness of the piazzetta. The latter is open on the side toward the lagoon and, therefore, appears to draw into the total spatial effect, not only the buildings of the island lying oposite, but also the remote distance.

124. STRALSUND, on the Baltic sea.

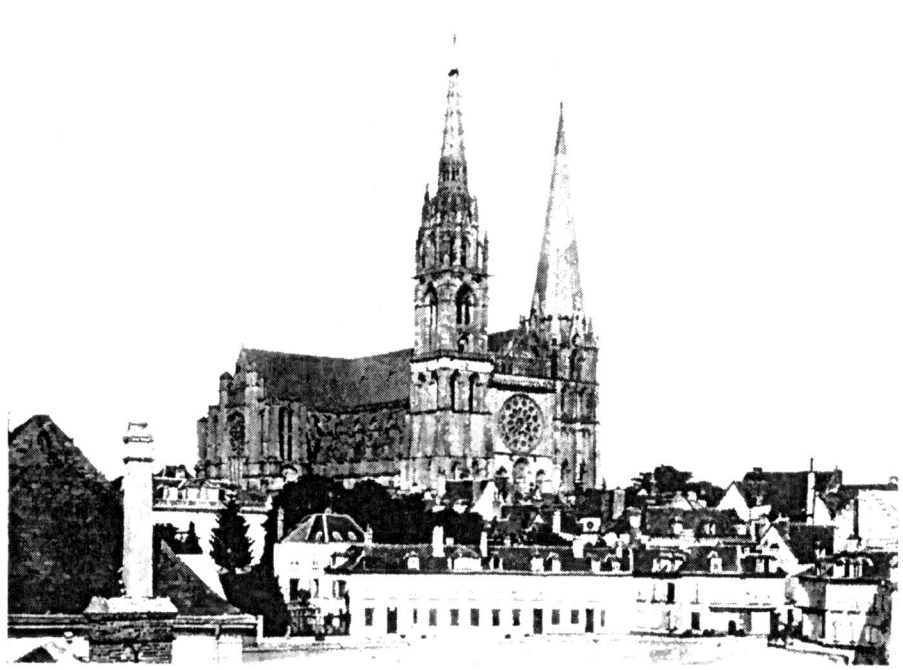

125. CHARTRES, Cathedral.

Spatial feeling is self-evident and existent in all periods of history, but spatial concepts and their expression have changed with the centuries

Narrow, high, enclosed space, for example, was the spatial concept of the Gothic, and it is expressed best in the narrow and high naves of the cathedrals *(ill 131)* In their loftiness those naves symbolize the aspiration of those times toward the supernatural The spatial expression they achieve is raised to the mystical by the manner in which light pours through the windows The same spatial concept expresses itself in city structure Here also narrow, high, enclosed space predominates, and all means are used to enhance the feeling of confinement The narrow high buildings permit bends in the streets *(ill 132)* The narrowness of the streets practically prevents any opening along the main street or the squares.

A new spatial concept entered city building as the supernatural spirit of the Gothic was followed by the strict logic of the Renaissance The Renaissance city, arranged geometrically, strove for rectangularity and clarity While the court of the Palazzo Farnese in Rome *(ill 133)*, for example, still gives an impression of spatial limitation, the Palazzo itself, comprising an entire block, stands free between the streets—a building of static character

Centric building was the ideal of the Renaissance. It was best expressed in the Santa Maria della Consolazione in Todi *(ill 135)*, an edifice of simple forms wholly symmetrical in plan as well as in inner and outer appearance The spatial concept of the Renaissance was centralistic, harmonious, and immovably static. The design of Santa Maria della Consolazione may be by Bramante who attempted to execute the same spatial concept in the church of St Peter's in Rome *(ill. 134)* Bramante's suggestion for the square of St Peter's is of unusual interest. In his design, the church stands free in the center of a large quadrangle surrounded by porticoes With its semi-circular extension, this square follows exactly his plan for St Peter's. Thus the total symmetry of the church is embodied in the square, achieving a spatial concept of magnitude and unlimited expanse

This centralistic concept is expressed also in Renaissance city planning. Fra Giocondo's design for an ideal city *(ill 136)* shows this clearly The circular city surrounds a central edifice from which the streets radiate. This concept of a city as a homogeneous entity in which all parts are subordinated to the whole was a new view in city planning Originally it was merely a formal concept. Later, with the development of firearms, it was generally adopted for reasons of

Spatial feeling and spatial concepts Gothic

The static concept of the Renaissance

Circular buildings

Circular cities

126. OLYMPIA, Temple of Zeus and the Hill of Cronos.

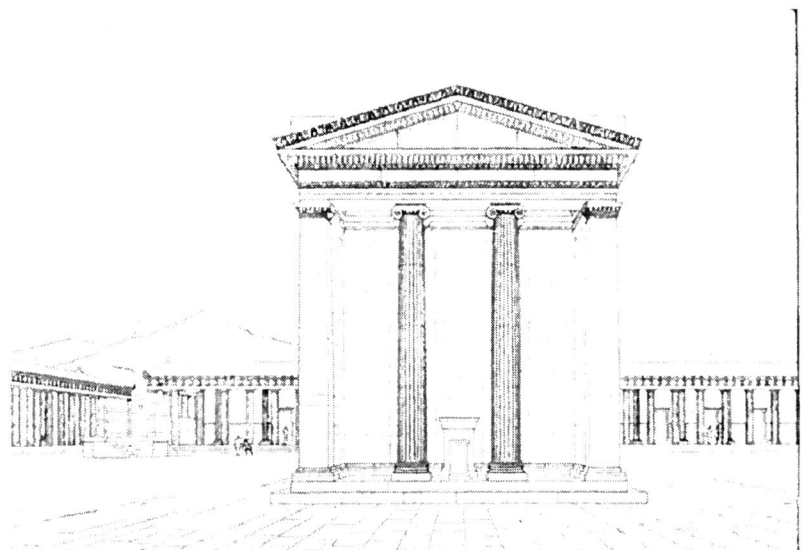

127. MAGNESIA, Temple of Zeus.

128. PRIENE, Temple of Aesculapius.

129. PIAZZA ST. MARK, Venice.

130. PIAZZA ST. MARK, Venice.

defense A fortress in the center of the city could command the whole circular settlement Palma Nuova *(ill 137)*, near Venice, was built according to a plan by Scamozzi in 1593. one hundred years after Fra Giocondo designed his ideal city It is a perfect realization of the Fra's ideal of centralistic city planning and it became the prototype of many cities founded during the Renaissance

The dynamic concept of the Baroque

The rational spirit of the Renaissance was completely displaced by the supernaturalism of the Baroque which was a product of the Counter Reformation The Renaissance's static concept changed to a dynamic concept of space This change is illustrated in the alterations of the cathedral and piazza of St Peter's in Rome *(ills 119 and 120)* The centric structure above the symmetrical Greek cross, with the dome dominating the whole, dates back to Bramante His square repeats the outline of the church, which is located in the center of the wholly symmetrical square This concept of the centric structure was maintained by Michael Angelo when he took over the construction St Peter's was almost completed according to Michael Angelo's plan when it was decided, under Pope Paul V, to base the plan on the Latin cross instead of the Greek Carlo Maderna added an oblong extension in front of the central edifice after the pattern of the church of Il Gesu The centralistic. static spatial concept changed thus for the dynamic. And when the piazza of St Peter's was formed in the same spirit by Bernini, church and square were fused into one homogeneity expressive of the newer concept, but diminishing the importance of the dome *(ills 119 and 120)*.

Under the influence of the Baroque, the city area no longer converged toward a center. It became instead a series of squares which, by reason of contrast, enhanced each other dramatically In such cities the spatial dynamic concept transcends the city area and gradually embraces the free space also. making it a vitally important part of the whole

Free space: A new city element

Free space as a new city element was discovered by Michael Angelo He used it for the first time in the structural formation of the Capitol square in Rome *(ills 139 and 140)*. The plan of this square shows that the side buildings diverge, thereby expanding the square toward the Senate house and narrowing it toward the opposite open side This causes a closing and opening of the square, with the spatial confinement being simultaneously maintained and suspended. Here we see for the first time how spatial order is possible without enclosures on all sides The spatial movement in depth is much increased by the divergence and the particular formation of the buildings, by the

131. INTERIOR OF A GOTHIC CATHEDRAL.

132. MEDIAEVAL STREET.

133. MICHELANGELO AND SAN GALLO. Palazzo Farnese, Rome.

134. DONATO BRAMANTE. Plan of St. Peter's Church and Square.

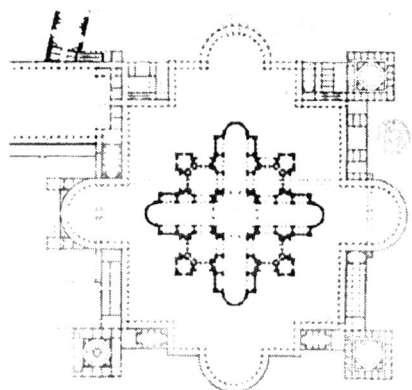

135. DONATO BRAMANTE. Santa Maria Della Consolazione at Todi.

136. FRA GIOCONDA. Design for an ideal city.

137. PLAN OF PALMANOVA.

horizontal aspect of the lateral buildings, and the vertical aspect of the tower at the rear

The same device of connecting the landscape spatially with architecture is illustrated in a painting by Perugino "Christ delivering the keys to St. Peter" *(ill. 138)* The triumphal arches to the left and right of the central building in the painting cause a movement in depth heretofore unknown to the Renaissance It anticipates, in a sense, the spatial feeling of the Baroque

Union of the city with the landscape

The union of the city area with the landscape around it was aided by changes in power politics It became possible to build unfortified cities Such cities as Versailles, Karlsruhe, and others founded in the Baroque period, show the connection of the palace—and later of the city—with surrounding open country by means of parks City space and free space, subordinate to one formative will, are developed according to the same architectural principles This new development is also a development of princely domination. Just as the state was subordinated in the period to an absolute system, so also the city became subordinated to an absolute artistic principle The city became an artistic homogeneity—a work of art

At the end of the Baroque period, as the classic revival began, a new and significant idea came into city planning which is influencing even our own times This idea was based upon the realization of the spatial concept of the Baroque without making the city and the landscape geometrical in the process This important contribution was made by the architects Wood, father and son, as they worked upon plans for the expansion of the city of Bath *(ills 141 and 142)*

During the eighteenth century Bath had become quite prosperous because of its therapeutic springs The population had so increased that it was necessary to enlarge the city No space for such expansion was available on the plain on which Bath stood The city could expand only on the sloping land to the north At first this extension was carried out in the conventional manner Closed streets and squares were planned Their spaciousness was unusual, and unusual also was their connection with green areas, and their architectural homogeneity The planners achieved harmony between buildings and topography, between the city and the landscape

As the expansion of the city went on, however, the problems it created were solved in an entirely new manner. During the Baroque period only princes had built their palaces in the open country But now, homes for the common people came to be built in the open. Free-

138. PERUGINO. Christ delivers the keys to St. Peter.

139. MICHELANGELO. Plan of the Capitol Square of Rome.

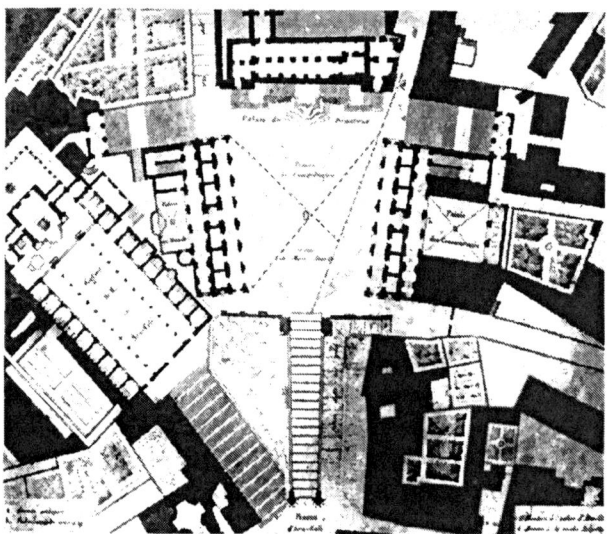

140. MICHELANGELO. View of the Capitol Square.

standing, large, crescent shaped apartment houses were erected on the slopes near Bath, and these structures were organically connected with the landscape. These buildings were no longer absolutely dependent upon streets. The streets led to the buildings, but they no longer determined their location. Buildings and streets have special functions to fulfill which may, but need not, coincide. Freed of the formalistic, super-architectural spirit with which the Baroque stifled the function of the dwelling, these buildings could develop according to their own laws.

The traditional confinement of the city was broken for the first time in Bath. Harmony was created here between the city area and the landscape by joining them and giving both city elements equal value.

Classic revival

The pomp of the Baroque was followed by the sobriety of the classic revival which derives its chief energy from intellectual rationalism. Two factors influenced the rise of this movement: the discovery of Pompeii during the 18th century, and the influence of the Roman concept of democracy upon the French. The Roman influence, giving rise to democratic principles, led to the French revolution.

Beauty at the expense of truth

The spatial concept of the classic revival, however, based as that revival was on pseudo-antiquity, was more closely related to that of the Renaissance than it was to the antiquity from which it thought to draw its inspiration. The extraordinary vitality which distinguished the Renaissance, however, was completely lacking in the classic revival. The tendency was toward imitation rather than creation. The strength of the spirit of the times lay in its ability to meet the dangers of life with discipline of spirit, and to oppose to external unrest an inward poise and steadfastness. But since this goal was sought through the sacrifice of truth and reality, the quest was shallow and was directed more often to "beauty" than to inner truth. The imitative tendency of the nineteenth century found its roots in this classic revival and the tendency has not been overcome to this day. Its expression in city building has led to decorative instead of structural results.

The imitative spirit of the nineteenth century

This decorative element in city building is, however, not the product of the nineteenth century classicism alone. It is as old as city building itself. Because decorative city building became general during the nineteenth century, however—because one misguided building attempt followed another—the cities developing so fast in those years became more and more chaotic. More buildings were erected during this period than had been built in the preceding thousand years. And because this unprecedented spurt in building coincided with the arti-

141. BATH. Panoramic view.

142. BATH. View from Hedgemead Park.

ficial concepts of nineteenth century pseudo-classicism the results were particularly bad City building came to be a conglomeration of quantity without quality, a lucrative business enterprise instead of a creative art And we have, therefore, a fatal heritage, whose liabilities weigh more and more heavily upon us and whose harmful effects can be eliminated only gradually through generations in the future

The esthetic and the scientific approach

At the turn of the century a decisive change took place Men began to explore the possibilities of finding new forms for implements and utensils, and of making those forms expressive of beauty Similar trends appeared in the planning and building of cities and houses This was an incomplete approach to the problems of the builder and the designer. Such problems could not be solved on the basis of formal aesthetic considerations So long as form was still considered, as the nineteenth century had considered it, as an arbitrary artistic element, independent of all the many social relations and requirements and their technological bases, the solutions sought continued to be elusive

Not until the first quarter of the twentieth century was there a consciousness of the social responsibility of architects, especially of planners of cities Then the growing recognition of the forces shaping intellectual, social and economic and technical changes was definitely brought into the field of city planning to effect there significant and lasting new concepts City planning became a science Man came to realize that, like any other science, it is rational and must be mastered in all its phases

Science and art

The rational elements of the new science were over-emphasized in some quarters. The erroneous view arose that city planning, having risen to the status of a science, was totally divorced from art, that the city planner should neither seek nor be allowed artistic freedom We know that this is completely fallacious reasoning. The dependency of city planning on a scientific basis does not limit its artistic expression On the contrary, it is the beginning of new possibilities, for the problem of city planning as a whole consists in the creative mastery of all conditions and means

Adequacy of the spatial concept and of the new city structure

Since the Gothic period, our spatial concepts have been moving steadily in the direction of greater freedom. We have become more and more concerned with widening and opening the city and merging it with open space Today our spatial feeling tends to openness, so does our city structure Different forces tend to dissipate the confinement of the city, to liberate the house, and with it, man; and to link man to nature once again.

The planning principles outlined in this study are adequate to this new spatial concept. The new settlement unit which we have constructed contains all the elements we need for its realization. Such a unit can be surrounded by gardens and parks. The mixed type of settlement permits the erection of free-standing buildings, each of which can develop functionally according to its own particular laws. Higher buildings within the "garden" parks, contrasting with the low one-family houses, may be used to create a feeling of spaciousness and openness. The narrow confined street and city area can give way to an entirely open and free city area. Just as the house fuses with the landscape, the room with the garden, the interior with the exterior, so also the city itself can merge with the landscape and the landscape can come within the city.

We have tried, in this discussion, to ask rational questions and answer them rationally. But a wholly rational discussion of the problems of city planning must always remain incomplete. The art of city planning is not susceptible of analysis by reason alone. Artistic ability, which cannot be taught, is beyond technical means. Though the proportions of the Doric temples may be determined geometrically, they cannot be formulated. Not in the measurable, but rather in the immeasurable, lies the essence of art.

Rational elements the base of artistic freedom

Only by mastering the technical means can the city planner realize his aims with artistic freedom. This freedom must be always linked with the useful and the necessary. It by no means is contrary to them, it is indeed fundamentally dependent upon them. Artistic freedom in city planning is not possible without this link with reality. All that is created by man is bound to time and space and can be executed only in time and space. Spiritual creativeness alone can turn the transitory into the permanent, the temporal into the eternal.

A NOTE BY THE AUTHOR

It has taken time to arrive at the basic principles of City Planning, and many years of thought and work to evolve a solution in accordance with them. The first diagrams I made, some 20 years ago, dealt overmuch with the metropolis and its traffic problems. In those days I made plans for skyscraper cities. Later I became interested in the considerably more important problems of sunlight, prevailing winds, small houses and gardens, and the human aspects of planning. I studied all the different problems involved, and developed planning principles out of the needs of life and the nature of things, and arrived at the solution presented in this book.

I began to write this book after teaching City Planning a number of years at the Bauhaus in Dessau. When the Nazis came into power I was forbidden to teach. There was then scarcely a chance to publish the book. Yet two parts of it, "Penetration of Sunlight into the Room" and "Penetration of Sunrays and Density of Population", were published in the *Moderne Bauformen* 1935 and 1936. Other parts of the book were used in addresses to the Chicago Chapter of the American Institute of Architects—"Literature of City Planning", January 1939, and "Cities and Defense", October 1941. A portion of the first was published in the *Architectural Forum*, August 1940. In 1939, at the request of Mr. S. Papadaki then editor of *Plus*, I wrote an article in which I used some of the material in this book. But *Plus* discontinued, and this article was then published in the *Armour Engineer and Alumnus*, December 1940, under the title "Elements of City Planning".

Since 1938 I have been teaching City and Regional Planning at the Illinois Institute of Technology, Chicago. Here an ever increasing number of students have become deeply interested in planning problems. Their mutual work has made it possible to develop certain planning ideas, and to apply my planning principles to various towns and cities.

L. Hilberseimer

Chicago, September 1943

CPSIA information can be obtained at www.ICGtesting.com
Printed in the USA
LVOW021233161111
255113LV00028B/9/P